Between Movement and Establishment

Between Movement and Establishment

Organizations Advocating for Youth

Milbrey McLaughlin

W. Richard Scott

Sarah Deschenes

Kathryn Hopkins

Anne Newman

Stanford University Press
Stanford, California

Stanford University Press
Stanford, California

Printed in the United States of America on acid-free, archival-quality paper

Library of Congress Cataloging-in-Publication Data
Between movement and establishment : organizations advocating for youth / Milbrey W.
McLaughlin . . . [et al.].
        p. cm.
    Includes bibliographical references and index.
    ISBN 978-0-8047-6210-6 (cloth : alk. paper)—ISBN 978-0-8047-6211-3 (pbk. : alk. paper)
    1. Youth—Government policy—California—San Francisco.   2. Youth—Government
policy—California—Oakland.   3. Youth—Services for—California—San Francisco.
4. Youth—Services for—California—Oakland.   5. Pressure groups—California—San
Francisco.   6. Pressure groups—California—Oakland.   I. McLaughlin, Milbrey Wallin.

    HQ796.B434 2009
    362.7—dc22
                                2008054139

Typeset by Thompson Type in 10/14 Minion

Contents

List of Figures and Tables

Figures

Tables

Acknowledgments

MANY PEOPLE MADE IMPORTANT and essential contributions over the course of this project. Primary financial support came from the Evelyn and Walter Haas Jr. Fund. Sylvia Yee and Cheryl Rogers of the Haas Jr. Fund have been enthusiastic about the project from the beginning; their direct appreciation of the critical role played by organizations advocating for youth grounded this study. A grant from the Spencer Foundation enabled us to complete our field research and writing. Conceptualization of our research benefited enormously from previous scholarship on local youth advocacy efforts and urban politics, most particularly that of Xavier de Souza Briggs, Dennis Shirley, Clarence Stone, and Mark R. Warren.

This project would not have been possible, of course, without the interest and generous cooperation of people involved with and knowledgeable about the conditions for youth in San Francisco and Oakland, CA (see Appendix). The many individuals involved in organizations advocating for Bay Area youth welcomed us into their organizations and their personal files and experiences. Their perspectives on and commitment to the well-being of urban youth form the core of this book. Deborah Alvarez-Rodriguez and Michael Wald helped us understand the broader Bay Area political and cultural contexts.

Research by Stanford colleagues Denise Gammal and Walter Powell expanded our thinking about nonprofits and understanding of the broad Bay Area nonprofit sector. Elisabeth Hansot and David Tyack generously reviewed multiple drafts of this manuscript. Their insightful comments always were right on target, and we benefited greatly from their willingness to talk through sticky issues and fuzzy arguments until clarity emerged. The helpful suggestions of several anonymous reviewers also improved this book. We are deeply grateful to all of you.

Between Movement and Establishment

Introduction

ORGANIZATIONS THAT ADVOCATE for urban youth can play a critical role for this vulnerable population. Youth growing up in the nation's big cities confront the same developmental tasks as do American youth everywhere. They must acquire the social skills, personal attitudes, and intellectual competencies that will carry them to successful adulthood. But too many urban youth must accomplish these goals in the context of deeply flawed institutions. The child poverty rate in the nation's large cities stands at 26 percent, well above the national child poverty rate of 17 percent, and 45 percent of urban youth live in families where no parent has full-time, year-round employment (Annie E. Casey Foundation 2004).[1] Other markers of institutional dysfunction signal particular challenges facing youth living in America's largest cities. Urban students are two times more likely to drop out of school than are youth in other settings.[2] Urban youth pay a "health tax" in terms of disproportionately high rates of asthma and of lead and asbestos poisoning; they have limited access to health care. Moreover, urban youth contending with these disadvantages must do so in settings that are often made unsafe by gangs and drugs.[3] Urban youth are more likely than nonurban youth to spend time in the foster care and juvenile justice systems or to live in zero-parent families. Data on every measure of child well-being—poverty, education, family supports, health, teen pregnancies, teen death rate, housing—indicate that too many young people living in America's large cities lack the opportunities and resources they need to become successful workers, parents and citizens (Annie E. Casey 2004, 2008; National Research Council and Institute of Medicine 2002).

The relative powerlessness of young people growing up in urban America means that more or different resources are not enough to address these challenges. Political and civic will are required as well. Unlike youth growing up in the suburbs, many urban youth have no effective parent advocate. And even when city parents have access to decision makers and time to represent their children's interests, they make up only a small segment of the electorate. Only around 15 percent of adult residents in the nation's urban centers have children in the public school system, and so big cities' voting population has scant direct investment in education and youth services. The interests of urban youth must compete for attention on a civic agenda with issues more compelling to voters—such as municipal transportation and public safety.

Without effective political activism dedicated to their interests, urban youth are likely to lose in the competition for community resources. Moreover, many urban voters have few positive connections to youth. They encounter the young people in their community only as fleeting faces on the evening news in stories of gang violence, or in statistics reporting school failures, teen pregnancy, or drug abuse. Negative media representation of urban youth as social problems to be managed aggravates the already difficult task of responding to their needs and improving the deficiencies in their institutional setting.

Antecedents to This Study

As often is the case, past research lays the groundwork for future investigation. This project grew from puzzles and questions prompted by three lines of our previous research, inquiries that were not explicitly related to one another but were mutually informative and generated new questions. One involved research into social policy implementation; the second examined the role of community-based organizations in the lives of urban youth; and a third the levers for and constraints on institutional change. We briefly highlight these three lines of inquiry, which together shape our investigation into how advocacy organizations can improve conditions for urban youth.

Policy Implementation

Research into policy issues, most particularly in education, taught that usual debates about "top-down" or "bottom-up" policy change largely misunderstand differences between macro level influences and levers and micro level opportunities for action (McLaughlin 1987, 2006; Scott & Meyer 1991). Differences among scholars typically center on which level of the system is more "important"—which has moral primacy and legitimate authority for action and is substantively prior (Lawlor, Ridgeway, & Markovsky 1993; Munch & Smelser 1987). These academic debates, primarily among sociologists, obscure two important points. One is that macro and micro levels of action are mutually contingent. Macro level policies both influence and depend on what happens on the ground. A second essential point is that micro is not a small macro. So-called "backward mappers," policy analysts who followed policy trails and consequences from the bottom to the top of the implementing system, framed their investigations in macro terms of policy tools and expectations. But macro and micro level actors have different "keyboards" at their disposal. Macro-level tools are the relatively blunt technical tools of policy; micro-level tools are adaptive and shaped by their specific contexts. Further, at the level of practice, important elements shaping implementation include those outside the formal policy system—such as community-based organizations, civic leaders, and community activists. Consideration of how policy choices are made and carried out at the local level requires a broader lens, one that looks beyond formal policy instruments and mandates to a view that better captures the nonsystem actors responsible for local preferences and implementation choices.

Social policy change is a problem of the smallest unit. Ultimately, policy consequences are tallied where policy is put into practice by those individuals who, in their classic study of policy implementation, Weatherley and Lipsky (1977) famously called the "street level bureaucrats." Choices and actions at the end of the policy implementation chain are of course influenced by official policy goals, regulations, and resources. But they also are shaped, in the final analysis, by the priorities, beliefs, and capabilities of the individuals who have to act on them. Choices made on the ground account to a significant extent for the observation that the "same" federal or state policy very often looks different in settings across the country. Implementation research poses questions about the nature of those local actors and elements that influence policy implementation on the ground. What factors affect local will, priorities, and capacity? How do political, organizational, and historical contexts matter to local policy adaptations? Exploring these questions is a crucial part of understanding how the local conditions that shape urban youth's experiences come to be and how they may be reformed.

Community-Based Youth Organizations

Research into community-based organizations engaging youth looked outside the "official" institutions through which youth move and into their neighborhoods and nonschool hours. We learned how critical these local, nonformal resources could be in the lives of youth struggling with challenges of poverty, neighborhood turmoil, and subpar schools (Deschenes 2003; Deschenes, McLaughlin, & O'Donoghue 2006; McLaughlin n.d.; McLaughlin, Irby, & Langman [1994], 2001). In many instances, these private or voluntary organizations provided the only handhold for youth attempting to navigate the tough corridors of their urban adolescence—Boys and Girls Clubs, local sports and arts groups, neighborhood centers. And, oftentimes, these community-based organizations served as a channel through which otherwise disenfranchised youth and their families could express their needs to city officials and influential citizens in moral rhetoric that compels attention (Newman, 2007). This research highlighted the important and particular role of "third sector" organizations—those local nonprofit or voluntary organizations that function independently of both market and state to take up the slack created by insufficient opportunities for employment or participation in a positive activity or to shore up the shortfalls resulting from failing schools and other youth-serving institutions.

In the course of research into community-based youth organizations, we encountered substantively different urban contexts for youth—from cities where youth were relegated to the end of the line in terms of community resources and viewed as problems, to urban settings where youth enjoyed a place at the community's decision-making table and status as an investment worth making. Where we found positive opportunities and resources for urban youth, especially youth from disadvantaged settings, we often also saw advocates working effectively in their behalf. Organizations advocating for urban youth seemingly made a difference in the nature and quality of opportunities and resources available to young people in the community. This observation raised many questions. How do these "third sector" actors successfully navigate their urban political and institutional contexts to secure resources for youth? What are the structures and strategies that enable youth advocacy organizations to mediate successfully the gauntlet of establishment politics in big cities? The effective presence of organizations advocating for urban youth, we expected, represented a particularly important but little-understood element of observed differences in the willingness and capacity of big cities to provide positive youth development supports.

We set out to learn more about these nonsystem actors and their community contexts. In particular, we wanted to explore their condition of "betweenness." Advocacy groups working to secure new or different resources for youth in their cities operate as intermediary organizations, moving be-tween established institutions and political arrangements and the individu-als or neighborhoods lacking access to or notice by community leaders. Our book's title, *Between Movement and Establishment,* signals the strategic posi-tion of advocacy organizations as both outsiders and insiders in conversation with mainstream interests. How do organizations advocating for youth man-age this mediating role in urban settings?

Determinants of Institutional Change

We also believed that an understanding of the structure and role of community-based advocacy organizations would benefit from insights from recent research on the ways in which organizations interact with their broader institutional structure, as well as from new work on the ways in which social movement or-ganizations contribute to institutional change.

Our previous work has examined the nature of institutional structures (Scott 2008a) and the ways in which institutional structures and organiza-tional forms are reciprocally related (Scott et al. 2000). Changing regulative and legal systems, normative structures, and cultural belief systems give rise to new forms of organizing at the same time they undercut support for exist-ing organizations. For example, new policies and programs at the federal level during the 1960s—the Medicare/Medicaid programs—stimulated the growth of hospitals in the United States as well as enabled the creation of new spe-cialized forms, such as kidney dialysis centers. Later retrenchment in fund-ing and the spread of neoliberal ideas gave rise to innovative forms such as health maintenance organizatons (HMOs). Could we observe similar connec-tions between institutional frameworks and community-based organizations working to improve conditions for urban youth?

There is also renewed interest in the distinctive role played by social move-ment organizations in effecting institutional change (McAdam & Scott 2005). In our study of advocacy organizations, we draw on these ideas to shed light on the ways in which problems and situations are "framed" and repertories of action constructed to exploit political openings and to motivate and enable social change and reform.

The institutional literature to date provides a good bit of insight into the processes by which new institutions arise (for example, DiMaggio 1991), but only a few studies have been conducted that examine how highly institution-alized systems of organizations lose traction and undergo substantial change (for example, Rao, Monin, & Durand 2003; Scott et al. 2000). We pursue this latter question in the present study. In our time, and particularly in urban America, apart from the family, youth concerns are primarily the responsibility of a number of venerable, established structures, including school systems, juvenile justice programs, and social welfare agencies. We ask how advocacy groups and community organizations work to introduce change and reform into these entrenched institutional arrangements.

Advocacy in the San Francisco Bay Area

In this book we bring together ideas and arguments from scholarship on public policy setting and implementation, organization theory, and social movements to shed light on the work of community-based advocacy organizations. We chose to focus on local organizations advocating for youth because of the strategic opportunities as well as the particular challenges associated with advocating for youth in the nation's big cities. To understand how they work to improve conditions in urban areas, we examine the efforts of two populations of organizations in the San Francisco Bay Area, focusing particular attention on the advocacy initiatives of three case study organizations: Oakland Community Organizations, Coleman Advocates for Children and Youth, and the San Francisco Organizing Project.

Oakland Community Organizations (OCO), a faith-based, membership organization, has been a presence in Oakland for more than thirty years. The San Francisco Organizing Project (SFOP), a faith-based, membership organization, like OCO, belongs to the PICO National Network. Coleman Advocates for Children and Youth in San Francisco, in contrast to SFOP and OCO, is an independent, secular advocacy organization that focuses exclusively on issues related to children and youth. Like SFOP and OCO, Coleman has enjoyed an unusually long life in the domain of nonprofit advocacy, with its founding extending back to the 1960s. Each of our focal organizations has played a somewhat different role in their community and has used somewhat different strategies to advance their goals. But each has been successful in framing an agenda for youth in their communities and garnering political and financial resources to support it. We explore these diverse ways of making a difference for youth and their contributions to a deeper understanding about the form and function of advocacy organizations working at the local level.

1 Organizations Advocating for Youth

ADVOCACY ORGANIZATIONS ACTING in the interests of youth play an especially vital role in our nation's urban centers. Because youth are nonvoters and must rely on others to speak on their behalf, advocacy organizations are critical representatives for them—particularly when it comes to America's poorest youth, who have little representation or effective voice.[1] As prominent members of the "third sector"—the nongovernmental or nonprofit organizations that operate between market and state to pursue a "third way" to address public problems—advocacy organizations undertake private action in the public good (Giddens 1998). Organizations advocating for youth share features of advocacy organizations generally; but, as we will elaborate, they also face particular challenges as they work on behalf of youth. In this chapter, we describe the opportunities and obstacles such organizations face as they strive to improve conditions for youth in urban areas, before turning in subsequent chapters to our contextualized case analysis.

Advocacy Organizations: Their Functions and Challenges

Organizations advocating for social change take up problems that individuals cannot resolve on their own and amplify the voices of underrepresented, marginalized, or special interests. In doing so, they contribute in unique ways to the representation of pluralistic interests in a democracy and enhance the character of civil society (Andrews & Edwards 2004; Fung 2003). Such groups have played pivotal roles in the development of various areas of human rights and social issues, including civil rights, women's rights, environmental issues, and, more recently, children's rights and child and youth services. By giving voice to these issues, advocacy groups have paved the way for more supportive legislation, worked to provide more and better services to their constituents, and struggled to reframe public opinion about the issues that shape debate, policy, and programs.

The word *advocacy* derives from the Latin word *advocare*—coming to the aid of someone (Reid 2000, p. 1), but advocacy activities are only loosely defined.[2] The term *advocacy* implicates a broad range of activities, causes, and organizations, from mobilizing political participation, to action on behalf of others, to service provision, and often is used synonymously with *lobbying*. Advocacy organizations and community organizers often function as educators, informing policy makers and citizens about the issues that frame their mission and providing individuals with the knowledge and skills they need to take part in the political process (Warren 2001). They can also serve as a check on the political establishment and provide a channel through which individuals can press for action on public concerns. Because advocacy organizations can express opinions and push for issues in a more powerful way than can most individuals acting alone, they can provide the benefits of direct citizen participation without the limitations of personal time, access, or resources. In this way, advocacy organizations potentially enhance both the quality and the consequences of representation and broaden political discourse.

Between Movement and Establishment

As our title suggests, we see a primary contextual factor shaping organizations advocating for youth in urban communities as their state of "betweenness." Advocacy occurs in diverse venues—at the grassroots, as gadfly at work with other community organizations, and as external critic or participant within public agencies at all levels of government. To be effective in any venture, they must engage society's institutionalized preferences and the organizations that enact them: the establishment. We base our examination of advocacy organizations on the idea that these groups exist in the middle of a continuum between social movements and stable organizations and institutions, which we call here "the establishment." The groups we study may have emerged from a loosely coordinated reform movement but have found ways to transform themselves into organizations with a relatively stable structure; or they may have developed from the efforts of a collection of entrepreneurial "do-gooders," one or more individuals committed to social change. Alternatively, they may be the franchise of a national organization that has decided to establish a branch in a particular community. Whatever the specifics of the origin, such groups have evolved from the stage of mobilization and movement formation to that of viable organization—with a locus of operations, a staff, a budget, and a director.

This transformation represents a dynamic process through which social movements assume some attributes of formal organizations to stabilize their reform efforts. Organizations specialize in erecting durable, reliable, and accountable systems that provide valued goods and services (Hannan & Carroll 1995). By contrast, social movements emerge out of unorganized, inchoate collections of individuals. They exist to challenge established systems of power and authority, and they seek to change the bases on which decisions are normally made and the ways in which activities are routinely conducted. Their aim is to destabilize existing governing structures and dominant social logics within a field and to substitute other players with different cultural frames and modes of acting.

Despite their independence from the establishment, social movements ultimately depend on action by governmental or other established structures such as corporations to create and oversee programs to meet their demands. Their work requires ongoing, open interaction among state, market, and nonprofit sectors and positions advocacy organizations and community organizers as links between and critical observers of institutions of government, business, and other nonprofits (Boris & Mosher-Williams 1998; Salamon 2002). In this way, they "deepen the ways in which people are represented and participate in democracies" (Reid 2000, p. 3). Others argue that "many of the innovations in American politics can be traced to decades of efforts by popular associations to link policy outcomes to citizen concerns" (Clemens 1997, p. 320).

However, movements that begin to enjoy some success find that they need to become more like organizations—locating a more reliable source of income, selecting and differentiating among participants, establishing ways to coordinate efforts—if they are to survive and persist as viable systems (Zald & McCarthy 1987b). Moving in the other direction, organizations, for their part, have had to become more flexible, focusing more on differentiated and specialized services, and more capable of responding to rapid changes in their environments. Just as movements have become more organized, organizations have become more flexible and movementlike in their structures and behavior (Davis et al. 2005).

This greater fluidity between movements and organizations leaves advocacy groups with an ongoing tension to negotiate. They are fundamentally *intermediary* organizations, and their function is to mediate between the weak and the more powerful, the unannointed and the legitimate, the have-nots and the haves, the disenfranchised and the entitled. They are subject to the danger of becoming radicalized to the point of engaging in illegal and rebellious actions—or to the opposite trap of becoming co-opted by the establishment and serving as an apologist for entrenched powers. Productive, responsible, and effective actions must be sought somewhere between these poles.

And, more so than most organizations, advocacy groups position themselves quite self-consciously between past logics and practices and future possibilities. In this sense of "betweenness," advocacy groups are condemned to sit on the cusp of social reform, reflecting on the past and attempting to shape the future. But while advocacy organizations struggle with their condition of betweenness, they also benefit from it. As nonsystem actors marginal to existing regimes, they are more likely to develop and advance alternative ideas and programs.[3]

Advocacy: Forms, Functions, and Challenges

Advocacy organizations working between movement and establishment embrace several different forms and functions (Andrews & Edwards 2004). Although each type of advocacy group differs in its general strategies and mission, each also pursues a collective good framed in terms of the public interest, but they do so in different ways. Some are membership organizations, some have no individual members but include only organizations, and others are a mix. Some are interest groups, lobbying on behalf of special interests, professional or personal—the American Medical Association or the National Rifle Association, for example—where members participate by means of a checkbook. Andrews and Edwards (2004) observe that interest groups often exhibit a social class bias in favor of the individuals or professions with easier access to resources and prestige. Some are social movement organizations, another type of advocacy group that typically operates outside the mainstream to press for change in established priorities and institutionalized patterns of decision making. Civil rights, feminist, and environmental groups exemplify social movement organizations.

Nonprofits working on behalf of groups not well served by either market or state comprise yet another form of advocacy—for example, the Child Welfare League of America, a group that functions to improve services and protection for foster children. These groups serve as watchdogs for their special interest groups but do not push for fundamental social change as do social movement organizations. Grassroots organizations in the community organizing tradition pursue another form of advocacy. They operate somewhat differently and often have a different purpose than professionally run advocacy organizations. Nevertheless, they serve important advocacy functions, particularly as they help community members become advocates for themselves. Typically, organizing groups act as generalists that mobilize and train community members to act in their own right to advance their concerns, whether it is with respect to housing, public safety, or education. Community organizing groups are often based in affinity groups such as churches (for example, the Industrial Areas Foundation; see Shirley 1997) or what Jenkins (2006) calls "cooptable social networks." Others are local affiliates of national groups, such as PICO (formerly the Pacific Institute for Community Organization), a national faith-based organizing network with twenty-nine organizations in sixty-five cities, or ACORN, which has 850 neighborhood chapters in seventy-five cities across the United States.

Advocacy groups also differ in their relationship to the establishment. Some advocacy organizations prefer to align themselves more with those groups that work outside of and, frequently in opposition to, the establishment, whereas others are more willing to move within the halls of power and create enclaves within the establishment that reflect their values and agenda. There are differing locations along the tension lines separating the empowered and the disempowered. Some organizations will be more likely to engage in adversarial and confrontational politics; others will be more prone to attempt mediation and compromise, and still others will seek alignments with entrenched powers that critics will label cooptation (or "selling out"). Alternatively, the same organizations can use all these positions, varying their stance by issue or over time.

Among the chief obstacles advocacy organizations of all stripes face is that of funding. Funding for nonprofit advocacy and organizing groups comes from a number of sources (see Reid 2001). Many organizations engaged primarily in providing service—nonprofit charitable organizations, faith-based groups—receive government funding either directly, through grants or contracts from public agencies such as health or social welfare, or indirectly, in their role as junior partners to recipients of government grants, such as those community-based youth organizations included in the federally funded 21st Century Community Learning Centers. Some social change advocacy groups make a public point of their refusal to accept public funding, under the belief that such support undermines their independence. The Children's Defense Fund's mission statement announces, for example, "We have never taken government funds."[4] Political advocacy efforts associated with professional or trade organizations are supported by members' dues. Foundation support has played a critical role for advocacy associated with social change agenda such as education reform, enhanced health care services, or environmental protection, though such sources tend to support moderate rather than more extreme advocacy positions.[5] Philanthropic support has been key to the growth of professionally staffed advocacy organizations at the end of the twentieth century and central to solidifying the gains made by social movement organizations, such as environmental and civil rights groups (Andrews & Edwards 2004) and organizations advocating for youth (Yee 2008).[6]

Regardless of funding source, nonprofit advocacy organizations and community organizing groups have few dependable, stable sources of support and for the most part survive through their own fund-raising efforts. Especially at the grassroots level, this funding picture creates a hand-to-mouth existence and limited life span for the average local advocacy group. Such organizations typically lack the size, infrastructure, or slack in resources to respond effectively to swings in philanthropic fashions, government initiatives, or donor interests (Galaskiewitz & Bielefeld 1998). Low-income constituents lack the deep pockets to provide significant financial support to the groups that represent them. Unstable funding for advocacy groups, particularly those speaking for poor and marginalized individuals, carries significant consequences for local political access and social resources. While large, national advocacy organizations such as the American Association of People with Disabilities or the Children's Defense Fund feature prominently in high-profile national policy debates and so are attractive to donors with similar concerns, the small, freestanding grassroots nonprofits that comprise the "backbone of U.S. civic activity" (Reid 2001, p. 121) remain the most vulnerable. In fact, local advocacy groups account for the lion's share of American's political participation. Research on political activity found that 92 percent of individual political activity (that included more than voting) was connected to such local groups (Reid op. cit.). And for these local groups, though funding is critical to their survival, success in securing support can be a two-edged sword when it may create conditions that deflect the organization from its mission or strings that compromise the organization's core principles. From this broad overview of the chief functions and challenges of advocacy organizations, we now turn more specifically to how organizations working on behalf of youth operate, the issues they address, and their evolving role in urban centers.

Advocating for Youth

Advocacy organizations working in the interests of youth vary in focus, location, size, and strategy. Some exist for advocacy purposes only; some are hybrids and also provide services and supports for their target population.[7] Some advocacy organizations are issue specific and focus, for example, on health issues—such as groups involved in promoting funding for AIDS research and treatment, for mental health, or for diabetes. Other advocacy organizations are constituency specific, advocating for rights and resources for groups possessing limited political voice in the American democratic system—gay, lesbian, and transgendered individuals, for instance.

Advocacy organizations for youth have proliferated at all levels of the policy system. At the national level, organizations such as the Children's Defense Fund and Voices for America's Children have vigorously pursued national policies and programs aimed at improving conditions for children and youth. State-level organizations typically target types of issues that have particular salience to a specific state. In California, for example, the California Association for Bilingual Education has worked since 1976 to promote educational equity for the state's large population of multilingual, multicultural students. Yet the majority of advocacy groups operating in America today are freestanding, grassroots creations working to effect change at the community level. In Chicago, for example, Designs for Change compelled the Chicago Public Schools to decentralize governance to school site committees. In Oakland, California, the group Books Not Bars pressured policy makers to abandon plans for an expensive new prison and direct funds instead to needed school reform.

Whatever form and focus advocates for youth assume, the need to change public perceptions of youth, especially poor urban youth, presents a fundamental challenge to their work. Negative media portrayals contest advocates' messages about what youth need and deserve and about the responsibility of government to meet their needs. These challenges facing advocates for youth are then compounded by ever-evolving and contested conceptions of the role of the state in child welfare and adolescent development, which we turn to next. We offer a brief policy history of child welfare programs and supports in the United States to understand the lineage of the contemporary advocacy organizations we study.

The Evolving Role of the State in Child Welfare

Public ideas about government's responsibility for the welfare of children changed in significant ways throughout the twentieth century. Only since the 1970s have the distinct needs of children been formally recognized by the legal system and public institutions (Rodham 1973). Changes in public ideas about children's needs and guardianship have in large part been a result of the efforts of child advocates. In the late nineteenth and early twentieth centuries, the well-being of children was held to be the responsibility of families, and children's interests were assumed to be synonymous with parents' interests. To the extent that public institutions were involved in providing for the welfare of children, they took a largely punitive stance toward misbehaving or troubled youth. Those lacking parental support became "wards of the state" and were provided only minimal care in almshouses and orphanages, where many died or encountered substantial abuse. In reaction to the mistreatment of children, anticruelty societies sprang up late in the nineteenth century to advocate for laws protecting the health and public safety of children, and by the beginning of the twentieth century more than 300 anticruelty societies worked on behalf of children (Carson 2001, p. xiii).

These advocates were central to the development of what Theda Skocpol calls a "maternal welfare state" in the Progressive Era, during which welfare policies for dependent citizens won out over proposals for a more paternalist social service regime and were justified as a "universalization of mother love" (Skocpol 1992, 1995). Maternalist policy victories included the creation of a Children's Bureau in 1912, which disseminated information on child rearing, sponsored health conferences and prenatal services, and conducted home visits. The Sheppard-Towner Infancy and Maternity Act of 1921, administered by the Children's Bureau, was the nation's first explicit social welfare legislation and aimed to reduce infant mortality. Advocates were also instrumental in passing the 1935 Social Security Act, which provided aid for widowed and deserted mothers and funds for states to develop child protective services. This legislation created a number of categorical programs targeting support for children lacking families (adoption and foster home care) and for "broken" families (aid to single mothers). Federal support for such programs waned after World War II, however. Grants-in-aid to states throughout the middle third of the twentieth century led to decentralized and uncoordinated services for children that varied greatly across states (Bremner 1974).

Despite federal retreat from the project of a fully developed maternal welfare state, the children's rights movement in the 1960s and 1970s did secure additional supportive policies and programs at the federal level. In 1963, a landmark national child advocacy bill was enacted: the first statute mandating child abuse reporting.[8] Other legislation followed (including Head Start 1964; Child Abuse and Treatment Act of 1974; Social Services Block Grant 1975; Family Preservation and Support Initiative, 1993) that recognized the welfare of children and youth as a concern of the government at federal and state levels and broadened the policy focus to include a range of factors that influence children's well-being, families, schools, neighborhoods, and communities (history from Carson op cit.). The early child advocacy organizations—the anticruelty societies—and their successors can take credit for launching the ongoing shift in the state's responsibility for the welfare of young people.

A Changing Youth Policy Agenda

More recently, youth advocates have continued to push for state support in light of changing conceptions about adolescent development and responsive policies. This evolving perspective about youth often means that organizations advocating for and with youth find themselves pushing not only for *more* resources but in many instances for *different* ones, as they embrace new conceptions of youth and their needs. Demands that established institutions work differently to better support the youth in their community often meet with stiff resistance. Contemporary shifts in thinking about youth that motivate advocates' current work also implicate established ways of operating and public investments. Along with changing ideas about the role of the state in the lives of youth and their families, ideas were shifting about the fundamental nature of adolescence and the policy issues presented by that age group. Throughout much of the twentieth century, policy and research conceived of adolescence as a time of upheaval and strain and regarded youth as a risk to themselves and to others. G. Stanley Hall's 1904 book *Adolescence: Its psychology and its relations to physiology, anthropology, sociology, sex, crime, religion and education* launched the study of adolescent development and set out a theory that conceived of adolescence as a period of "storm and stress." Hall saw adolescence as a stage in human development when people evolved from being untamed animals to being civilized. Adolescence was understood as a time of "overcoming one's beastlike impulses" (Lerner 2005).

Many adolescents, in this view, exhibited "deficits" in their behavior. Millions of public and private dollars were spent to address the problems thought to be caused by youth's alleged deficits—dysfunctional behaviors such as unsafe sex, teenage drinking, drug use, academic failure, crime, and violence. Researchers, too, used this model of adolescent development to understand youth's behavior and conceived of a young person's second decade in individualistic terms of invariant, stage-based development. This view paid scant attention to interactions with adolescents' highly varying social and institutional contexts. Thus a significant body of science related to adolescent development supported policy and programs that set out to "fix" discrete individual problem behaviors through intervention, remediation, or punishment.

Beginning in the late 1980s, both youth policy and research on adolescent development entered a new phase, one that departed from a narrow emphasis on remedying "deficits" with uncoordinated institutional supports and instead focused on the broader context of healthy development and enhanced integration of youth services (Pittman, Irby & Ferber, 2000). Reformers and practitioners experienced in working with young people pointed out that the needs of youth are complex and interwoven. They contended that policies and programs intended to benefit youth should strive for continuity across sectors (such as education, social service, and juvenile justice) and over time. This view contrasted sharply with traditional Balkanized youth services and institutions that operated in isolation from one another, with little communication or coordination of resources.

The early 1990s saw a similar shift in models underlying the scientific study of adolescence. Neuroscientists, physicians, developmental psychologists, and others engaged in clinical research on adolescent development began to move to an ecological model that viewed youth as embedded in multiple contexts that influence their behavior and development—most especially contexts of families, communities, schools, and peer networks. Research began to examine how elements in a young person's environment—family background, neighborhood poverty, public resources—influenced their development for better or worse. As a dynamic model of person-environment gained ground, many researchers, like practitioners, began to replace a deficit perspective with a youth development paradigm that incorporated contextual factors and assumed variability and plasticity in human development (see Public/Private Ventures 2000). This shift carries important implications for policy and practice: A youth development perspective takes a comprehensive rather than a compartmentalized view of the supports and opportunities youth need to thrive and features positive rather than deficit-focused supports for development. A youth development stance thus advocates for greater integration and coordination among those youth-serving institutions traditionally operating in isolated silos.

Simultaneously, articulate advocates for positive youth development were at work at all levels of government. Karen Pittman, Executive Director of the Forum for Youth Investment and a major voice for a changed policy stance, popularized her slogan "problem-free is not fully prepared" and rallied supporters from all segments of the youth-serving sector to press for a more comprehensive, positive policy approach to youth programs. Leaders in youth development urged movement away from an "anti" stance—antidrug, anti-gang, antidropout, anti-teen pregnancy—to focus on resources and opportunities that could assist young people in taking positive steps toward healthy futures:

> The (youth development) movement's fundamental assumption [is] . . . that enduring, positive results in a youth's life are most effectively achieved by tending to basic needs for guidance, support and involvement, and not by surgical interventions aimed at removing problems. (Public/Private Ventures 2000, p. 9)

Programs and policies consistent with a positive youth development point of view acknowledge the broader social and institutional contexts that actively influence individual outcomes and development. This changed perspective directs attention from a single-minded focus on individuals to include families, schools, and other community-based resources as targets for intervention and opportunities to enhance youth well-being. In doing so, a positive youth development stance broadens the playing field for youth advocates as they seek a variety of resources across sectors—supportive adults, an engaging school environment, opportunities for youth leadership in local government, for instance—in addition to seeking remedies for problems.

Influential voices from many sectors have demanded this reinterpretation of youth's needs and have reminded policy makers that "quick-fix" programs seldom result in enduring benefits for youth or society. They have called for a comprehensive system of integrated and ongoing resources for young people and a shift away from categorical, domain-specific resource streams. Health, welfare, education, housing, and other programs, too long functioning in isolated silos, required reconfiguration to more effectively serve youth. Researchers engaged in questions of adolescent development buttressed this policy position with evidence about the value of a comprehensive web of programs and opportunities at the community level—findings supporting the generalization that the more supports youth have, and the more they are aligned and integrated, the better youth outcomes are likely to be (National Research Council & Institute of Medicine 2002).

Challenges to a Youth Development Stance

Ideas about youth and society's responsibility for them influence the changing role of the state in policies affecting youth. Though many policy makers and practitioners embrace youth development principles for ideological reasons, deeply rooted establishment constraints associated with funding streams, oversight, and responsibility have slowed the broader policy uptake. In addition, conceptions of youth policy remain contested. Organizations advocating for and with youth encounter ambivalence or disagreement about social investment in youth. Adolescents, some feel, have grown beyond the protection society assures its most vulnerable young; others go so far as to describe youth as "superpredators . . . the youngest, biggest, and baddest generation any society has ever known" (Bennett, Dilulio, & Walters 1996).

Challenges to enacting a youth development perspective also stem from the relatively rigid institutional boundaries, professional assumptions, and partisan battles for resources. Entrenched logics of action, diverse institutional histories and mandates, and distinct sources of authority separate rather than integrate youth-focused resources. Educators, for example, draw famously tight lines around schools. Youth advocates have struggled, with little success, to bring educators into young people's broader domain and link them to after-school and other community-based activities. In this fragmented institutional context, organizations advocating for youth find it difficult to bring all the players and establishment interests to the table to negotiate their collaboration.

Though not all organizations advocating for youth operate within a youth development framework, most seek resources and policies supported by positive youth development principles. These organizations are at the heart of much of the policy change that affects youth, and they continue to take on these challenges in their work.

Organizations advocating for youth thus operate in the context of a changing social logic about what youth need to thrive and how best to provide those resources, and they can become critical actors in reframing opportunities and resources for youth. Although youth development cannot yet be called a coherent "organization field" with the stability and recognition of established fields such as medical care, indicators suggest that a social movement is taking hold that lends authoritative support to advocacy for positive youth development resources.[9] We next describe this movement's progress and setbacks at different levels of government.

Responses to a New Youth Policy Agenda

Much of new youth policy and legislation since the 1960s has focused on the unique rights of children (for example, protection from abuse and rights to shelter and education). However, efforts to promote policies that embrace a positive youth development approach began to gain ground in the 1990s at all levels of the policy system.

At National and State Levels

A key turning point in the framing of national policy for youth occurred in the 1990s, as service providers, funders, and analysts began incorporating data from studies that identified important predictors of youth behavioral outcomes across service sectors. The 1997 21st Century Community Learning Center's support for after-school programs constituted prominent federal response to this evidence. In 1998, the Mott Foundation partnered with the U.S. Department of Education to provide grants to schools, community and faith-based organizations, and youth development agencies to provide high-quality, expanded learning opportunities outside of regular school hours. In his 1999 budget proposal, President Clinton detailed an $800 million increase to the program as part of a historic initiative to improve child services. Support from the White House, the efforts of grassroots groups and advocates, as well as the tremendous response from the field, helped the program grow to $846 million in the 2001 federal budget. The federal No Child Left Behind Act, passed in 2000, continued momentum for after-school services; the program reached a level of $2.7 billion in fiscal year 2007. Nonetheless, progress toward a youth development agenda that integrates federal programs serving youth has moved at a glacial pace.

Although advocacy organizations have proliferated and additional federal programs have been generated at the national level, an important countertrend has been underway since the early 1980s. For ideological and economic reasons, the movement known as "devolution" has gradually shifted discretion and funding for social welfare programs to state and community levels. Federal programs are increasingly implemented by states and local communities, under the assumption that states and communities are better able to target local needs. Although this strategy allows for some local discretion, most programs remain categorical with funding restricted to targeted problems and populations. In many ways, these categorical restrictions impede youth advocates' efforts to coordinate and integrate services across sectors.

Despite the fragmentation of services and funding at the federal level, some states have developed the capacity to collaborate across service sectors and geographic regions in accordance with a positive youth development perspective. For example, at least twenty-eight states have established collaborative youth councils in an effort to coordinate youth programs and services (Foster, Gieck & Dienst 2005). New York and Iowa are among a handful of states that have advanced statewide policy for youth expressly based in a youth development stance. These states have been able to leverage funding for youth programs, forge links across political silos, and move the center of youth policy debates from a punitive to a more positive developmental outlook.[10] However, most states continue traditional operations, and there has been little movement across categorical lines or agency boundaries to take up a new youth policy agenda. States, by and large, have not to this point become major players in the design of youth development programs and services and youth advocates struggle to broker collaborations across sector and special interest boundaries. In many states, political interests remain tied up in categorical concerns tied to subgroups of youth defined by special needs or ethnicity.

At the Local Level

The most important action for youth takes place on the ground, in neighborhoods and communities. Communities have become integral to reform efforts in large part because families experience the direct effects of failing schools, ineffective drug control programs, and overcrowded jails and juvenile halls at the local level. It is individual parents and kids who suffer from the fragmentation of services, when real problems are artificially disaggregated into distinct and uncoordinated slices and when actual needs fail to map on to categorized, specialized services. And it is here, because of the emergence of vigilant local advocacy groups, that parents and youth experience the empowering effects of participating in actions aimed at improving their well-being and opportunities.

The most innovative and consequential developments for youth are found on the ground, in communities across the country. Youth advocates point to a number of significant changes in policy investments and programs at the local level as evidence that organizations advocating for youth are making concrete differences. Increased public and private investment in after-school programs provide the most dramatic example of attention to youth's needs more broadly considered. Groups such as LA's BEST (Better Educated Students for Tomorrow) in Los Angeles and The After School Corporation (TASC) and Partnership for After School Education (PASE), both in New York City, provide substantive and political leadership around youth development. National youth organizations such as Boys and Girls Clubs of America and Girls, Inc., have moved from the backwaters of youth policy to gain support from both public and private funders as partners in community youth development.

Some public funds at the local level support an approach promoted by youth development activists. The Beacons programs, begun by the Youth Development Institute of the Fund for the City of New York and now operating in cities around the country, offer all-year programming for youth and in many instances to parents and community members. Change in youth policy can also be seen in other cities around the country. Communities such as Savannah, Georgia, Hampton, Virginia, and Redwood City, California, have adopted youth development goals for their youth programs and have used "youth mapping" and "youth budgets" to document the nature and cost of community resources for youth. They place youth in key decision-making roles and support them in carrying out these responsibilities. These examples represent the commitment of significantly more resources and improved organizational relationships to advancing positive youth development principles; nonetheless, they do not yet represent mainstream practices.

Youth Advocacy on the Ground

Organizations advocating for youth at the local level provide the structure for micromobilization to take place. At this level, one does not see social movements on a grand scale. At the local level there are smaller groups organizing around issues of local concern, although, as we will emphasize, such groups are attentive to and influenced by wider social forces. This micromobilization occurs in grassroots organizations and by way of "any small group setting in which processes of collective attribution are combined with rudimentary forms of organization to produce mobilization for collection action" (McAdam, McCarthy, & Zald 1988, p. 709). As a site for these processes, organizations advocating for youth and community organizers serve as the bridge between different levels of the system—between community members confronting their problems and agency officials from whom they seek assistance or, at a higher level, to elected officials who oversee and allocate resources. In this manner, these organizations often serve as a vital link between the citizen and the state—or between movement and establishment, as our title highlights.

Analytical Levels

We have already pointed out that local organizations are connected to wider systems of organizations. As detailed in the next chapter, we make use of analytical distinctions developed by organizational sociologists to distinguish among the different levels at which organizations operate. This provides us with a more precise language for discussing the linkages between micro and macro levels of activities. We view advocacy organizations as operating simultaneously in interaction with their immediate exchange partners and targets—their "organization set"—in relation to other organizations in the community engaged in the same type of work—their "organization population"—and in relation to wider circles of organizations, including state and national levels that play a role in youth concerns—their "organization field" (Scott & Davis 2007, chapters 9 and 10). Increasingly in modern social systems, local organizational structures and activities are embedded in and penetrated by distant processes and forces. All of the organizations we studied relate to and collaborate with other organizations. Some are connected to large, relatively stable networks that provide support in the form of information, training, and financial resources. And every organization attends closely to what other similar organizations are doing—via direct observation, newsletters, mass media, and the Internet—as they decide how to configure and reconfigure their structure and what strategies and tactics to pursue.

Themes and Contributions

Our focus on organizations advocating for youth provides a useful lens on a relatively under-studied area—youth policy at the local level—as shaped by their local context and more distant forces. Young people grow up in communities, not in programs or categorical initiatives, and local decisions about the resources associated with youth-focused policies and programs—whatever their origin—ultimately matter most in the kinds of experiences they have and the opportunities afforded them. Communities are the settings in which the situated and specific needs of youth can be understood and addressed; communities are the places where professionals, politicians, and civic leaders can establish priorities for investments in their young people, define locally meaningful indicators of positive outcomes, and push for greater integration of resources across sectors, agencies, and age groups. Communities offer the occasion to embed youth programs and resources in a broader local youth development agenda. The local level is where categorical resources are unbundled, monitored, and used. Decades of implementation research demonstrates that, despite the rhetoric, regulatory systems, mandates, and other trappings that accompany categorical state and federal policies, the "policy" that ultimately matters most is the one made and enacted by local officials and service providers (McLaughlin 2006; Pressman & Wildavsky 1973; Weatherley & Lipsky 1977). Youth advocates must confront and maneuver around particular obstacles as they navigate establishment interests to generate supports for young people.

Our local vantage point illuminates an important gap as well. At the local level, many advocacy and community organizing groups press for services in areas where government and the market have fallen short of need, give voice to local concerns, and encourage changes that benefit community residents. Although the lion's share of advocacy efforts occur at the local level (Reid 2001), little systematic attention has been paid to activities at the local level. Most research undertaken on advocacy organizations has focused on national-level groups and their impact on policy formation, especially as seen in congressional debates (see Andrews & Edwards 2004; Boris & Mosher-Williams 1998).[11] Yet, as we have seen, action and actors at micro or local levels differ in consequential ways from those at macro, or state and national, levels. Local political contexts differ as well in terms of partisan alignment, issues, and access (see, for example, Stone 2001). The experiences of the youth advocacy organizations featured here provide insight into the character of advocacy on the ground—its politics, processes, and parameters. What kinds of agenda are local advocacy groups suited to advance? What are the opportunities and constraints particular to the local level? How do local groups engage pluralism and privilege in advocacy for youth?

The focal cases presented here provide concrete examples of strategies and tactics organizations advocating for youth employed in the different urban contexts of San Francisco and Oakland, California, and so contribute important perspective about how it is possible to advance a positive policy agenda for urban youth. These Bay Area settings present different political opportunity structures, material conditions, youth demographics, and cultural constraints. In short, our approach calls attention to the ways in which *localness* affects the organizations studied.

This research on local youth advocacy also presents an opportunity to consider critical questions that are unexamined by the general literature on advocacy organizations. To understand the built-in tensions confronting advocacy organizations functioning as intermediary organizations, we ask two foundational questions about the work of advocacy and community organizing groups: *What are the structures and strategies that enable organizations advocating for social change to mediate the quicksand of social reform—to operate between movement and establishment? And, what are the opportunities and challenges particular to advocacy for youth at the local level?* The general literature on advocacy organizations provides little guidance on questions of *how* they operate to affect public opinion and public policy. Sociologists have looked at questions of individual participation in social movements and advocacy groups; political scientists have focused on how political institutions and culture influence advocacy and its outcomes (see Andrews & Edwards 2004; Child & Grønbjerg 2007). Neither line of inquiry has considered how advocacy organizations move between citizens and the state, between the powerless and the powerful. In our analyses, we ask how advocacy organizations manage their condition of *betweenness* as they work in the space separating movements and the establishment.

These cases also introduce an issue central to the outcome of advocacy efforts but about which little is known, what we call the *handoff*. Each of our cases uses "outsider" strategies in its efforts to change policy and secure new or different resources for youth. As such, advocacy groups are "frontloaded"; they rely on political, organizational, or other inputs to change the routines of governments and policymaking (Fung 2003). Scholars who examine advocacy efforts, for example, feature influence on agenda setting, shifts in priorities and resource allocation, and entrée to decision makers (see Andrews & Edwards's 2004 synthesis). Yet social policy studies underscore the discomfiting reality that policy adoption (or passage of legislation or acceptance of a new program) does not portend implementation consequences as intended by reformers. Though an essential first step, much more is required to move policy or practice in the desired direction, especially at the local level—will, capacity, and, especially, tenacity. Advocacy groups' nonsystem or third-party status is both a strength—they can push issues in ways elected officials or bureaucrats cannot—but also a liability in that they cannot honcho the critical implementation phase. No studies of advocacy efforts have, to our knowledge, looked beyond political or bureaucratic acceptance of advocates' demands for change to consider what happened next. Did anticipated changes result? Was implementation true to advocates' mission? What standing do advocates' causes continue to have on the public agenda?

Social movement scholars focus on the mobilization of marginal people and groups around the pursuit of a common issue. Organization scholars concentrate their attention on the operation of established organizations by authoritative officers (McAdam & Scott 2005). Little attention is afforded to the process by which an issue passes "from the streets to the suites"—from the rallies and protest movements occurring in the neighborhoods into the corridors of power and the boardrooms of the establishment.[12] Once an advocacy campaign succeeds at the local level, organizations advocating for urban youth "hand off" their mission to bureaucrats or politicians to carry out. New kinds of actors with different repertories of action take over. Although we do not follow advocates' agenda into the suites, we do attend to issues local advocates confront as part of the hand off. We consider the constraints and opportunities they encounter as they strive to ensure positive establishment response to their efforts and continued fidelity to their intent.

Youth advocacy and organizing work happens in a particular time and place, within a specific organizational field, and in particular political and social environments. We examine the ways in which the contexts within which organizations work shape what they are able to do on a local level. All of these organizations are immersed in a rich, rapidly changing lattice of ideas, models, opinions, and pressures. We turn in the next chapter to consider in more detail three contexts that affect youth advocacy on the ground and to describe our approach to understanding how the structure and strategies of these organizations work between movement and establishment to create improved opportunities for youth in urban areas.

2 Understanding Advocacy in Context

TO COMMEMORATE SAN FRANCISCO Mayor Gavin Newsom's first 100 days in office in April 2004, hundreds of supporters gathered to acknowledge his accomplishments on behalf of the city's children and youth and to appeal for continued support. Staff members from many of the city's child advocacy and youth-serving nonprofits were present at the Civic Center, but these adult advocates were peripheral—figuratively and literally—to the gathering's focal point: several hundred young people seated in rows centered in front of the stage, holding signs with slogans including "My parents need to work. Child care now!" and "Who's for Kids and Who's Just Kidding?" The mayor and other public officials stood before these precocious and strategically placed activists, trying to convince surrounding adults that the children at the center of the gathering were central to their thinking as well.[1]

This "2004 Rally for Kids," organized by Coleman Advocates for Children and Youth, was the result of a long-term effort—which began months before the election had been decided—to get the new mayor to prioritize children's issues. Following Newsom's win, Coleman sent an open letter to him from an ad hoc committee of children's organizations, setting forth immediate priorities for Newsom to address to keep San Francisco a child- and family-friendly city. The requests included preserving children's services despite the city budget crisis; appointing a new agency head for the Department of Children, Youth, and Their Families (DCYF) and a new Chief Probation Officer who would be community minded; and expanding health coverage to young adults ages eighteen through twenty-four.[2] The letter closed with one additional request: that the mayor report back to the community after his first 100 days in office on his progress toward realizing these goals for children and families. The letter suggested a date of around April 15 for this public report; Newsom not only complied with that exact date by appearing at the "2004 Rally for Kids," but his remarks to the community that day indicated that he had already begun work on many of Coleman's priorities.

In such ways, advocacy organizations can shape their context. All organizations shape the wider systems by which they are shaped, although some organizations are more active and influential than others. This relationship between organizations and their environment holds true for the advocacy and organizing groups in our study. These organizations attempt to alter political, social, and economic conditions just as these forces simultaneously shape organizations' goals, tactics, and resources. As Coleman's rally with Mayor Newsom suggests, making advocacy and organizing issues prominent through a public forum and taking advantage of political change have helped modify the political climate in San Francisco by giving children and youth a political presence. We believe that taking context into account helps us understand how the organizations in our study operate and how they have been effective or not in their efforts to promote supportive environments for youth. We have already described some of the conditions that organizations advocating for youth confront: changing perspectives on adolescent development, institutional silos, funding challenges, and political obstacles, along with some examples of support for youth development. Here we focus on three of the most prominent contexts—organizational, historical, and political—to understand how they influence, and are influenced by, the organizations we study. In doing so, we draw variously on organizational, social movement, and political science theories.

Three Facets of Context

Organizational Context

We place great emphasis on the organizational context within which organizations that advocate for youth function. Regardless of the level at which individual units operate—local, regional, state, national, international—each must relate to other types of social entities, in particular, other organizations. Moreover, every level of organizational unit serves as at least a potential context for each of the lower levels. Organizations are surrounded, penetrated, and constituted by wider relations and forces that both empower and constrain them. The three organizational context levels that matter most to our study are the organizational set, organizational population, and the organizational field. In addition, the structure of a particular organization provides a context affecting the actions of all its participants. Until the 1960s, students of organizations focused most of their attention on activities within a single organization and did not venture beyond this boundary.

Organization Sets   As students of organizations began during the 1960s to attend more to the importance of the environment within which the organization operated, analysts such as Blau and Scott (1962) and Evan (1966) pointed out the utility of examining a single "focal" organization and its immediate exchange partners and/or competitors. For example, as described just above, Coleman Advocates collaborated with various other advocacy organizations as they confronted the mayor's office to demand reforms in various city departments and programs. This *organization set* level of analysis encourages the exploration of exchanges among diverse types of organizations (see Williamson 1975), the political processes that emerge when resources are exchanged among unequal partners (see Pfeffer & Salancik 1978), and the types of strategies organizations may employ in relating effectively to their environments (Lawrence & Lorsch 1967; Porter 1980; Thompson 1967). We apply the organization set level in the examination of our three focal cases as they relate to other organizational players (see Chapters 6 and 7).

Organization Population   Stimulated by the work of human ecologists (especially Hawley 1950), organizational scholars during the 1970s called attention to the importance of considering the fate, not simply of a single organization, but of a collection of organizations sharing the same structural features—the equivalent of a species. This "organizational ecology" perspective focused attention on the *organization population*, a collection of organizations sharing the same structure and dependent on the same environmental resources (see Aldrich 1979; Hannan & Freeman 1977, 1989). Members of a population are "commensalistic"—competing for the same resources but also gain legitimacy from the presence of other organizations of the same kind and often cooperate to improve their collective adaptation (Astley 1985). The behavior of an organization is greatly affected by the existence and activities of other organizations belonging to the same population—in our case, other advocacy and community organizing groups. Many of the most important patterns of competitive and cooperative action are determined by the nature of the population of which the organization is a member.

While our study examines in greater detail the structure and work of three advocacy organizations, we also gathered information on the larger population of youth advocacy organizations in the two communities. Many of these organizations concentrate their advocacy efforts on one or another specific set of youth in the community (for example, Asian or African American youth) or carry on their advocacy activities in connection with some type of service program (for example, foster care). We examine these populations found in our two study communities in Chapters 4 and 5.

Organization Field   Because of the number and variety of different organizational and contextual influences on the groups we study, we use the organizational field as the primary level at which to focus our analysis. An *organization field* refers to "those organizations that, in the aggregate, constitute a recognized area of institutional life: key suppliers, resource and product consumers, regulatory agencies, and other organizations that produce similar services or products" (DiMaggio & Powell 1983, p. 148). In the case of advocacy for youth, this field would include not only advocacy and organizing groups, but funders, public agencies, governance systems, and other nonprofit organizations working with and for the youth of a community. In short, it encompasses both the organization set and the organization population levels but adds to this mixture regulatory and funding organizations. By situating organizations in their larger interorganizational context, it encourages attention to important, but often overlooked, features that shape actions and outcomes. For example, funding or regulatory structures may be at state or federal levels, far removed from the communities they affect, and organizations may acquire information and ideas—from newsletters or websites—about how to organize and how to conduct programs from other organizations scattered around the world. The field perspective also allows us to compare and contrast the strategies and structures of both community organizing and professional advocacy groups enabling us to see the connections, traveling of ideas, and reverberations of their efforts both on the ground and across communities, connections that in other studies might be overlooked. Fields undergo changes over time as they develop, mature, decay, and undergo reorganization. These change processes are described below as we discuss the concept of field "structuration."

Many fields are constructed around consensually defined products or services, such as computer companies or banking firms, but others arise from contentious issues and conflicts. For example, Hoffman (1997) studied the field created by the rise of the environmental movement as it battled the chemical industry and lobbied the federal government to adopt and enforce new pollution standards. As Hoffman (1999, p. 352) elaborates:

Where some may define a field around companies with a common product or market . . . I suggest that a field is formed around the issues that become important to the interests and objectives of a specific collection of organizations. Issues define what the field is, making links that may not have previously been present.

In our study of advocacy organizations, we draw heavily on this issue-based conception of field boundaries. Organizations are of interest, not simply because they engage in vital exchanges with youth advocacy organizations (members of the organization set), and not simply because they carry out some of the same types of advocacy activities (members of the organization population), but because they provide funding for, or attempt to regulate the activities of, or are the targets of the reform efforts of youth advocacy organizations (members of the organization field).

Several concepts are particularly important to analysis at the level of the organization field. First among these is organization archetype, meaning "a "set of [organizational] structures and systems that consistently embodies a single interpretive scheme" (Greenwood & Hinings 1993, p. 1055). An organization population contains a collection of organizations adhering more or less closely to a given archetype. A field will contain a limited number of organization archetypes. In Chapter 5, we identify four archetypes found within the population of advocacy organizations of our two communities.

A second concept is an organization's repertoire of action, understood as the ways in which similar types of organizations carry on their work. Just as an individual organization is associated with a distinctive mode of acting, so a field contains a limited number of such repertories. As Hoffman (1997, p. 148) observes, "In setting strategy and structure, firms may choose action from a repertoire of possible options, but the range of that repertoire is bound by the rules, norms, and beliefs of the organizational field."

Institutional logics are another field-level component. These logics, as defined by Friedland and Alford (1991, p. 248) are "a set of material practices and symbolic constructions which constitutes its organization principles and which is available to organizations and individuals to elaborate." That is, in addition to a limited repertoire of activities, a field is characterized by shared conceptions of the work to be done or the types of problems confronted. Thus, two broad types of institutional logics we will encounter in this field are those associated with community organization—cultivating participant skills and creating opportunities for democratic involvement—and with policy advocacy—

bringing pressure to bear on political leaders and holding them accountable for promises made.

Finally are organizations' governance systems: regimes or control systems that exercise oversight and enforce compliance at the field level. As defined by Scott and colleagues (2000, pp. 172–173), "*Governance structures* refer to all those arrangements by which field-level power and authority are exercised involving, variously, formal and informal systems, public and private auspices, regulative and normative mechanisms." Many of these structures reflect the power and actions of wider national and state-level systems; others are field specific. Public systems are always accompanied, and sometimes undermined, by private governance systems—some formalized as associations, others operating through more informal means. Governance structures are invariably shaped by the views and interests of the more powerful field participants. These organizations work to shape rules and logics so as to preserve the stability of the field, as well as their own dominant role in it (Fligstein 2001a). In the youth development field at the community level, organizations such as school districts and systems of juvenile justice exercise disproportionate influence on how youth are viewed, managed, and "treated."

Each of the above concepts should be viewed as subsuming clusters of variables that differ in value over time and across fields. There may, for example, be more or less consensus on the institutional logics employed in a field. This variance is captured in the general concept, "field structuration," but this concept is best explicated after discussing the importance of attending not only to the organization, but also to the political and historical context.

Political Context

Advocacy organizations, at national, state, and local levels, primarily exist to influence political decisions and to shape policies and programs. It is important, however, to emphasize that, in countries like the United States, politics is not monopolized by public institutions and officials—the formal apparatus of the nation-state. Citizens have and exercise the right to assemble, petition, and protest conditions affecting their well-being and do so visibly through structured community organizing groups. An influential third sector—composed of voluntary associations and nonprofit organizations—acts in various capacities, as a watchdog, goad, mobilization agent, political educator, and institutional entrepreneur, providing an independent forum and voice speaking truth to power. Free, albeit commercially driven, media encourage transparency and dissent, allowing ideas across the political spectrum to circulate and be considered. Private, for-profit organizations also attempt to influence political decisions, and many offer programs and services affecting the public good. While all of these and other devices and safeguards can hardly be said to function flawlessly at all times, they do provide vital opportunities for supporting opposition and reform of public institutions and widen access to the political process.

Advocacy and community organizations devote much effort to the shaping of public policy. This effort inevitably involves at least two major phases: (1) attempts to formulate goals and mobilize interest and energy around a program or plan; and (2) if successful, efforts to guide and monitor the implementation of policies and programs. Almost always, the players in these two phases vary, as do the rules of the game (Bardach 1977; Wilson 1973). We are aided in our examination of mobilization processes by a variety of arguments and concepts formulated by political sociologists, in particular, ideas associated with social movement theory (Davis et al. 2005). Movement scholars have identified three concepts of particular interest to the study of advocacy organizations.

First are emergent forms, which are forms of organization that enable suppressed or marginal actors to come together in the pursuit of common objectives. Whereas most conventional students of organizations attend exclusively to established forms, movement scholars have demonstrated the value of extending interest to newly emergent forms. Conventional modes of organizing may be unavailable to disadvantaged groups. For example, at the turn of the twentieth century, women in the United States were denied the vote and thus forced to turn to alternative modes of political expression (Clemens 1993, 1997). Movement theorists attend to the various types of collective vehicles by which such groups mobilize to engage in concerted action. Often the building blocks are friendship networks or other informal systems. Various grassroots settings—work, neighborhood, church, prison—may play a critical role in facilitating the connection of people who then discover common interests.

Second are framing processes, understood as the "collective processes of interpretation, attribution, and social construction that mediate between opportunity and action" (McAdam, McCarthy, & Zald 1996, p. 2). Movement analysts have proposed the concept of *cultural frames* to capture the beliefs, assumptions, and definitions that shape participants' interpretations of situations, and the more active notion of *framing processes* to emphasize that cultural frames are not fixed but constantly being shaped and modified. As Benford and Snow

(2000, p. 614) comment: the notion of framing "denotes an active, processural phenomenon that implies agency and contention at the level of reality construction." As we will see, the framing of problems and of policy options is one of the most important activities undertaken by advocacy organizations in their work to mobilize collective action. We explore these concepts as they relate to our case study organizations in Chapter 7.

And third are political opportunities, meaning the openings and inconsistencies presented by existing governance structures that allow for the introduction of novel ideas, excluded groups, and suppressed interests. Whereas, as noted above, organization theorists (and conventional political scientists) attend to the structure and functioning of established governance systems, social movement scholars search for ruptures and weaknesses in reigning power systems that offer possible routes to power for excluded groups (McAdam & Scott 2005). More positively, policy scholars speak of "windows of opportunity" that can open to support fundamental political and social reforms (Kingdon 1984).

To the extent that mobilization efforts prove to be successful, established governing systems are confronted by new demands and enjoined to enact and implement new policies. A large scholarly literature has grown up since the 1970s to discuss the ways in which existing (and sometimes, newly created) authorities implement new policies and programs (see, for example, Bardach 1977; Peterson, Rabe, & Wong 1986; Pressman & Wildavsky 1973). While this literature increasingly recognizes the difficulties and challenges posed in carrying out new policies and programs, to date relatively little attention has been devoted to what we term the "handoff" process—the ways in which external reform groups who have been successful in passing a new law or initiative work to ensure that the original intent of the reform is reflected in the programs that are implemented. Our analysis will deal with this important moment of transition (see Chapter 7).

Advocacy organizations often employ a limited range of strategies or tactics as they attempt to initiate or reform specific policies or programs. However, other organizations, particularly community organizers, embrace a longer-term approach as they endeavor to build the capacity of neighborhood groups or foster the growth of youth leadership. As part of their repertoires, some organizations focus primarily on outcomes—on achieving specific, palpable objectives—whereas others focus more on process—not attending so much to what was accomplished as to the ways in which the capacity of the community for self-governance has been enhanced and political intelligence cultivated.

Some organizations are more confrontational, while others seek compromise and inclusion in the inner circles of the establishment. Advocacy organizations and community organizers may choose to operate independently, or they may prefer to cultivate wider networks of support. However, irrespective of such tactical and strategic choices, all such organizations confront a volatile political environment. The political aspects of fields are ever changing. They are regularly punctuated by election cycles; they are conditioned by changing issues and disturbed by unexpected events, both within the field and in the wider environment. Both problems and solutions go in and out of favor. All too often agencies and advocacy groups discover that they are no longer the "flavor of the month."

As noted, the policy process involves two phases, and while advocates and community organizations participate actively in phase one, the second phase—that of policy implementation—extends into the realm of established organizations. When new initiatives or laws are passed and new programs launched, they commonly fall under the jurisdiction of existing political bodies that assume responsibility for and authority over agencies empowered to implement the policies and oversee program operations. A large policy and political science literature details the extent to which government organizations operate somewhat autonomously of other institutions (Evans, Rueschemeyer, & Skocpol 1985) and examines the kinds of incentives and constraints that guide the decisions and actions of officials (Fesler & Kettl 1991; Rainey 1991; Wilson 1989). However, although there exist some independence and insulation of these agencies from external pressure groups, a substantial change beginning during the early decades of the twentieth century and building over time involves the increasing ability of various interest groups to penetrate, monitor, and influence ongoing program activities, as we discuss below.

Historical Context

Social events occur not only in specific places but in particular times. We collected most of our community-level field data during the years 2003 through 2005. Had we done the study in 1960 or in 1980, our findings would have been different. It is important that analysts specify the conditions and types of actors operating at the time events of interest are occurring. It is also important to take into account the historical processes leading up to the conditions and events observed. As we have noted in Chapter 1 and will elaborate below, ideas concerning youth—who they are and the nature of their needs—have changed over time. Many institutional and organizational arrangements were constructed in earlier times and continue to reflect these varying cultural frames and social logics. The origins and development of the newer challenging frames and logics, and the organizations they nurtured, also need to be examined.[3] The following review provides a brief summary of some of the more salient historical changes that have influenced the current structure of advocacy groups in American society.

Changes in Advocacy Groups

Several scholars have provided expert guidance to changes over time in the forms and processes of political action. We focus particularly on work examining changes in interest and advocacy groups—important foci for interest aggregation and mobilization—within the United States during the twentieth century. Three trends are identified representing changes affecting the wider societal level. In this sense, they are exogenous to the specific field of youth development.

Inventing Alternatives to the Politics of Parties   As we know from the *Federalist Papers* and Madison's early concern with factions, interest groups have existed since, and indeed prior to, the founding of the republic (Berry 1989). But, as Clemens (1997) describes in her revealing history of the evolution of interest representation during the period 1880 to 1930 (especially the Progressive Era), interest groups that had earlier been viewed as narrow and corrupt expressions of "special interests" came to be seen as legitimate modes of political participation. Changing political norms endorsed a "hybrid regime of party and extrapartisan organizations" (pp. 3–4). Through the organizing efforts of farmers' and, particularly, women's groups, new legitimate modes of political expression were cobbled together. Excluded at that time from the franchise and other conventional modes of participation, women "created alternative channels for attempting to influence policy outcomes" (p. 3), becoming more directly involved in legislative activity:

> Guided less by loyalty to party than in the past, voters learned to monitor the legislative process, to intervene in shaping policy, and to hold their representatives accountable at the polls. The new currency of political influence included procedural mastery, technical expertise, and the ability to mobilize public opinion. These new organizational capacities were accompanied by new patterns of political action. (Clemens 1997, p. 1)

These are among the basic techniques employed by the advocacy organizations that are the subject of our study.[4]

From Lay Membership to Professional Staff   The historically prominent role of membership organizations in the United States, documented as far back as midnineteenth century by Tocqueville, has been the starting point for much contemporary analysis of American exceptionalism in its approach to social life (Lipset 1996). However, the landscape of civic engagement has changed. Membership organizations have declined in strength during the past century. Putnam (2000) has assembled a variety of types of data to document what he regards as a precipitous and alarming withdrawal by individuals in the United States from social life in this country. And Skocpol (1999, 2003) has assembled data on the largest American membership associations as of the 1950s, to examine membership trends.[5] Her sample includes labor and farm organizations, veterans' and male service clubs like Rotary and Kiwanis, female organizations such as the American Association of University Women and the League of Women Voters, and a number of fraternal organizations. Beginning during the 1960s, most of these associations have suffered substantial membership losses—ranging in the period 1955 to 1995 from a 13 to a 92 percent decline. Only four experienced membership gains.[6]

In their heyday, these large membership associations shared a number of characteristics. Although many recruited members across class lines, most were organized along gender or racial lines. The majority were multitiered, with units organized at local, state, and national levels. More important, most of these associations were organized and largely staffed by volunteer members, not professional administrators, and so provided important opportunities for civic participation and for leadership training and mobility. Using data on the membership of the state senate of Massachusetts as an example, Skocpol (1999) shows that in earlier periods, very high proportions of senators claimed membership in one or more of these associations, whereas this is no longer the case.

Although membership organizations declined in strength, the last quarter of the twentieth century witnessed an "explosion" of advocacy organizations (Berry 1995). With the social upheaval of the 1960s, new social movements and forms of participation emerged and "membership federations were no longer where the action is" (Skocpol 1999, p. 467). This explosion of "rights movements" in the 1960s—spreading like wildfire from civil rights to women's rights to gay rights to environmental protection and other causes—dramatically altered the landscape of American political participation (Andrews

& Edwards 2004; Jenkins 2006). While some "new" traditional forms of membership participation were created during this period, for example, the Southern Christian Leadership Conference (SCLC) and the National Organization for Women (NOW), most of the organizations formed after 1970 assumed a new template: that of the professional advocacy organization.

The newer forms substitute professional staff for voluntary leadership and transform the role of members from active participants to "consumers with policy preferences" (Skocpol 1999, p. 492). Members may attend programs or "events" organized by staff, but for many participation is limited to financial support—"checkbook" activism. While this mode of organizing does not apply to all of the newer advocacy organizations, including some of those in our own study, this new organizational vocabulary applies to many of those founded since 1970 and affects the operation of all. These changes have raised contemporary concerns about the health of American democracy. Social scientists, notably Robert Putnam (2000), assert that Americans are increasingly withdrawing from civic life, as documented by declining voting rates and dwindling participation in social and political associations. Although these national-level trends offer cause for alarm, it is not obvious that they reflect important developments at the community level, where involvement and participation in civic matters can still be observed.

Changes in Mission and Function   The "cycle of protest" (Tarrow 1994) that commenced during the 1960s in this and other Western countries was fueled by a range of emotion-laden issues, from the anti-Vietnam War actions to the civil and women's rights crusades. Employing data assembled for the United States by the *Encyclopedia of Associations* during the period 1955 through 1985, Minkoff (2002) reports a substantial increase in the total number of women's and racial-ethnic organizations founded commencing during the late 1960s and early 1970s. She observed that the majority of these organizations fused traditional service provision with advocacy, creating the rapid growth of "hybrid" forms. Minkoff suggests that this might be viewed as a bridging strategy, building community support on "the legitimacy of established organizational forms and taking advantage of previously institutionalized resource flows" (2002, p. 384; see also Minkoff 1994).

The other type of change observed in comparing newer with earlier populations of organizations involves a shift in mission from serving "role-based" to "identity-based" interests of members. In general, nineteenth-century organizations were rooted in roles, variously serving workers, or farmers, or parents and teachers, or automobile drivers. More recently, a higher proportion of associations and advocacy groups are being organized around issues of *identity*, including gender (women and gays or lesbians), ethnicity (blacks, Hispanics, Asian Americans), and alcohol or drug abuse issues.[7] This transition is described by Armstrong (2002) in her studies of the gay and lesbian population of organizations in San Francisco. She notes a fundamental transformation, during the late 1960s and early 1970s, in the underlying logics guiding the political activity of these groups. She argued that many of them shifted from an "interest group political logic" to an "identity political logic" (p. 371). The former presumes a level playing field and a network of competing interest groups. The goal of organizations representing gay interests is to lobby for antidiscrimination laws and improved opportunities. And, for these organizations, a professional staff structure is the preferred mechanism. By contrast, identity-based groups are primarily concerned with reducing alienation and improving opportunities for authentic self-expression among their members. Rather than lobbying for political advantage, these groups "focus on identity preservation, elaboration, celebration, and display" (p. 372). Instead of seeking unity among all members within a social category as a means of increasing political power, as interest groups would attempt, identity groups are content to protect, advance, and find occasions for expressing the identity of a particular subgroup. Hence, these latter groups exhibit varied forms of organization but tend to be smaller, more informal, and less reliant on professional staff.

We would expect these broader trends to be reflected in the characteristics and postures of the organizations we examine in the field of youth development. Indeed, as we will show, first, all of the organizations in our study populations embrace some portion of the vocabulary of interest-based organizations seeking in one way or another to advance the cause of their constituency. Virtually all of them attempt to *directly* affect the political process—by proposing legislation, mobilizing citizens, educating members, and extracting promises from political officials and attempting to hold them accountable. In this sense, all of the organizations in our populations reflect the general societal trend during the past 100 years that supplement (and sometimes replace) a reliance on the politics of political parties with more direct political influence approaches.

Second, most of the advocacy organizations in our study do not rely on lay members for leadership but rather depend on the organizing and mobilizing skills of a cadre of professional leaders. However, there are important exceptions and caveats to this generalization, as we will see in subsequent chapters.

Third, only a few of the members of our populations of advocacy organizations focus on identity as opposed to interests as a basis for organizing. We will describe these exceptional cases in the following chapters, as appropriate.

In these and related ways, the youth development field has been shaped by wider historical developments occurring in the wider society. We turn now to a brief review of some of the factors at work over time within the field of youth development.

Changing Institutional Logics

An explicit focus on youth development did not emerge on the U.S. scene until the late 1980s, although, of course, there had been some attention to the distinctive problems of children and youth much earlier (see Chapter 1). A focus on youth development does not represent so much a new target for reform but a new stance: in our terms, a new *institutional logic.* Changes in logics entail a revision in our interpretation of a social situation and what it requires. Here we observe attempts to reframe the understanding of youth and their needs and, consequently, alteration of the approaches employed to address them.

We believe it useful to identify three dominant institutional logics that have been employed with respect to youth in this country. All still have their advocates and adherents and the logics are often blended, but they may be characterized distinctly. First is the view of *youth as problems*—that they are victims, deviants, or "stubborn" (Deschenes, Cuban, & Tyack 2001; Sutton 1988). Within this frame, attention is focused on only selected youth—those viewed as troubled or out of control. Logics and repertoires of action center on what can be done *to* these individuals. Illustrative approaches include punishment, incarceration, and providing controlled environments, such as mental health facilities or foster homes.

Second is the view of *youth as clients,* meaning they are recipients of professional services. Here the focal population is somewhat broadened to include "exceptional" youth, both those with special needs such as autistic or mentally retarded youth or, at the other extreme, those viewed as particularly gifted or talented. Here the logics and modes of intervention center on what can be done *for* the individual. The orientation emphasized more positive approaches, such as therapy, education, or recreation, but remains primarily paternalistic.

Finally is the view of youth as *valuable potential resources* to be cultivated and empowered. Here the purview is greatly broadened to include the full range of youth, not just those with special needs or special gifts. Logics, which emphasize leadership, empowerment, and the cultivation of a wide range of physical, intellectual, and social skills, center around what can be done *with* young people; in particular, what they can be helped to do for themselves.

While, as noted, all three logics are in play at this time—indeed, the first two logics undergird the established sectoral structures embodied in juvenile homes and detention facilities, conventional schools, and welfare approaches—the youth development arena endeavors to advance the third logic, stressing the capabilities of youth for self-development and self-fulfillment.

As we will describe, our advocacy populations represent a "mixed bag" of logics. None embraces a pure version of the "youth as problem" logic—which would be characteristics of some more punitive juvenile justice and educational policies. Many of our population organizations embrace the second "youth as client" logic, in particular those that combine advocacy with service. Others embrace, to a greater or lesser extent, the youth development logic of "youth as resources" to be nurtured and empowered. A considerable number of the smaller organizations in our populations express this logic in their work with distinctive collections of youth—Asian, African American, women, gay-lesbian-transgender—offering them training in leadership, community organizing, and varying modes of self-advocacy.[8]

Field Structuration

While not a felicitous term, *structuration* is a concept coined by Anthony Giddens (1979, 1984; see also Sewell 1992) to emphasize the truism that social structures are not static frameworks but ongoing processes. Giddens points to the dualistic nature of structures: They serve as both the products of past actions and the context for present actions; structures also combine both symbolic and material elements. Social structures exist only to the extent that they are constantly reproduced, and every enactment works, to a greater or lesser extent, to modify the structure.

DiMaggio and Powell (1983; DiMaggio 1983) have applied the conception of structuration to organizational fields to emphasize the extent to which fields undergo change in the characteristics of organizational actors, their level of interaction and sharing of information, their beliefs and institutional logics, and their governance arrangements. Such change may reflect "top-down" processes—reflecting dominance or status processes from more powerful or superordinate units. Familiar examples of top-down processes are federal regulations, state-level funding flows, or the imitation by some organizations of the behavior of more "successful" organizations. Alternatively "bottom-up" processes may be at work, reflecting adverse response from subordinate units or the mobilization of suppressed interests (Scott 2008a, pp. 190–193). For example, governance arrangements may evolve out of repeated interactions among community-level organizations, or neighborhood groups and church communities may come together to form a coalition to advance their interests.

By definition, structuration processes involve the passage of time, so that a historical perspective is central to structuration analysis. And given our focus on advocacy groups, political and organizational processes are of central interest in attempting to explain how contending groups attempt to structure attention and effort and resources to advance interests they believe to be of vital importance. In Chapter 8, we describe in more detail structuration processes affecting the youth development field at the local and the national level.

In this chapter, we have introduced a number of concepts that we will employ to examine, in their organizational, political, and historical dimensions, the contexts that confront, shape, and serve as the targets for organizations advocating for youth. We next turn to the salient demographic and political features of San Francisco and Oakland as a background for examining the community-level structure of organizations supporting youth.

3 Conditions for Youth in San Francisco and Oakland

IN THE PREVIOUS CHAPTER, we described the major contexts that shape and are shaped by organizations advocating for youth. We now turn to the specific local landscapes in which the organizations we study do their work: the cities of Oakland and San Francisco. We first look to the state level to better understand the policy climate and advocacy activity with respect to youth, as both organization populations in this study share the context of California. With few significant statewide policy achievements to improve programs and services for youth, California has experienced a policy displacement from the state to local communities, making the environment in San Francisco and Oakland all the more important for understanding how the organizations we study operate.

The California Context

The absence of a cohesive and supportive set of policies for youth at the state level in California, whether a result of the structure of the state system or the ineffectiveness of state advocacy organizations, contributes to the challenges as well as the importance of advocacy for youth at the local level. California, despite repeated attempts, has yet to establish a coordinating structure or plan at the state level or to pass youth policies that cut across departmental lines and embrace a more preventive, positive developmental stance.[1] Nonetheless, state-level actions have an impact on the institutions and settings within which California youth grow up, especially in big cities such as San Francisco and Oakland.

The initiative process in California allows voters to put legislation to a direct public vote if at least 5 percent of the electorate signs petitions of support. Proposition 13, which passed in 1978, proved to be quite an effective and powerful initiative proposed by voters. The proposition both lowered property taxes and put a limit on future increases. The effect drastically reduced revenue for local school districts that depend on these taxes, creating distressed schools across the state. Economically strapped communities experienced significant reductions in education budgets and had few local resources to take up the slack. California is now derisively portrayed as having gone from "first to worst," once ranking at the top among states in test scores and per-pupil spending and now ranking at or near the bottom along these measures.

In reaction, state advocacy organizations have led grassroots organizing campaigns to improve conditions at local schools and to reduce funding disparities between individual schools and school districts. Additionally, Proposition 187, which passed in 1994, attempted to deny undocumented immigrants access to most government services, including education. The initiative brought about an anti-immigrant sentiment that led to increased violence in schools and neighborhoods. Although not intentionally aimed at youth, the policy created a groundswell of action and contributed to youth movements advocating social justice and combating issues of racism and violence. Proposition 21, or the "Gang Violence and Juvenile Crime Prevention" initiative, also had a visible impact on the communities we study. The measure passed in 2001 and became widely known as the "three strikes" law, leading to more incarcerations and longer prison time for youth defendants.

On a more positive front, Proposition 10, or First Five initiative, has raised millions of dollars from tobacco taxes for early childhood development. Arnold Schwarzenegger, prior to becoming governor, was able to attract media publicity and raise enough money to campaign for children's after-school programming, resulting in the passage of another voter-approved bill, Proposition 49. This After-School Education and Safety Program, which passed in 2002, earmarks money for after-school programs. Other important victories have occurred, such as the passage of "express lane eligibility" to streamline the process by which poor and working families qualify for health care. State-level advocacy groups such as the California Coalition for Youth and the California Center for Civic Participation and Youth Development have achieved largely symbolic victories as a result of their promoting the importance of youth participation in policy and program development.[2]

The foundation-funded California Children's Policy Council advocated, in the early 1990s, for new state legislation to coordinate the delivery of social services to children most in need. The diverse group of members, representing government, advocacy, service providers, and university interests, were, however, unable to agree on a clear mission or whether they should become an independent advocacy organization, which ultimately led to the councils' demise (Einbinder 2000).

Activists promoting a youth development agenda at the state level have sought out and worked with a few sympathetic lawmakers in state government. But despite a variety of innovative and determined efforts at the state level, policy makers have experienced frustration in their individual attempts to reform the structure and function of youth-serving agencies.

State-level efforts aside, in many ways the local level is a more practical venue for advocacy activity: This is where families and youth experience problems with public institutions most deeply. It is here that families and youth interact with a variety of services and have to navigate the many governmental and nongovernmental bodies that support youth. Hence, the local city context is where the tension between social movements and the establishment is strongest—in our specific case, where the mobilization of families meets the fragmentation of youth policy.

San Francisco and Oakland

San Francisco and Oakland offer particular political, institutional, and economic contexts for youth advocacy. Both cities have innovative approaches to youth services and are recognized as pacesetters in the youth development movement. For example, both cities have passed significant legislation to dedicate public funds to services for children and youth; San Francisco is additionally recognized for providing health care to low-income children and youth, while Oakland has gained national attention for offering health and social services through school-based health centers (J. B. Johnson 2005; Siler 2005). However, significant cultural and historical differences distinguish the context for advocacy in the two cities.

San Francisco has been called the capital of America's progressive movement (DeLeon 1992, quoting Nancy Pelosi, p. 2). Its progressive ideology and populist values promote an expanded role for government in addressing liberal causes such as neighborhood preservation and grassroots voice, public accountability for ethnic and cultural diversity, and a social justice agenda. Observers note that, in San Francisco, everyone is a minority; majorities are made not found (DeLeon 1992). Oakland exhibits little of San Francisco's populist ideology and struggles to address racial and economic inequalities—aspects of the city shaped by federal welfare and urban policies of the 1960s and 1970s

Table 3.1 Race and Ethnicity in Two Cities and Associated Counties[a]

	San Francisco (city and county)	Oakland	Alameda County
Total population	776,733	399,484	1,443,741
White	50%	31%	41%
African American	8%	36%	15%
Asian or Pacific Islander	31%	16%	20%
Latino or Hispanic of any race	14%	22%	19%
Two or more races	4%	5%	4%
Foreign-born population	37%	27%	27%

[a] U.S. Census 2000.

(Self 2003). Issues of class and race dominate Oakland politics, and the city is deeply segregated; the "haves" live in the hills and the "have-nots," approximately two-thirds of the community and primarily of color, live in the economically distressed flatlands.[3] Flatland residents regularly express reactions to neglect and economic exploitation by powers outside their control, in particular state and federal welfare policies (Self 2003). If San Francisco is seen as a city that values *human* development, Oakland's priorities privilege economic development—a focus that has a negative impact on flatland residents.

Many of the differences between the cities as contexts for youth and advocacy also are rooted in an overarching structural distinction between the two cities: San Francisco is distinct among American cities as a city/county hybrid; Oakland is the largest city within Alameda County.[4] Because many services for youth are coordinated at the county level, youth and organizations advocating for them have different access to services and programs in the two cities.

Demographics

San Francisco and Oakland both rank among the most ethnically diverse urban areas in the country. San Francisco's largest ethnic group is Asian; Oakland's, African American (see Table 3.1). African Americans came to work in the Port of Oakland during World War II; the city has the largest concentration of African Americans among any northern California city. Oakland has undergone waves of recent immigration, over 30,000 people between 1990 and 2000.[5] Other demographic changes created contentious ethnic divides between black residents and Latinos, who began to arrive in larger numbers in the 1980s.[6] However, San Francisco has a much larger foreign-born population,

Table 3.2 Demographics for Residents Under Eighteen

	San Francisco	Oakland
Population 0–17 (2000)[a]	121,802	99,759
Percent of population under 18	14%	25%
Households with residents under 18[b]	19%	33%
Race and Ethnicity 0–17 (2000)[a]		
African-American	11%	39%
Asian and Pacific Islander	38%	15%
Hispanic	22%	30%
White	23%	11%
Two or more races	6%	5%

[a]Annie E. Casey Foundation 2004a.
[b]Annie E. Casey Foundation 2005.

more than three times that of the country as a whole.[7] The diversity of both cities is reflected in the advocacy and community organizing groups that focus their efforts on particular racial and ethnic populations, such as Community Educational Services in San Francisco, which focuses on Chinese American students, or School of Unity and Liberation in Oakland (SOUL), which targets Oakland youth of color.

In both cities, the youth population differs in some important ways from the overall population. (See Table 3.2.) White residents comprise almost half of the population of San Francisco, yet less than a quarter of the city's youth are white. A pressing concern in San Francisco is the fact that it has the smallest percentage of children (19 percent) of any major U.S. city,[8] and it is the only major city that has recently experienced a decline in its child population while simultaneously experiencing an overall population increase.[9] Many families leave the city due to the high cost of living (Crawford 2005). This out-migration has been particularly pronounced among San Francisco's African American population; there were 43 percent fewer African American families with children in the city in 2000 than in 1990 (Blash et al. 2005). After African Americans, families with children under six are the most likely group to say they will move out of the city in the next three years (Blash et al. 2005). In response, San Francisco Mayor Gavin Newsom has appointed a special twenty-nine-member Policy Council for Children, Youth, and Families to address how the city can keep families with children as residents.

Attending to the needs of San Francisco's children might seem an easier task since there are simply fewer children to worry about. But the low percentage of children in San Francisco makes it easier for voters to overlook their needs in the service of other causes. As Margaret Brodkin, former Executive Director of Coleman Advocates for Children and Youth said of San Francisco, "You have liberal politics but you don't have many kids so it's a different kind of dynamic, like 'Why should we care?' "[10] Youth issues have not typically been at the top of the city's priority list, in part because of the size of the constituency and its lack of political power but also because the city over the past decade has had other major issues to focus on, including gay rights, the 1990s bursting technology bubble, and a lack of affordable housing.

Oakland, by contrast, has both a higher percentage of households with children and more children in need. Although Oakland's overall population has remained relatively stable over the last decade, the youth population has increased significantly in certain neighborhoods of the city with the large influx of Latino and Asian families. The city's population of children and youth is close to the national average of 26 percent.[11] Oakland organizations, therefore, are not required to expend as much energy to focus public attention on youth but, as we will see, they do confront racial politics. They must also contend with a child and youth population that is more economically distressed.

Economics

San Francisco has a relatively wealthy adult population, with the third highest median income ($60,031) in the United States in 2004 (J. Johnson, 2005). It is a major commercial center with a thriving financial district and a large philanthropic community. Housing prices are four times the average cost of similar housing in other U.S. cities (Alameda County Public Health Department, 2004). The city's lack of moderately priced housing may be one reason San Francisco's poverty rate is among the ten lowest in the country's big cities (J. Johnson, 2005). Families able to afford expensive housing and private schools continue to live in the city, while those in the middle income brackets find it difficult to remain there (Crawford 2005). Thus, the relatively few children in San Francisco are doing well by standard metrics of child welfare compared to other big cities. San Francisco has the smallest number of children under 18 living below the poverty level out of twelve major cities,[12] and few of San Francisco's children (16.1 percent) live in areas of concentrated poverty.[13] However, San Francisco's dwindling middle class means that the city's income distribution is somewhat bimodal—the wealthy and the poor, who are disproportionately families with children.

The Oakland housing market is less pricey, but many low- and moderate-income families are still unable to buy or rent a home and so leave the city. Even though average incomes increased between 1990 and 2000, the home-ownership rate in Oakland fell during that decade to 41 percent, making Oakland rank eighty-seventh in homeownership among the 100 largest cities (Brookings Institution 2003).

The low rate of homeownership in Oakland reflects the city's high poverty rate. Oakland is ranked tenth in the nation for child poverty levels and has more than twice as many families living below the poverty level as does San Francisco; moreover, Oakland has over three times the number of children and youth living in areas of concentrated poverty as compared to San Francisco (see Table 3.3). The bulk of the city's youth live in the lower-income areas of East Oakland and are Latino or African American (Gibson & Associates 2005b). Other parts of the city with concentrated poverty include West Oakland (with poverty rates greater than 40 percent), San Antonio, downtown, Chinatown, and Fruitvale—neighborhoods that comprise the economically marginalized "flatlands" of Oakland that border the Bay. Advocacy organizations working on behalf of youth in Oakland confront a more economically deprived and racially divided constituency than do their counterparts in San Francisco.

Government

San Francisco is governed by a Board of Supervisors, while Oakland has both a city council and a Board of Supervisors for Alameda County. Alameda is split into five large districts that are governed by a five-member Board of Supervisors. The geographic region of Oakland spans the boundaries of three of the counties districts. San Francisco, a smaller city geographically, is split into eleven small districts. Both cities also have youth commissions that serve as advisors to the mayor, though San Francisco's commission plays a more active role in city politics than does Oakland's.

The political decision-making process in each of these cities creates opportunities and barriers for youth advocates. San Francisco has a reputation for significant public access to the political process through its Sunshine Ordinance, which requires that most government meetings be open. This requirement works to the advantage of advocates. However, it is also a city with an uncommonly large number of commissions, which slows down the policy process because interest groups can continue to call for additional hearings.

Table 3.3 Poverty in Two Cities

	San Francisco	Oakland
Families living below poverty level[a]	8%	16%
Population under 18 living below poverty level[b]	14%	28%
Population under 18 living in neighborhoods of concentrated poverty[c]	16%	58%
Single-female heads of households living with children under 18[d]	39%	56%
Percentage of families receiving public assistance[e]	24%	47%

[a]U.S. Bureau of the Census 2000.
[b]Annie E. Casey Foundation, KIDSCOUNT 2000.
[c]Annie E. Casey Foundation, KIDSCOUNT 2000. Concentrated poverty is defined as areas where 20% or more of the population is below the poverty line.
[d]Lopez2001.
[e]U.S. Bureau of the Census 2000.

In Oakland, by contrast, the political atmosphere is more relaxed, giving residents access to their politicians rather than access to just the policy-making process. As one Oakland official described it: "In San Francisco the protocol is so intense . . . Oakland is more casual. People have much more access to the chief of police, for example, and it operates more like a small town."[14]

In 1998, Oakland voters approved a "Strong Mayor" initiative which gave the city a stronger executive branch (Walker 1998a,b). According to the Economic Development Alliance for Business, former Mayor Jerry Brown's "pro-business climate" aimed to lower the cost of doing business to attract new companies to Oakland and has attracted some new industries. *Forbes Magazine* rates Oakland among the best U.S. cities in which to do business.[15] Still, the city's unequal income distribution across the population continues to be greater than that of the county, the state, and the nation (Alameda County Public Health Department 2004). Moreover, advocacy organizations have sometimes challenged the city's progrowth policies when they have conflicted with their campaigns to improve resources and services for youth.

Funding for Youth

Funding for youth services in both the public and nonprofit sectors is varied and complex, coming from many different revenue streams and levels of government, as well as from private foundations. Federal and state dollars for child and youth services have been on the decline, so local municipalities have assumed more responsibility for funding these services. Although it is an incomplete account of resources that are spent on services for children and youth—leaving out funding for educational and juvenile justice systems, for example—each city's dedicated funds for such programs (through the Department of Children, Youth and Families in San Francisco [DCYF] and Oakland Fund for Children and Youth in Oakland [OFCY]) offer a sense of the relative resources available. OFCY's annual budget of about $10 million is used to provide programs and services for about 20,000 children, which amounts to about $500 per child annually. DCYF in San Francisco has a significantly higher budget; it spends about $44 million to serve 28,000 children annually, which amounts to over $1,500 per child.

The number of foundations in San Francisco and Oakland provides an important but imperfect indicator of support from the third sector. San Francisco has a larger philanthropic community than Oakland, with 769 foundations, in contrast to only seventy-nine in Oakland.[16] These numbers do not provide an accurate guide to the respective philanthropic communities, however, because many of these foundations make grants across cities, regions, and states.[17]

Public Support Systems for Youth in San Francisco and Oakland

Figure 3.1 depicts an array of government agencies and third sector organizations that serve youth in Oakland and San Francisco. Local systems that support youth's healthy development operate within a broader context of state and national agencies and categorical programs. Local public sectors—including education, social services, public health, juvenile justice, and community development—and generalized governmental units at the city and county level provide the lion's share of services and set the prevailing tone for the treatment of youth in each city.

Both San Francisco and Oakland have multiple departments and agencies that affect conditions for youth. (See Tables 3.4 and 3.5.) The Robert Wood Johnson Foundation's Urban Health Initiative found in Oakland alone at least thirteen different public agencies delivering services to children, including two federal agencies, one state agency, six county agencies, and four city agencies. Two more independent agencies operate outside of the city government: the Oakland Unified School District (OUSD) and the Oakland Housing Authority.

In San Francisco, at least 11 county- and city-based agencies or commissions serve youth.[18] The well-being and safety of youth pose significant, though

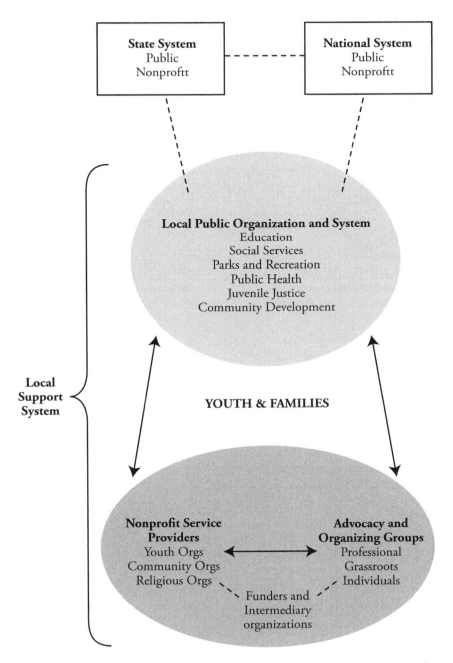

Figure 3.1 Field-Level Diagram of Institutions and Organizations Supporting Youth. The light shaded area includes *public* agencies analyzed in this chapter; the dark shaded area includes private organizations discussed in the next chapter.

Table 3.4 Public Agencies Serving Oakland Youth

Federal	State
Social Services Agency (SSA)-OASDI and SSI	California Youth Authority
Health and Human Services (HHS)	
County	**City**
Social Services Agency (SSA)	Life Enrichment Agency
Health Care Services Agency	Police Services
Probation	Community and Economic
Sheriff's Office	Development Agency
District Attorney	
Public Defender	Oakland Fund for Children and Youth (OFCY)

County and *City* headers are italicized; *Federal* and *State* are italicized.

Table 3.5 Public Agencies Serving San Francisco Youth

Federal	State
Social Services Agency (SSA)-OASDI and SSI	California Youth Authority
Health and Human Services (HHS)	
County and City	
Department of Children, Youth and Their Families	
Children and Families Commission	
Human Services Commission	
Juvenile Probation Commission	
Juvenile Probation Department	
Child Support Services	
Department of Human Services	
Recreation and Park Department	
Department of Public Health	
San Francisco Unified School District	
Youth Commission	

somewhat different, issues in each city. Though Oakland might struggle with more entrenched poverty and fewer resources than San Francisco, youth in both cities have serious needs in the areas of housing, education, employment, health, and safety. In Oakland, 56 percent of children live in families where no parent has full-time, year-round employment; in San Francisco, that figure is 45 percent.[19] Family economics pose serious problems for youth in both cities.

Foster care placements in Oakland have been declining in recent years, and teen pregnancy in Oakland dropped by half between 1990 and 2002 (Gibson

& Associates 2005a). While youth arrests decreased 12 percent between 2000 and 2003, homicide continues to be the leading cause of death for the city's youth between fourteen and nineteen years old (Gibson & Associates 2005a).

Violence plagues both cities, though Oakland's problems are much more severe. In terms of crime and violence, in 2007 Oakland was rated the fourth most dangerous city in America;[20] San Francisco doesn't make the top fifty. Both cities struggle with a significant gang problem. Safety concerns are the impetus for many of the campaigns that advocacy and organizing groups in both cities undertake, including efforts to improve after-school programming and violence prevention programs.

The most prominent specialized *public* institutions concerned with the safety and well-being of youth are Department of Children, Youth and Their Families in San Francisco, and Oakland Fund for Children and Youth (schools, health, juvenile justice, and social services). For the most part these agencies deliver services in traditional ways, but there is some recent movement to employ youth development practices in both cities.

DCYF and OFCY

Despite having so few children, San Francisco has created significant public structures dedicated to children and youth in the city. According to Coleman Advocates, in 1991 San Francisco became the first U.S. city to set aside funding for children each year in the city budget. This new policy, known as the Children's Amendment, or Proposition J, was enacted through a voter-led initiative that ensured a dedicated 2.5 percent of the city's property tax for services for children and youth.[21] The amendment was reauthorized in 2000, and the set-aside was increased to 3 percent. The public agency in charge of administering these funds is the city's Department of Children, Youth and Their Families (DCYF). DCYF provides grants to community-based organizations and city agencies (200 in 2003–2004); creates partnerships across the city to support youth in their employment, education, health, and safety; and is conducting an evaluation and planning initiative to make the best use of The Children's Fund. DCYF also coordinates the Citizens' Advisory Committee, which advises on the use of the fund, and the Mayor's Children's Cabinet, a partnership of departments and agencies providing youth services. The Fund's youth evaluation component, Youth IMPACT, is part of the Department's effort to bring youth voice into the planning process, evidence of the city's growing interest in youth development. According to one resident, DCYF "creates a forum where everyone has to come play," in contrast to Oakland where the city is interested in "just serving. . . . It's every man for himself."[22] In an ironic twist, however, San Francisco's Mayor Gavin Newsom has quipped that the city has developed all these resources, but with the declining child population there will be no youth left in the city to benefit from them (Crawford 2005).

Following on the heels of San Francisco's voter-approved Children's Fund, in November 1996 over three-quarters of Oakland voters approved the Kids First! Initiative, or Proposition K, an amendment to the City Charter that created the Oakland Fund for Children and Youth (OFCY). Like San Francisco's Children's Fund, Proposition K earmarks 2.5 percent of the city's unrestricted General Purpose Fund to support direct services to youth under twenty-one years of age. The Planning and Oversight Committee, with representatives from the city and local community-based organizations, including youth, acts as an advisory body to the fund and provides recommendations to the mayor and city council.[23]

Education and Schools

San Francisco and Oakland both struggle to provide a more equitable public education system by raising the achievement of minority students and distributing district resources to address the special needs of youth at risk. San Francisco, as a result of a 1983 desegregation consent decree, operates a lottery system for school assignments to balance student populations across the city's schools. Although the lottery achieves greater racial and ethnic parity within and across schools than would a system of neighborhood schools, the lottery also deters families who do not want their children to endure long bus rides from sending their children to public schools—a reality that has prompted families who cannot afford private school tuition to leave the city (Crawford 2005). The San Francisco Unified School District has lost about 4,500 students in the past six years and is expected to lose another 4,000 more in the next five years—significant numbers given its total enrollment of about 57,000. Declining student enrollment, coupled with state funding cuts and rising employment costs, caused the district to close five schools in 2005 and was projected to lead to another ten to twenty school closures in the upcoming year.[24]

Oakland Unified School District (OUSD), which serves a higher proportion of non-English-speaking learners than both the county and the state,[25] also is experiencing enrollment declines and school closures. OUSD enrollment has declined by 6,000 students since 1999, prompting the controversial closure of about seven underenrolled and low-performing schools in 2005, with more school closures likely in upcoming years.[26] Between 1997 and 2000, OUSD went through major administrative turbulence (three superintendents in three years) accompanied by controversy both locally and nationally over the use of "Ebonics" (black English) in the classroom. In June 2003, Governor Gray Davis approved a $100 million loan to OUSD because of its serious financial troubles and appointed a state administrator for the district, making Oakland the sixth district in California to be taken over by the state.

Both districts serve a significant number of low-income students; more than half of the students in both districts are eligible for free or reduced lunch (55 percent in SFUSD and 72 percent in OUSD).[27] Both school districts are plagued by low achievement and other systemic problems, but Oakland youth are dropping out at a greater rate; OUSD has a little over half the graduation rate of San Francisco (43 percent to 78 percent). However, these district averages mask the substantial differences in school quality and student outcomes between schools. In Oakland, for example, the graduation rate at Skyline High School, in the "hills," is 85 percent, and 45 percent meet course requirements for the University of California; the "flatlands" high school Business, Entrepreneurship School of Technology graduates 69 percent, and only 21 percent of these students meet University of California course requirements. Overall, OUSD high school performance is poor. The most highly rated school received only a 5 (of 10) on the Greatschools rankings; most of Oakland's high schools hovered around a rating of 3.[28] In San Francisco, though the overall performance of SFUSD's high schools is stronger than Oakland's, disparities across high schools are starker. High-performing Lowell, rated 10 by Greatschools and CA's number-one urban high school by the state's academic performance index, serves a predominately Asian population.[29] Across town, Mission High School, with a Greatschools rating of 4, enrolls primarily students of color (Latino and black) and has failed to meet its annual yearly progress goal for three years running; student achievement in English language arts, mathematics, history, and science all fell below both district and state averages.[30] Despite its poor student outcomes relative to SFUSD, Mission High School nonetheless outperformed most of Oakland's best-performing high schools.

Promising Initiatives: A Youth Development Stance

Despite the challenges of declining enrollment and other issues, both districts have undertaken some promising initiatives. The San Francisco Beacon

Initiative, for instance, a partnership between DCYF, the school district, the Juvenile Probation Department, community organizations and private foundations, encompasses eight school-based centers that provide neighborhood-focused youth and family services. Oakland's small schools reform, the focus for our case advocacy organization, has attracted national attention and serves as a model for other districts. With the recent addition of school-based health centers around the district, state and national attention has been paid to envisioning schools as a locus for community activity and social services. A few Oakland schools have been able to recover costs lost from state and federal reimbursement dollars by enrolling and serving low-income eligible families that otherwise would not access services in accredited health care programs on school sites. Given the systemic problems that plague both school districts, many advocacy and organizing groups in both cities have made education reform a central issue in their work.

Health

San Francisco's Department of Public Health is home to the city's Community Health Network (CHN), which encompasses the city's health care providers. Through the CHN, the city offers a variety of services to children, youth and families ranging from prenatal care to dental services. The health department also has services designed specifically for youth offered at four adolescent health clinics in the city. These services include mental health, family planning, HIV testing, and health promotion and life skills training.[31]

San Francisco also has worked toward expanding health care coverage for uninsured children and youth. Healthy Kids, established in 2002, provides low-cost insurance to children and youth not covered under other insurance programs but whose families have incomes below 300 percent of the poverty level. Special attention is also paid in San Francisco to the health of the city's young gay and lesbian population, with a number of organizations dedicated to reaching out to this population. Recently both Mayor Newsom in San Francisco and Oakland's Mayor Ron Dellums explored the idea of universal health care coverage for all city residents, an easier task in San Francisco because of its larger revenue base, populist values, and fewer uninsured residents. Thus, in Oakland, where reforming health care policy at the city and county levels has proved difficult, community and school health care clinics have received special attention for addressing the shortage of school nurses and families' lack of access to decent heath care.[32]

Public health services in Oakland are provided through the Alameda County Public Health Department. This countywide department includes a Community Health Services Division (CHS), which works at the neighborhood level in cities across the county to provide services and health-related public education. The city of Oakland does provide some health services through its Department of Human Services; its children and youth services division provides Head Start, family literacy programs, "Safe Walk to School" (a program that employs adult monitors before and after school to ensure the safety of youth traveling to and from school), and a summer lunch and nutrition program, in addition to administering the Oakland Fund for Children and Youth.

The city of Oakland, with funding from the Robert Wood Johnson Foundation's five-city Urban Health Initiative, initiated Safe Passages, a partnership of city leaders, county agencies, and Oakland schools. The collaborative redirects Oakland's public and private resources to implement strategies to keep kids in school and engaged in positive activities. With the use of four core strategies—early childhood, middle school, youth offenders, and after-school—Safe Passages aims to intervene with kids at critical times when youth are vulnerable and susceptible to getting into trouble, to help them stay focused and provide pathways for healthy and safe development.

Juvenile Justice

Both San Francisco and Oakland are working to restructure their juvenile justice systems to balance the competing need for rehabilitative services and public safety—a longtime concern of many advocates for youth. The disproportionate representation of minorities in the juvenile justice system—especially African Americans—is an issue of particular concern in both San Francisco and Alameda counties and has promoted community calls for reforming the entire process from arrests through detention and probation practices. Given the high costs of incarcerating youth and the detrimental effects of detention (high rates of recidivism; isolation from public institutions, including schools; stigmatizing impact on youth), both cities are trying to implement community-based, rehabilitative alternatives to large detention facilities.

Although San Francisco has its own probation department and Oakland's is part of Alameda County, the two systems have the same basic structure. San Francisco's Juvenile Probation Department encompasses probation services, a short-term juvenile hall facility, and a longer-term residential facility for male juveniles. The Alameda County Probation Department similarly operates a short-term juvenile hall and a longer-term residential facility for male juveniles.

In 1996, San Francisco initiated a major reform effort and spent over $20 million in state and federal funds to implement new programs and services through the Mayor's Criminal Justice Council and the Juvenile Probation Department. Despite this unprecedented investment in reform, however, the city's juvenile detention population increased, and the disproportionate confinement of African American and Hispanic youth worsened (Macallair & Males 2004). The Juvenile Probation Department, however, has taken promising steps toward implementing more effective, community-based programs for youth to meet the special needs of youth offenders, including education and mental health services. The city also has adopted successful strategies from other communities, most notably Orange County's "8 percent plan," that focus on the small group of youth who are at the greatest risk of becoming serious and chronic offenders (Mayor's Office of Criminal Justice and Juvenile Probation Department 2006). This strategy centers on offering intensive, comprehensive services for this population ("wraparound services") rather than sporadic interventions.

The Alameda County Juvenile Justice system, which handles Oakland's youth offenders, faces many of the same issues that San Francisco deals with— the detrimental effects of institutionalizing youth and the overrepresentation of minorities; in both communities reformers call for more local, community-based programs to replace large, county-level detention facilities. Oakland's youth comprise about 48 percent of the county's total juvenile probationers— the greatest concentration of any city in Alameda by far (Alameda County Probation Department 2005). The separation of city and county government structures makes the coordination of services even more difficult in Oakland, and an independent study of Alameda's system highlighted the need for greater coordination among service providers including mental health, substance abuse, education, social services, and community-based organizations (Huskey & Associates 2004). Alameda County's existing Juvenile Hall has been deemed unfit by the County Board of Supervisors and the State Board of Corrections due to overcrowding and its location on an active earthquake fault line. The county plans to build a new comprehensive facility with mental health and educational services and 540 beds to meet the County's needs—a figure that is lower than projections made before the county focused on alternatives to detention.

Social Services

Both San Francisco and Alameda Counties are also striving to reform their child welfare systems to improve outcomes for foster youth. The educational and employment outcomes for foster youth are significantly less promising than that of the regular youth population; emancipated foster youth are more likely to drop out of high school, be unemployed, and rely on welfare. Reform to this system reflects a shift in emphasis to family preservation and away from removing children from their homes if it is not absolutely necessary.

San Francisco's number of children in placement (about 2,400 children) has declined along with the city's child population. Although family preservation is now a priority, there is a large number of adolescents in custodial care from when the county removed children from homes of substance-abusing parents—particularly during the crack cocaine epidemic in the late 1980s and early 1990s. Given that almost half of the children in foster care are thirteen or older, the county is focused on preparing youth for emancipation by concentrating on improving education, job training, and independent living skills programs for youth. This is a challenging task given the logistical barriers to interagency collaboration, the high mobility of foster youth that can impede their educational progress, and the social stigma sometimes attached to foster youth. Because the city's caseload is relatively small and concentrated in particular neighborhoods, resources can be targeted to particular parts of the city. Alameda County focuses on preparing youth in foster care for emancipation. To this end, it has an independent living skills program like that of San Francisco that helps youth gain employment skills, find housing, and complete high school and apply for college; it also provides health services.

The demographics, institutions, and political dynamics discussed in this chapter provide the community context for advocacy efforts in San Francisco and Oakland. From this general discussion of the landscape in San Francisco and Oakland, we now move into a specific discussion of the organizations in these communities that make up the advocacy and organizing groups striving to improve conditions for children and youth.

4 Populations of Organizations

MOST STUDIES OF ADVOCACY ORGANIZATIONS focus on either the very macro or the micro level: They analyze trends at the national level across decades (Berry 1995; Cigler & Loomis 1998; Gormley & Cymrot 2006; Minkoff 1994; Skocpol & Dickert 2001) or document the work of individual organizations (Delgado 1986; Shirley 1997; Wood 2002). In this chapter, we focus on an often neglected meso level—the *populations of advocacy organizations* that exist in communities. Considering entire populations at this level allows us to better address a question we posed in Chapter 1: What are the structures and strategies that enable organizations advocating for some social good to mediate the quicksand of social reform—to operate between movement and establishment? In this chapter, we identify a collection of organizations advocating and organizing for youth in San Francisco and Oakland and examine the differing approaches they employ to address problems or improve conditions for youth. This multifaceted assemblage of organizations drives much of what is happening in youth development and youth policy in the Bay Area. Our populations of advocates are positioned as mediators between social movements and established organizations: They strive for social movement goals such as racial and economic justice but turn to structured forms such as government bureaucracies to implement their work. They are, as we have noted earlier, an important bridge between citizens and the state.

We first introduce our populations of organizations, including the methods used to identify and describe our populations as well as the specific characteristics, such as budget, staff, and constituency, that complete an organization's profile. Next we look to existing types of organizational structures and examine how our populations map onto this organizational typology. Finally we turn to the historical context of these organizations, looking to founding dates and historical eras as a way to understand how the populations of advocates have shifted over time. The next chapter takes up the analysis of these populations.

Recognition of the existence of multiple, diverse organizations pursuing broadly similar objectives motivated our population-level analysis; we wanted to include the full range of organizational structures, targets, and tactics that represent the total population of advocates working for youth at the city level. Being attentive to this diversity, however, rendered our analytic work difficult. Even the primary term for identifying our population of organizations was controversial: some of the "advocates" in our study do not consider themselves advocates working on behalf of a constituency but instead see themselves as facilitators who help others become self-advocates championing their own cause. San Francisco Organizing Project (SFOP) and Oakland Community Organizations (OCO), for instance, members of the PICO National Network, are organizing groups that engage community members around specific issues generated from local concern. More often than not, though, the issues that OCO and SFOP community organizers identify as community concerns have an impact on youth and result in advocacy campaigns, such as a youth-led research project to expose concerns about neighborhood safety or a political rally to demand accountability from public officials regarding school district reforms. PICO's strategy centers on the democratic participation of community members, which enables citizens to choose issues and press for policy reform alongside staff members. Other organizations that provide services for youth engage in advocacy only in relation to the types of services they offer. With varying models of action and theories of community change within our populations, we witness as much disagreement as agreement about the goals, targets, and tactics of reform, and such differences influence the extent and nature of the relations these organizations develop with each other. As we will highlight in this chapter, we find more evidence of independent than of interdependent work among these organizations. This fragmentation and complexity might appear to challenge the wisdom of our decision to analyze these organizations as a single population within each city. We, however, prefer to treat it as a reflection of the nascent state of the field of youth development—a field driven by a broadly shared goal, which is presently advanced by myriad and often competing and isolated actors.

Identifying Members of the Populations

The local San Francisco and Oakland advocacy organizations we identify share the following core characteristics: They advocate or organize communities for youth (as opposed to children) exclusively or in conjunction with providing services for youth, such as after-school programs; they are regarded as legitimate and recognized actors in their fields; and they primarily operate on a citywide level rather than at a neighborhood, regional, or state level. The city level affords us a view of organizations interacting with local government and is, in a practical sense, the level at which many youth services are provided. We define advocacy work in these organizations as either working to change local support systems for youth or empowering others to participate in the political process themselves through advocacy or youth organizing activities.

Because youth advocacy organizations come in so many sizes and shapes, it is not a straightforward exercise to determine which organizations to include in the populations. Though other studies of advocacy organizations using IRS Form 990 data have defined them as any 501(c)4 organization and any 501(c)3 reporting expenditures for lobbying (DeVita, Mosher-William, & Stengel 2001), we concluded that neither this definition nor a keyword search using GuideStar, an online database of nonprofit organizations, could accurately locate which organizations were engaged in advocacy because of the mismatched organizations that our search captured.[1]

We therefore employed a two-pronged approach to identify the two local populations. Local nonprofit executives, foundation officers, and other leaders knowledgeable about youth advocacy identified prominent organizations—the recognized players within the community. Their responses allowed us to build a snowball sample and conduct interviews with nominated leaders of local organizations. Further research on prospects from GuideStar allowed us to identify which of the organizations met our criteria for inclusion in the two city populations.[2] Organizations whose advocacy or organizing efforts were fleeting, episodic, or marginal to their core organizational activity were excluded. In this manner, we identified nine organizations in San Francisco and eleven organizations in Oakland that had communitywide recognition for their advocacy work with youth and that were described as being dedicated to improving conditions for youth through advocacy activities, including rallies, leadership development, public education, litigation, and budget analysis. Finally, we validated our final population lists by vetting them with a foundation officer in each community, leading advocates in both communities, and city officials.

Organizational Populations in San Francisco and Oakland

The populations of youth advocacy organizations we identified in these cities include a mixture of small grassroots organizing groups and well-established, well-funded professional advocates, as well as organizations that do case-by-case advocacy for individual children and youth. They vary a great deal along numerous dimensions (see Tables 4.1 and 4.2 and Chapter 5). Some reside within the specialized sectors, such as education or juvenile justice, while others are generalists, operating across sectors. They exhibit a wide range of sizes, with annual budgets ranging from under $200,000 to over $8 million, and they range in founding dates from 1967 to 2001.

In their structures, some organizations are independent and others are linked to networks; some are nonprofit and others are government-sponsored. Some are run mostly by professionals, while others rely on volunteers or members. They target different levels of the policy system that affect youth and carry on different types of advocacy. And they vary in the scope of their advocacy targets: Some may advocate for better lunches in schools, while others attempt to change funding structures for youth development across an entire city.

In general, the service providers in our populations (such as EBAYC, Huckleberry, and Larkin Street) are larger both in staff and budget. Larkin Street Youth Services has an annual budget of $8.7 million, and Huckleberry Youth Programs has a budget of $4.5 million. In contrast, all of the general advocacy organizations in our study operate on budgets of under $1 million. The staff size in advocacy organizations in our populations tends to be under fifteen, while the service organizations can have up to fifty staff members.

The organizational units vary in other ways. In our populations, we include some independently operating organizations as well as some subunits of organizations, such as Books Not Bars, a program of the national advocacy organization Ella Baker Center for Human Rights. The populations consist of organizations dedicated to reform at the city level, and a few have branch offices elsewhere or are part of countywide coalitions that have a specific focus on the city. And we have organizations with professional advocacy programs and staff and some with youth-led structures. Interestingly, *none* of these organizations was officially listed as being a 501(c)4 organization—an organization legally permitted to engage in political lobbying campaign activities.

Organizations advocating for youth engage in a wide variety of activities. Youth organizing and leadership development is the largest category of activity in these two populations, with eleven organizations using this strategy to

Table 4.1 San Francisco Population of Organizations Engaged in Advocacy for Youth[a]

	Founding date	Annual budget	Staff size	Constituency	Main advocacy activity
General					
Coleman Advocates for Youth	1975	$700,000	6	SF children and youth	Budget and legislative advocacy; youth empowerment; public education
San Francisco Organizing Project (SFOP)	1982	$500,000	5	SF community; member congregations	Grassroots organizing; education advocacy
San Francisco Youth Commission	1995	$200,000	3 staff; 17 commissioners	SF youth	Legislative consulting to Board of Supervisors
Specialized					
Center for Young Women's Development (CYWD)	1993	$550,000	17	Low- and no-income, high-risk young women; street workers	Justice system advocacy; youth employment; leadership development
Lavender Youth Recreation and Information Center (LYRIC)	1988	$1.46 million	10	Lesbian, gay, bisexual, transgender, queer, and questioning youth 23 and under	Improved environment and opportunities for LGBTQQ youth
San Francisco Court Appointed Special Advocates (SF CASA)	1991	$800,000	14 staff; 200 volunteers	Youth in the legal system; foster youth	Individual advocacy in legal system
Service					
Community Educational Services (CES)	1969	$720,000	5 (2 PT)	SF public school students, particularly Chinese American	Youth-led advocacy in schools
Huckleberry Youth Programs	1967	$4.4 million	65	Homeless, runaway, and foster youth	Legislative and policy advocacy regarding housing and foster care for youth
Larkin Street Youth Services	1984	$8.7 million	114 staff; 300 volunteers	Homeless, runaway, and foster youth	Housing and educational advocacy

[a]Data in all tables (4.1 and 4.2) come from diverse sources, including organizations' websites, annual reports, IRS 990 Forms, and interviews with organization staff. Data presented were collected between June 2003 and August 2005.

Table 4.2 Oakland Population of Organizations Engaged in Advocacy for Youth

	Founding date	Annual budget	Staff size	Constituency	Main advocacy activity
General					
Kids First	1995	$360,000	15 youth organizers 5 adult staff (3 PT)	80 active youth, Oakland community	Youth organizing and training; school reform
Oakland Community Organizations (OCO)	1972	$700,000	11	Oakland community, schools, member	Grassroots organizing: education advocacy congregations
Oakland Youth Commission	1996	$183,000	1.75	Mayor and City Council, youth, schools	Facilitation of youth events, hotlines, and resources for youth; youth leadership
Specialized					
Asian Youth Promoting Advocacy and Leadership (AYPAL)	1998	$725,000 from 6 collaborative organizations	9 staff from 6 partner agencies	Primarily Asian youth in grades 9–12.	Asian youth leadership training; community organizing; advocacy skills
Books Not Bars [A program of the Ella Baker Center for Human Rights]	2001	$635,711	6	Youth, county officials, Oakland community	Direct-action mobilizing; media advocacy; public education; policy reform and legal services
Leadership Excellence	1989	$400,000	5 staff; 8 volunteers; 5 youth advisory board members	African American youth in Oakland ages 15–18	Grassroots community organizing; leadership skills for African-American youth
School of Unity and Liberation (SOUL)	1996	$350,000	5.25	Oakland youth of color, low-income youth	Training center for youth organizers; cultural and social justice activism
Youth ALIVE!	1991	$1 million	13; 2–4 students and summer interns	Youth in schools served (~500 per year); other organizations that use their model (in CA and US)	Violence prevention; public education advocacy; media advocacy
Service					
East Bay Asian Youth Center (EBAYC)	1976	$2.5 million [organizing budget is 20–25% of total]	50 staff (22 FT)	Three schools in Oakland and one in Berkeley serving about 700 families	Staff and separate funding to engage families in advocacy and community organizing
First Place Fund for Youth – Foster Youth Alliance	1998	$1.3 million	18	Foster and transitional youth ages 16 to 23, 14 Foster Youth Alliance member organizations	Foster care youth services; collaboration and advocacy with county agencies
Youth Together	1996	$650,000	6–10 FT; 1–5 PT; 4 paid youth organizers	300 students at five high schools; other schools	Youth organizing; social justice/education justice

improve conditions for youth. It makes sense that advocacy organizations and organizing groups dedicated to youth issues would devote significant time to empowering youth and cultivating democratic participation in social reform initiatives. Many organizations are trying to recruit and train the next generation of leaders, and many of these organizations have had significant legislative victories. Other types of strategies used by youth advocates include public education and budget advocacy. In addition, organizations in our populations engage in housing advocacy, cultural awareness activities, and advocacy for lesbian and gay youth, among others.

Most members of our service population work in schools, with the exception of Huckleberry and Larkin Street, which provide services for homeless, runaway, and foster youth. Community Educational Services, Youth Together, and EBAYC help youth advocate for changes in schools through school-based teams that promote youth leadership to achieve social justice goals in the public education system.

Finally, we emphasize again that not all of our organizations identify themselves as advocacy organizations. The large service providers see their service to youth as their primary activity, although their advocacy efforts are just as well known if not equally effective. The community organizers in our population take on a particular cause with regard to youth and advocate in significant ways to promote that cause. SFOP, OCO, and Youth Together, for example, lead communities and youth to organize around specific campaigns originating from constituents' concerns. They view their advocacy efforts on behalf of youth as supplementary to or as arising out of a broader organizing mission. Another, but different, issue is posed by the youth commissioners, who are not typically classified as advocates because they operate as insiders within city government. Nonetheless, in their role within the community, they function as advocates when presenting youth concerns and needs to government bodies.

Organizations Excluded from the Populations

A review of the populations indicates that some notable candidates are missing. One absent category includes affiliates of some of the larger, more traditional, and most recognizable youth-oriented organizations, such as the Boys and Girls Club and the YMCA/YWCAs. These organizations did not appear on any informant's list of organizations recognized as advocating for youth at the local level even though they do offer important programs and activities for young people, many of which embody youth development principles. Such more traditional membership-based organizations stress participation and services to their clients over advocacy on behalf of excluded or disadvantaged youth.

A second category includes the organizations that appeared in our Guidestar searches but for many reasons, including the fact that they failed to surface in our interviews with informants, did not fit our criteria for the populations. Examples of these organizations include Communities in Harmony Advocating for Learning and Kids (CHALK), Chinese Newcomers Service Center, Earth Island Institute, and Health Initiatives for Youth. A third category consists of county-focused organizations in Alameda County, such as Alameda CASA, which align with some population organizations (in this case, SFCASA) but work primarily at the county level.

Finally, a few organizations excluded from the list are those that have a strong presence in San Francisco and Oakland but primarily operate throughout the Bay Area and/or at state and national levels. These organizations include Youth in Focus, Youth Leadership Institute, Californians for Justice, California Tomorrow, Legal Services for Children, Youth Law Center, Action Alliance for Children, the Center for Third World Organizing, and Children Now. These organizations range in the type of advocacy they employ (including youth-led research, youth organizing, litigation, public education campaigns, media alerts and analysis, and organizing training). They also vary in their length of existence and expertise.

Types of Advocacy Organizations

To better understand the local youth advocacy landscape, we classified our organizations roughly into three separate, but in some cases overlapping, categories according to their primary activities and organizational focus as follows.

General Advocacy Organizations These organizations devote their efforts primarily to youth advocacy, youth empowerment, or grassroots organizing. They are "general" in two senses: (1) They operate across more than one sector, and (2) they devote energy both to more localized reforms and also attempt to stimulate systemwide change. They seek to improve conditions for youth by searching for solutions in public and private arenas and in various youth-serving sectors, including health, education, recreation, and justice. They also aim to give youth a voice in the democratic process through youth-led campaigns—especially because youth cannot vote. This set of organizations includes Coleman Advocates, the San Francisco Youth Commission, the Oakland Youth Commission, San Francisco Organizing Project (SFOP),

Oakland Community Organizations (OCO), and Kids First. Note that this category includes both private nonprofit and public organizations.

Coleman Advocates for Children and Youth is a highly visible citywide advocacy organization with an over thirty-year history in San Francisco. Coleman's professional staff has historically focused on budget advocacy and policy reform, and the organization also includes youth and parent empowerment groups that determine and execute their own campaigns. SFOP and OCO, both members of the PICO National Network, each represent 40,000 families through congregation-based organizing in San Francisco and Oakland. Their model is dedicated to developing local leadership and responding to issues that resonate with the concerns of individual families through democratic participation. These three organizations are the focus of our in-depth case studies and are the subjects of Chapters 6 and 7.

The youth commissions are affiliated with the Board of Supervisors in San Francisco and the City Council in Oakland. Representatives and the mayors appoint youth to these bodies. The commissions attempt to introduce youth perspectives in each city and enable the regular involvement of youth members in policy discussions. The commissions not only advise city government on proposed legislation affecting youth, but they also have the ability to introduce their own legislation and speak out on other issues affecting youth across their city. The youth commissions are potentially powerful vehicles for youth empowerment, as they give a diverse group of youth the opportunity to interact with legislators, affect policy and legislative decisions, and gain experience in local government.

Specialized Advocacy Organizations   A second set of organizations in our populations is concerned with advocacy in a specific area or for a specific group of youth; for example, foster care, education, and youth represented in the media. These organizations may or may not include youth as direct participants in their advocacy work—that is, some advocate "for" rather than "with" youth. Members of this category include Asian Youth Promoting Advocacy and Leadership (AYPAL), formed from a collective of local Asian organizations; the Center for Young Women's Development (CYWD); San Francisco Court-Appointed Special Advocates (SFCASA); Lavender Youth Recreation and Information Center (LYRIC); Books Not Bars, a program within the larger nationally recognized Ella Baker Center for Human Rights; Leadership Excellence; Youth Alive!; and the School of Unity and Liberation (SOUL), formerly a program of the Youth Empowerment Center. This category contains a diverse group, both in structure and focus, of organizations and coalitions of organizations supporting youth. CYWD, for example, supports and advocates for young women in the street economies and in the justice system of San Francisco through peer-to-peer counseling and networking; its staff consists entirely of young women, many of whom have been through the justice system. SFCASA, a local affiliate of the national CASA organization, connects adult volunteers with youth in the foster care system to act as advocates in individual cases. LYRIC is a community center in San Francisco for lesbian, gay, bisexual, transgender, and questioning youth, focused on community building, health, and education and employment opportunities.

Service Organizations with Advocacy Program   The third set of organizations in our populations devote most of their resources to the provision of services but also engage in some advocacy work as part of their service mission. Some organizations sponsor youth-led advocacy programs; others take up advocacy campaigns as they affect their core service programs. Community Educational Services (CES), Larkin Street Youth Services, Huckleberry Youth Programs, East Bay Asian Youth Center (EBAYC), First Place Fund for Youth's Foster Youth Alliance (FYA), and Youth Together are examples of these types of organizations in our populations. EBAYC, CES, and Youth Together work primarily in schools. EBAYC runs after-school centers, while CES and Youth Together work on youth-led needs assessments and advocacy within schools. Larkin Street and Huckleberry work primarily with homeless and runaway youth in San Francisco, and First Place Fund works with foster youth in Oakland; all three organizations provide emergency services and crisis intervention, housing, mental health support, and education and employment opportunities, while helping individual clients navigate the maze of social services. First Place Fund's facilitation of the Foster Youth Alliance has been its core advocacy work; the alliance seeks to hold Alameda County accountable to foster care youth and their issues, though it focuses its activities primarily on Oakland.

The service organizations that operate within schools work with students on educational advocacy and improving conditions within their schools; campaigns include defusing racial tension within the student body or advocating for the improved cleanliness and safety of the schools' bathrooms. In these cases, youth-led advocacy is a central organizing tactic. Larkin Street and Huckleberry involve youth in their efforts too, but they primarily advocate on behalf of their homeless and runaway youth, filling gaps in services and attempting to change public policy.

A critical part of understanding these organizations involves the history and development of their service-provision and advocacy campaigns. We next examine the social, political, and economic conditions at the time these organizations were founded, which provide insight into organizations' growth and survival.

Populations through Time: Three Periods

The first thing to highlight is that all the organizations making up the populations in our study are survivors; they have stood the test of time (at least to the point of our study) and have avoided fading out of existence or losing relevance in the advocacy community. They also all came into existence after 1965. Organizations established earlier—for example, the YMCA, YWCA, and Girl and Boy Scouts—provide services and facilities to youth and are based on the membership of young people, but they do not assume advocacy functions. They are cut out of a different cloth. Organizations created during different eras look and act differently. Organizations are "imprinted" or "time-stamped": They must be constructed out of materials—types of personnel, technologies, modes of organizing—available at their time of founding. Stinchcombe (1965) has observed that organizations of the same type tend to be founded in clusters or bunches. Moreover and more remarkably, organizations tend to retain their birthmarks throughout their life course. Thus, earlier forms, such as the Y and scouting programs, that have survived into the present tend to continue to operate in ways similar to their predecessors. This is not to imply that organizations do not evolve and adapt over time,[3] but they are unlikely to change in fundamental ways.

We identify three discernible periods in the history of these populations. These periods link our population organizations to state and national contexts in key ways and indicate some patterns in the development of local child and youth advocacy.[4] The environmental influences stemming from changes in the national political climate and national advocacy and organizing scene in each period set the tone for the development of the organizations over time.

1965–1978: Activist Era of Governmental Programs Combating Inequality and Expanding Rights

With the passage of the Elementary and Secondary Education Act of 1965 to combat poverty and inequality in schools and the U.S. Supreme Court decision of *In re Gault,* which set the standard for due process procedures in the juvenile courts in 1967, the federal government weighed in on the struggle for reforming institutions affecting youth. It is not surprising, then, that the history of our community organization populations begins in the late 1960s, when two of the organizations—Huckleberry Youth Programs and Community Educational Services (CES)—were founded. Huckleberry began as a home for runaway youth, while CES was founded by activists in San Francisco's Chinatown to secure funding and programs for that neighborhood's youth.

During this same time, the War on Poverty and the Great Society provided a historical turning point that changed relations between government and nonprofits. From 1965 to 1970, the federal government increased spending on social services from $812 million to $2.2 billion, and with that the number of nonprofits, including advocacy organizations, grew significantly (Smith & Lipsky 1993). Beginning with the community action agencies, nonprofit organizations were established as the key players linking local community needs and interests with federal funds, in areas ranging from antipoverty action programs to model city, community mental health, and area agencies for the aged (Musto 1975; Piven & Cloward 1971; Sundquist 1969). A major logic underlying all of these efforts was to encourage extensive participation in the programs by those affected—"maximum feasible participation" (Moynihan 1970).[5] President Lyndon Johnson's War on Poverty also created many programs focused on youth employment. In our local populations, two primarily service organizations were founded during this period—Community Educational Services and Huckleberry Youth Programs. Other youth advocacy organizations created during the War on Poverty did not survive long. Some disappeared altogether, while other organizations left behind their activist "ragtag" culture to become more stable, direct-service organizations.

Later during this period, the 1976 Tax Reform Act redefined lobbying to more explicitly identify the types of activities in which nonprofits (those that have tax-exempt funding) were allowed to engage. The law in effect allowed more organizations to participate in advocacy. The subsequent period marks what some scholars have described as an era of "advocacy explosion" (Berry 1995; Skocpol 2003). It was at this time that the children's rights movement came to the forefront of politics with landmark Supreme Court cases that began to consider children as rights bearers, including *In re Gault* noted above, and *Tinker v. Des Moines* (1969), which upheld children's right to freedom of expression in public schools. In 1975, the first nonprofit law firm for youth in the country was founded in San Francisco to serve youth around the Bay Area.

Our local populations in the early 1970s mirrored the level of advocacy activity at the national level. Local youth advocates created organizations that emphasized youth as persons with entitlements. Coleman Advocates, founded in 1975, emphasized youth rights to improve the foster care and juvenile justice systems. Huckleberry Youth Programs took a very early and radical position to serve runaway youth rather than return them to their homes; the endorsement of this model from civil rights lawyer Willie Brown, who later became the mayor of San Francisco (1996–2004), signaled the emergence and visible presence of a citywide children's movement in San Francisco. This same time witnessed the founding of Oakland Community Organizations (OCO) in 1972 and East Bay Asian Youth Center (EBAYC) in 1976. OCO was the first organization to spark the initiation of the widely known national network of community organizers, PICO (formerly Pacific Institute for Community Organizing), where local affiliates around the country share the same organizing model. At the national level, the Children's Defense Fund was founded in 1973, and the national movement to appoint volunteer advocates to represent youth in court, CASA, began in 1977. Congress also passed the Child Abuse Prevention and Treatment Act in 1973. Although there is no discernable financial or structural connection between federal programs such as the War on Poverty and the founding of these organizations, the organizations, from their inception, were positioned between broader social movements and the need to find a stable organizational home for their constituents.

1979–1990: The Era of New Federalism

By 1979, more than 260 programs administered by twenty agencies that benefit children and youth had been created (U.S. Department of Health, Education and Welfare 1979, cited in National Academy of Sciences 1982). These include programs that directly serve youth and those that benefit youth more indirectly through aid to parents, service providers, and other adults. Also included in this account were various programs ranging from those that provide supplemental income or institutional support to those that research problems facing children and families. Nevertheless, during the 1980s child poverty soared. The highest rates occurred among younger children, rates higher than any time in the previous period (National Academy of Sciences 1982). At the same time, the Reagan years produced an era of fiscal retrenchment in which advocates and service providers witnessed deep cuts in child and youth services at the federal level and increasing devolution of responsibilities—but not always funds—to states and localities.

The transfer of responsibility to the states under the New Federalism movement presented funding challenges to service providers and advocates at the local level but also presented political opportunities to expand advocacy efforts because of the need for more state and local services. In our communities we observe during this period an expansion of state and local advocacy efforts, with Oakland mandating a youth commission in 1985 and San Francisco creating the Mayor's Office of Children, Youth and Their Families in 1989. Five organizations in our populations were founded during this era. SFOP, part of the PICO National Network, was founded as a multi-issue and multifaith organization. Other organizations during this time emerged in response to local policy issues. For example, in San Francisco, Larkin Street Youth Services was founded to provide more services for homeless and foster care youth needing training and support to sustain their lives; and LYRIC (Lavender Youth Recreation and Information Center) was formed as an organization reflective of San Francisco's progressive cultural and social landscape. The organization provides a safe space and organizing structure for gay, lesbian, bisexual, and transgender youth.

Existing organizations also began to look beyond a narrow focus on individual services. Coleman Advocates, for example, which began with a focus on juvenile justice, expanded to a broader agenda as they came to recognize how systemic and widespread youth problems were. At the same time, at the national level, the Child Welfare Act was enacted to reform social services for children.

In this era, the majority of the organizations and advocates in our populations were founded in San Francisco, not Oakland, and many of the organizations target issues with policy relevance to the progressive San Francisco community. Oakland's diverse population, fractured political context, and larger geographic landscape strengthened local neighborhood organizing during this time but perhaps also provided a more challenging context for advocates seeking citywide reform.

1991–2005: Emergence of the Youth Development Movement

At the national level, principles distinguishing a youth development stance were being developed and promulgated, with the appearance of several publications devoted to explicating the foundations of youth development precepts and policies (Pittman & Cahill 1992; Pittman & Wright 1991). Several state-level propositions passed in California, creating community-based responses in the Bay Area that ultimately resulted in the creation of more stable forms of organization. The responses to particular policies at the state level, however, were markedly different than the broader children's rights organizations that formed at the national level. For example, Proposition 187, passed in 1994, reflected and fostered an anti-immigrant sentiment that led to increased violence in schools and neighborhoods. Although not intentionally aimed at youth, the policy created a reactive groundswell of action and contributed to the creation of youth empowerment organizations, especially in Oakland. Organizations such as Youth Together, focusing on racial injustice, developed as a way to organize in opposition to Proposition 187. In more recent years, however, this organization has turned its attention to youth-driven school reform with a youth development approach. This period witnessed an increase in youth advocacy in the Bay Area region with seven organizations founded and a citywide children's fund created in San Francisco and in Oakland.

The adverse fiscal climate of the 1990s affected advocacy efforts. Advocates of all kinds working at the turn of the twenty-first century had to fight many defensive battles, reacting to particular policy proposals or trying to defend programs they had previously worked hard to put in place (Gormley & Cymrot 2006). With a lack of resources or staff capacity to propose more proactive solutions, many advocates settled for calling attention to unmet needs, unresolved problems, or missed opportunities.

Many of the more positive efforts to foster reform that gained attention from public and private as well as local and national funders during this time focused on public schools. In the 1980s community groups were not heavily involved in efforts to improve schools. But national mapping projects conducted by New York University's Institute for Education and Social Policy, Research for Action, and the Cross City Campaign for Urban School Reform have documented a recent surge in the number of local community groups involved in advocacy and organizing around school issues. By one account, over 200 community groups throughout the country have organized around local school reforms (Fruchter 2001). ACORN (Association of Community Organizations for Reform Now), for example, was central in leading efforts in New York City to prevent the takeover of failing public schools by the Edison Corporation, a for-profit school-management firm. Other organizing groups not in our populations, such as the Industrial Areas Foundation (IAF), the Gamaliel Foundation, and the National People's Action (NPA), also became involved in school reform efforts at this time. And two of our focal organizations, SFOP and OCO, both part of PICO, became involved in school issues during the 1990s.

Many advocacy groups and community organizers were drawn to issues of education by first addressing issues related to time spent *out* of school. During the 1990s, local, state, federal, and foundation funding for after-school programming increased dramatically. Efforts to increase the provision of after-school programs—what some have facetiously termed "more school after school"—led some organizations to confront the underlying issue: the ineffectiveness of their local schools.

Other movements to reframe policy issues and perceptions of youth were also underway. A clearer youth development stance emerged, in part as a reaction to the media's characterization of youth as "superpredators" and other negative social constructions of youth. The founding of organizations in our populations such as Kids First, Oakland Youth Commission; First Place Fund/FYA; SOUL; Youth Alive; and Youth Together reflect the growing trend to empower youth through service and advocacy and to include youth voice as a critical component to local advocacy efforts. It is also in this period that Coleman Advocates established its youth and parent organizing groups, thereby adding both youth and parent empowerment as complements to its staff-led advocacy efforts.

During this era, ideas about children's policy and news of successful campaigns traveled rapidly from San Francisco to Oakland. The Proposition K initiative in Oakland was patterned on San Francisco's Proposition J or "Children's Fund," and the creation of Oakland's youth commission followed San Francisco's successful implementation of its commission.

Over time, it appears that organizations advocating and organizing for youth have increasingly been founded in response to specific events and legislation at the state or local level. Between 1998 and 2000, there were pockets of increased funding for children statewide, such as Children and Families First and a fund for homeless foster youth. The passage of Proposition 21, the "Gang Violence and Juvenile Crime Prevention" initiative, led to reactive campaigns like "Books Not Bars" and helped create a network of organizations in Oakland. In our populations, SOUL, Youth Alive!, Kids First, and others were involved in campaigns against the proposition, which enforced tougher penalties for juvenile offenders in California.

Youth Together began in 1996 as a response to the 1994 passage of Proposition 187, which denied specified services to illegal immigrants. SOUL was part of a merger in 2000 of four organizations that were all working against Proposition 21, creating the Youth Empowerment Center. Other organizations gained traction in a specific time period around a certain initiative and then shifted focus once initiatives were won. For example, People United for a Better Oakland (PUEBLO) was very active with EBAYC in spearheading the Kids First Coalition in the mid-1990s to gather signatures to put Oakland's Measure K on the local ballot. The organization now serves as a watchdog to police activity and more recently came close to closing its doors due to fiscal mismanagement. Kids First became a 501(c)3 organization after Measure K passed; the organization turned its focus to securing free bus passes for students and surveying and reporting local high school students' opinions about their school climate. Other organizations have shifted their balance of advocacy and service work; Huckleberry and Larkin Street, for instance, were founded largely for advocacy purposes to serve and protect homeless and foster youth and now primarily do service with advocacy campaigns as they relate to their service missions.

The current populations in San Francisco and Oakland, shaped by the social and political initiatives of major reform eras since the 1960s, are wide ranging and changing in nature as funding and political opportunities in the two communities shift. Although organizations that advocate for youth share the goal of improving conditions for youth, the fragmented nature of youth services compels organizations to work within or across several service sectors—a reality that often splinters advocates' common concerns into discrete, and sometimes disjointed, program areas. Moreover, the typically uncoordinated public and private services located within education, health, social services, and juvenile justice provide advocacy organizations with many types of constituents—various targets to reform and an extensive list of policy issues to address. Some organizations target public transportation systems to secure free bus passes for students as one way to support youth from low-income families; others work with superintendents and school boards to reform school district policies; still others rally on the steps of city hall to win more public funding for youth programs.

The population description in this chapter examined these wide-ranging advocates with regard to their organizational types and the historical, political, and social climate of their founding eras. We turn in the next chapter to analyze the particular campaign strategies organizations undertake to make for effective advocacy work, in particular three key dimensions affecting our populations' work—organizational structure, targets, and tactics.

5 Structure, Targets, and Tactics

ORGANIZATIONS ADVOCATING FOR YOUTH engage in a balancing act to advance their goals: On the one hand, they adopt organizational structures to give their efforts credibility and stability, while on the other hand they preserve aspects of a radical stance to remain independent of the institutions they seek to reform. Working between marginalized populations and the powers that be, they experience an inherent tension in their intermediary position.

This tension may be even greater for advocates attempting to improve support systems for youth. Many public policies are still framed around punitive stances toward youth, as illustrated by recent gang violence prevention acts and proposals for expanding jails in the Bay Area. The reframing—or social reconstruction—of targeted populations is an integral part of the policy process. As Schneider and Ingram (1993) emphasize, it matters greatly whether the target population of a policy is construed as deviants or victims; and many advocates in our study strive to shift public perceptions away from negative constructions of youth to advance supportive rather than punitive youth policies.

In addition to the framing of youth themselves, advocates frame the problems that affect their constituents and the possible solutions (Campbell 2005). These frames "mediate between opportunity structures and action because they provide the means with which people can interpret the political opportunities before them and, thus, decide how best to pursue their objectives" (Campbell 2005: p. 49). Because most policies for youth still center on negative constructions of them, the organizations in our population tend to be reactive rather than proactive. That is, many of the activities initiated by members of our organizational populations involve mobilization of forces to oppose existing or proposed programs rather than the advocacy of a new venture.

In this chapter, we consider key dimensions operating at the organizational level that influence what reform initiatives advocates for youth undertake and how they go about their work. We focus on three dimensions that help to explain the nature of advocacy efforts: organizational *structure*, *targets* selected for reform, and *tactics* used to execute campaigns. Although these dimensions are analytically independent, they interact in complex ways to influence what advocates do and how they do it. For example, an organization that relies heavily on volunteers instead of professional staff (structure) might identify citizens (targets), attempting to teach them leadership skills (tactics). Another organization that is professionally managed might provide leadership training to citizens as a utilitarian tactic (rather than a target) to get a certain piece of legislation passed.

Organizations that target different young people and different issues exhibit a variety of organizational structures as a result, and these structures influence what an organization is able to do. Even though all the members of our populations share some of the same organizational features—for example, the use of a professional staff—and subscribe to broadly similar objectives, they differ in the structural forms they devise to carry out their work. This structural variety becomes more evident as advocacy organizations mature from loose social movement groups into more formal organizations. The different paths they take suggest their position, interests, and mission in the intermediary space between movements and established structures. We therefore turn first to organizational structure.

Organizational Structure and Archetypes

In Chapter 4 we classified the members of our population in terms of their primary goals and activity—service delivery, advocacy for a specialized population or cause, or general advocacy for youth (Tables 4.1 and 4.2). Here we focus on organizational form. The form that advocacy organizations adopt can be thought of as *archetypes,* a concept that emphasizes the basic model or template which underlies the structural features of the organization (Greenwood & Hinings 1993). We see four discernable types of advocacy organizations. First is a *professional service structure.* This structure characterizes organizations that operate primarily as service units and whose advocacy efforts are subordinated to and associated with the services they provide. Representative organizations in our population adopting this form include Huckleberry Youth Programs, Larkin Street Youth Services, First Place Fund for Youth, EBAYC, and LYRIC. Service organizations are, on average, larger than the other subtypes, both in terms of budget and staff. Most of their resources are devoted to service activities, with advocacy efforts occurring episodically and engaging only a subset of the organization's staff and resources. In addition, these organizations typically depend on substantial grants from governmental sources for delivery of services. And like the larger human service organizations at the state level, these local organizations are well versed in the programs, policies, and agencies that have health and human service oversight (DeVita et al. 2004).

The second organizational type we identified in our population is a *professionally directed advocacy structure*. This structure is exhibited by organizations placing primary emphasis on advocacy for children and youth and whose efforts are directed by professional leaders with substantial autonomy in defining objectives, strategies, and tactics. Within our population, organizations such as Coleman Advocates and Books Not Bars of the Ella Baker Center for Human Rights exhibit this structure. These organizations tend to have relatively high visibility throughout the city, recognizable to government officials, funders, grassroots groups, and community members. As such, they also tend to obtain access to donors, advocacy networks, and governmental officials, and they have the flexibility to navigate among various service providers and city agencies to advance their cause. These organizations are as likely to act as political insiders as they are to take action in citywide public education initiatives or use media blitzes—often with a negative portrayal of city government—to fuel a campaign.

The third organizational type in our population is *professionally enabled, volunteer-staffed structure*. This includes organizations emphasizing the education and empowerment of volunteers (youth or adult) who are significantly involved in defining and implementing the organizations' objectives. These organizations employ their professional staff as facilitators, rather than as operatives. Lay people, who may or may not be compensated, are expected to take the lead in setting objectives and/or in carrying on organizational programs. Organizations exhibiting this form include OCO, SFOP, the Center for Young Women's Development, and Kids First. Many of these organizations encourage youth to do some or a great deal of the work, so they need to incorporate oversight and management of youth volunteers into their structure with outreach workers, membership coordinators, and more. Kids First, for instance, in its program that advocated for free bus passes, operated with only 1.25 adult staff; the rest of the work was carried out by youth leaders. The Center for Young Women's Development is staffed by individuals who have experienced firsthand the problems youth encounter in the street economy.

The fourth and final organizational type we identified is the *representative public forum*. This includes organizations that operate under the auspices of a governmental body whose members are expected to officially represent the interests of their "constituents"—in this case, the youth of the participating communities. A small administrative staff assists the representative group to perform its functions—which include holding hearings and providing advice on proposed legislation. The most difficult problems posed for this form are how to insure the representativeness of the representatives and how to achieve some balance between working within while at the same time remaining independent of the governmental system. Within our populations, the San Francisco and Oakland Youth Commissions embrace this form. The youth are appointed by supervisors from various geographical regions of the city, to help ensure diversity, and they serve as advisors to the Board and city government. In San Francisco, the Youth Commission is an autonomous city agency located within City Hall, and in Oakland the Commission is housed within the Department of Human Services.

While structures influence (and are influenced by) the choice of targets and tactics, the latter are even more highly interdependent. We next turn to how targets and tactics shape the advocacy efforts of organizations in our population.

Advocacy Targets and Tactics

Although the overarching mission of advocacy organizations' efforts is to improve conditions for youth, they direct their reform campaigns at specific targets—for example, legislation, public structures, government services, or community members themselves. Here we define targets as the policies, programs, or people meant to be affected or changed by specific advocacy and organizing activities. Possible targets include the juvenile justice policies that an organization objects to, the elected official who does not pay enough attention to youth issues, the foster care services that an organization wants to improve, or members of the community within which the organization works.

An organization's choice of targets is a critical part of its overall advocacy strategy and reflects how an organization frames a problem it wants to address. If an organization wants to work at the policy level, for example, it can either target the officials involved in creating and implementing public policy or it can launch a community empowerment and education campaign to mobilize a community's response to a policy. By contrast, an organization that focuses on leadership development and capacity building might provide political education to citizens or teach public officials about youth-related issues.

These targets then also lead to specific choices about advocacy tactics, understood as the ways in which advocates execute their campaigns to affect designated targets. Decisions about which tactics to use typically derive from decisions about targets. For example, organizations seeking to improve aspects of public education must tailor their activities to fit the structure of public school governance, which will result in the use of tactics that might not be effective in other sectors, such as juvenile justice reform or health care campaigns. Advocates' intermediary position between more activist social movements and established organizations also influences their decisions about tactics: On the one hand, they have to be confrontational enough to prompt change, but on the other hand they cannot be too radical as to be dismissed entirely.

Although structures, targets, and tactics can be analyzed distinctly, they are fluid, interdependent, and, in some cases, overlapping categories. Keeping this in mind, we describe the targets that advocates in our population identify, the tactics they employ to execute their campaigns, and conclude with a consideration of the interactions between targets, tactics, and organizational structure.

Targets

Organizations advocating for youth vary in the substantive focus of their efforts—their targets. Many factors determine what kinds of targets these organizations choose, ranging from an organization's mission to the political opportunities and structures available to it. Organizations' choice of targets, therefore, is driven by ideology about community change, strategic political calculations, and organizational capacity and expertise. Targets also reflect the particular contexts within which an organization chooses to work (for example, a school district or a mayoral election), and as such, influence the types of tactics it employs. Targets change over time as contexts and opportunities change.

The populations of organizations advocating for youth in San Francisco and Oakland focus their efforts on three main categories of targets: (1) public officials and policies, (2) service sectors, and (3) community members (see Figure 5.1). The public officials and policies category includes elected and appointed officials whose behavior advocates seek to change and the policies these officials

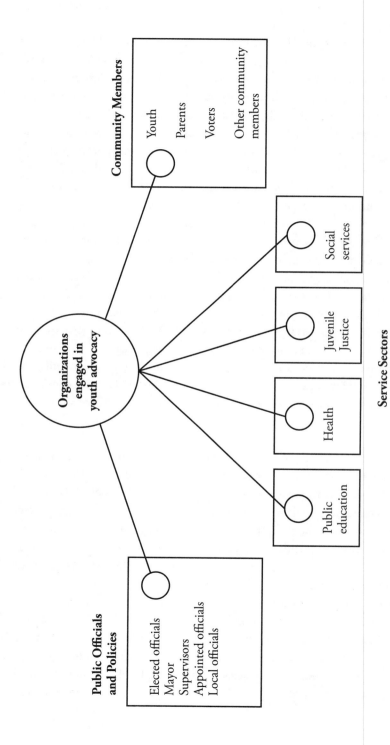

Figure 5.1 Youth Advocacy in Local Communities: Major Targets for Reform. Interior circles within major targets represent specific campaigns that advocates undertake in these arenas. Some of the advocacy organizations are themselves colocated within the various targeted service sectors.

design and support. The service sectors category encompasses the four public sectors that are the most common targets of the population organizations' efforts: the public education system, social services, public health programs and providers, and the juvenile justice system. Finally, the community category refers to the youth, parents, and citizens whose opinions, leadership, and involvement have an impact on youth advocacy. Advocacy organizations conduct specific campaigns (represented in Figure 5.1 by circles) to influence the services, structures, and framing of youth and youth development issues in each of these categories. Some organizations choose to locate themselves within a particular sector so as better to inform and concentrate their reform efforts, while others advocate across sectors. We next describe the three main targets toward which organizations in our population direct their efforts.

Public Officials and Policies

In the political sphere, advocacy organizations attempt to improve local conditions for youth by targeting local policy and the public officers who oversee programs so that local government better meets the needs of the community's youth. Some advocacy efforts target public officials and government bodies directly to bring about policy change, while others try to educate public officials, including mayors, city counselors and supervisors, and school boards, to frame public discussions about youth and youth policy. Two of our organizations in the population are located within the public sector itself: the youth commissions in San Francisco and Oakland, although they primarily target City Hall and advocate on behalf of youth throughout the city and are a recognized component of city government.

To effectively target a policy or individual within a political context, organizations must learn the contours of the local political terrain, what politicians want to hear, and how to appeal to voters. Kids First offers an example of how advocates target policy makers and voters to change public policies to better support youth. Kids First originated as a campaign to pass Oakland's Measure K, which set aside 2.5 percent of Oakland's general fund for child and youth services and established the Oakland Fund for Children and Youth. The campaign was initially conducted by a coalition of organizations that banded together to support the legislation, which passed in November 1996, after which Kids First became an independent entity. The organization is now known as a youth organizing group that has multiple targets: campaigns for free and affordable public transportation, improved relationships with police, and student-driven school report cards. But in its original mission, Kids First framed its advocacy campaign as a ballot campaign in order to secure resources for children and youth.

The only public organizations in our population, the youth commissions in Oakland and San Francisco, also target public officials directly—the City Council and Board of Supervisors, respectively. Youth commissioners give input on all legislation affecting youth and can propose their own legislation. The San Francisco Youth Commission, for example, held a public hearing about building a new skate park after finding out that youth were being arrested under the city's skateboarding laws. A distinctive tactic available only to this type of organizations is the ability to call for a hearing as a public body—an opportunity not available to other organizations in our population. The target and the context shaped the way the commissions could form their campaign.

Advocates also target policy makers in less direct ways as they attempt to reframe discourse and policy for youth and gain the attention of public officials who do not actively work to make youth a legislative or fiscal priority. SFOP and OCO regularly hold meetings with officials to educate them about salient issues. Such meetings may be directed to a particular policy issue or may aim to inform public officials more generally about youth's needs to raise their awareness and understanding. Similarly, soon after a new mayor was elected in San Francisco, the executive director of Coleman Advocates took him on a tour of city parks selected to help him better understand the ways in which parks are a critical asset to children and families in the city. Kids First and Youth Together often hold more focused meetings, such as mayoral forums or town hall meetings, around a particular issue. The knowledge gained from these discussions is also useful for policy formulation: Advocates learn what public officials want to hear and thus how they can best target policy and policy makers to improve conditions for youth.

Although candidate forums and legislative lobbying provide advocates an opportunity to proactively shape political discourse and policies, more often than not advocates' political tactics are reactive: That is, they launch campaigns to block policy detrimental to their cause. Our population organizations, more so than our focal case organizations, engage in *reactive mobilization:* They recognize threats to their goals and rally public support to challenge and thwart the perceived threat (McAdam & Scott 2005: pp. 18–19). In general, reactive mobilization may be easier for advocates to undertake; often, citizens can more readily rally around a policy they oppose than agree on a specific, alternative program. Feasibility issues aside, the prevalence of reactive mobilization in our population may reflect another reality: Because the youth development movement is relatively young, the bulk of public policies are still framed around the deficit model that construes youth as problems to be fixed. Advocates thus find themselves in situations where they are continuously confronting and attempting to respond to adverse policy initiatives.

Service Sectors

Because services for children and youth are still delivered largely through the work of public agencies, advocates also target individual government departments. The educational system provides the most common target for our population organizations because it reaches and affects the most youth. Other key sectors that advocates target include juvenile justice, social services, and health.

Each sector provides a distinctive institutional environment. Each is made up of a particular constellation of organizations displaying particular modes of interaction and governance mechanisms. Many members of our advocacy population attempting to influence these systems locate themselves within these subfields. For example, the Center for Young Women's Development (CWYD) and SFCASA operate largely within the juvenile justice system. Organizations such as Kids First and Community Educational Systems work within and on the educational system. Each must concern itself with the particular features of these institutional landscapes, determining where the power is located, who is allied with whom, and how decisions are made. Each must master the specific institutional logics characteristic of each sectoral arena.

The nature of targets interacts with various aspects of organizations' structure. Decisions about how to structure an organization typically derive from the goals of the organization and decisions about which sectors to address. For example, organizations seeking to work with community members to improve aspects of public education must tailor their management and activities to both fit the needs and skill set of their constituency as well as the realties of public school governance, resulting in tactics that might not be effective in other sectors. However, if an organization's structure is that of a faith-based organizer concerned with leadership development, it is less likely to be able to focus its efforts on a single sector.

When organizations target service sectors, they must also make decisions about which level of that sector to push against to stimulate reform. For example, if an organization wants to take on issues in public education, it must decide at which level to work: individual classrooms, schools, or districtwide practices and policies. Two of our focal cases, SFOP and OCO, chose to undertake education reform at the districtwide level before our data collection period, in both instances to institute a small schools policy. But most of the other organizations within our populations targeting education did so through youth-led organizing campaigns within individual schools. Community Educational Services, for example, works with individual teachers in middle and high school to incorporate youth voice into school decision making. The organization teaches youth how to identify and act on specific problems that need to be addressed in their schools. Issues have ranged from a lack of toilet paper in the bathrooms to tensions between Chinese and Latino students to girls not feeling comfortable speaking in class. Youth Together also targets high schools in Oakland, Berkeley, and Richmond to promote multiracial justice and unity and to train young people in nonviolent solutions to conflict. It convenes stakeholders within the school community to support youth-led campaigns to improve school conditions and opportunities to learn. These two service organizations are combining their mission to improve leadership development with efforts to address specific problems in the schools with which they work.

Kids First, on the other hand, is a general advocacy organization that has targeted schools from several different angles: high-stake testing reform, police presence in schools, and a Student Power Campaign that aims to increase student decision making and leadership at several school sites. These separate campaigns embody the organization's efforts to target three levels of the system simultaneously: the individual, the group, and the school system itself.

These campaigns are largely youth run, overseen by only one full-time staff person. Advocates in the justice system are concerned with the welfare of individual youth, but their choices about how to use their targets—individuals or institutions—to achieve their goals suggest important differences in how context matters. SFCASA, one of about 900 affiliates of the national Court-Appointed Special Advocates program, carries on "individually tailored advocacy and mentorship" in the Juvenile Dependency Court.[1] Volunteers are assigned one child and are trained extensively to ensure the child is getting the support and resources he or she needs. At the same time as they are advocating for their clients in the legal system, they are also advocating for youth individually in the schools and in the mental health system. In addition, SFCASA tries to broadly educate community members about both how abuse and neglect have an impact on adult outcomes and about homelessness, special education, unemployment, and delinquency as these conditions affect the youth with whom they work. Because of their interest in being effective advocates for the welfare of their individual youth clients, SFCASA realizes its need to go beyond legal concerns to understand youth's lives in a broader context and to adopt more general educational goals.

In contrast to SFCASA's focus on individual clients, Books Not Bars, a local program of the Ella Baker Center for Human Rights, has targeted institutions in the justice system through its campaigns against a "super-jail" to house youth in Alameda County and more general system reform through a youth leadership and organizing program and a family support network. It promotes alternatives to an "abusive and ineffective prison system" that "is destroying low-income communities and communities of color." Books Not Bars aims to provide communities with good jobs, education, social services, and a healthy environment through "Three Rs": reallocating public resources away from incarceration, removing the profit motive supporting prison development, and restoring communities. Having adopted the super-jail as a target for reform has meant that Books Not Bars needed to seek support from county leaders and politicians, as well as from citizens, for its alternatives. Books Not Bars is compelled to address different targets than SFCASA, which concentrates on the welfare of individual youth.

Social services, including welfare, foster care, and child protective services, provide another large arena of targets for youth advocacy organizations, with members of our population organizations trying to affect their service delivery systems in many ways. In general, these organizations attempt to influence established public structures to change their ways of doing business so that youth are cared for more effectively. Their advocacy is a by-product of their roles as nonprofit service providers themselves, which enables them to see directly the effects of the system on the youth with whom they work. First Place Fund for Youth's Foster Youth Alliance, for example, seeks to improve the quality of services for youth in foster care. Larkin Street Youth Services views its advocacy agenda as identifying and filling gaps in services for youth, changing public policy and models of care for homeless and runaway youth, and inspiring youth to improve their own situation. They work to increase awareness within the social services system about the needs of eighteen- to twenty-three-year-olds, and they have focused on fostering the development of housing specifically for youth.

Community Members

Although some members of our populations direct their efforts to community members as citizens to enlist them in a specific campaign, others promote individual leadership development, community development, or some combination, as central to reform. In so doing, they focus on youth, parents, and other community members to help them develop skills to become effective self-advocates.

Targeting community members is likely to be more process than outcome oriented. Unlike organizations that attempt to back specific reforms or address specific issues, many organizations targeting community members take a longer view of system change. The pace of change is apt to be slower when organizations seek to train youth or adults to identify concerns of interest to them and gain skills at pursuing these interests. Alternatively, the mission they pursue is different—focused more on individual outcomes than on specific policy outcomes or handoffs. Organizations that directly reach out to their constituents enable youth or parents to advocate on their own behalf. In a sense, such organizations seek to transform parents and turn youth into an interest group capable of making claims to further their own needs.

Kids First, for example, believes that adult-driven solutions to curb violence in schools can go only so far. In the view of its executive director, ultimately, youth themselves must be seen as "legitimate partners" and become engaged in the reform process if reforms are to succeed.[2] Huckleberry Youth Programs is similarly concerned that youth be included in decision making. And at the Oakland Youth Commission, the coordinator notes that youth need to be engaged in issues important to their lives and believe that their efforts may ultimately make a difference in others people's lives. Otherwise, he suggests, "You aren't going to retain young people if you bring them in a room to comment on policy." Intergenerational work may also be included in the work of these organizations. Kids First trains parents to work to reduce tensions between adults and youth and to gain intergenerational support for campaigns, and Youth Together emphasizes youth–adult partnerships to promote change.

Youth organizing is one way that organizations combine advocacy and service. It extends the advocacy work to the people who know the most about the conditions youth face and gives them a voice in reform efforts. Coleman Advocates includes a youth organizing component, Youth Making a Change (YMAC); Community Educational Services has a youth radio program; and

Youth Together helps students run their own educational justice campaigns. The organizations targeting the education sector, including Youth Together, Kids First, Community Educational Services, and Youth Alive!, as described above, have a combined advocacy-service mission with students working on school reform inside schools. Other organizations weave organizing throughout their service work. EBAYC, for example, provides direct service to families, but also works to "engage families in transforming their communities." They see their services as essential because of the discrimination, poverty, and problems in accessing school services that their families face, but in their advocacy work they address these issues more generally by "challenging people to get engaged in their environment." EBAYC's executive director believes "it would be a good thing if more service organizations went that way."

Tactics

Advocates used five general categories of tactics to advance their reform agenda: political campaigns, accountability measures, efforts to build civic capacity, research, and policy formation. These tactics often resemble and reflect the organizations' intermediary role: They range from outsider strategies such as public rallies and marches to insider meetings with elected officials; the organizations in our population employ these strategies both in reaction to unwanted policies as well as in more proactive ways to introduce new courses of action (see Table 5.1).

Political Campaigns   Electoral politics provide advocates high-visibility opportunities to directly change policies and power structures. As we highlight throughout, the localness of city-level advocacy work makes this both possible and effective because advocates can communicate directly with voters and elected officials—an advantage not available to social movements operating at the national level, where strategies necessarily have to be more general to appeal to a diverse set of actors in different settings (Tarrow 1994). Working at the community level allows advocates to develop and use their local knowledge of constituents' needs and their access to power holders to advance their cause—an advantage that is especially salient during local elections.

When advocates engage in political activities, they employ both insider and outsider tactics. They have to strike a careful balance: If advocates are too confrontational, their efforts may be disregarded, but if they are too timid or establishment oriented, their efforts will result in institutional reproduction rather than change (Clemens 1997). Between these extremes is a wide

Table 5.1 Youth Advocacy Tactics by Targets

Tactics	Targets		
	Public officials and policy	*Service sectors*	*Community members*
Leading political campaigns	Endorsing of ballot initiatives; holding public meetings with officials; sponsoring candidate forums during election cycles	Mounting proactive and reactive campaigns to improve public services.	Mounting campaigns driven by community input; staging protest marches; holding public meetings with officials that include youth or adult community members
Holding public officials accountable	Soliciting and recording candidates' campaign promises; analyzing budgets of city agencies; monitoring and publicizing elected officials' positions on salient issues	Analyzing school budgets; tracking and publicizing the performance of specific public agencies such as fire and police departments	Holding public rallies; conducting research meetings with officials; writing community petitions
Building civic capacity	Fostering transparency with local government by sponsoring public forums; improving access to policy and data	Empowering low-income youth to develop leadership skills (e.g., through advocacy within schools) and find employment	Canvassing community to identify needs; providing leadership training to empower citizens to be self-advocates
Conducting research	Gathering and analyzing data on community problems; disseminating findings in public forums (publicized fact sheets; public meetings and rallies)	Gathering, analyzing, and disseminating data about service provision, budgets, and needs within public sectors; using Internet forums and service meetings to disseminate information	Facilitating youth and citizen-led data collection about community problems (e.g., youth-led projects to collect information about conditions in schools)
Forming policy	Framing issues to get public officials' attention and to prompt their creation of new policy to address problems; proposing new legislation	Framing issues that affect specific public institutions (e.g., petitions to school board or probation department)	Developing policy proposals from community input

spectrum of possibilities for confronting and partnering with government officials and institutions to promote reform. This middle ground is where the bulk of advocates' political strategies fall. For most advocacy organizations, their relationship to government is a conditional one that depends on who is in office, what issue is at stake, and what "insider" relationships the organization has developed.

Local elections present advocates with an opportunity to use outsider strategies to influence election outcomes, affecting who is elected as well as what issues candidates address in their campaigns. By holding candidate forums during elections, for example, advocates can galvanize public support and shape the public agenda to focus on constituents' concerns. Mayoral candidate forums organized by SFOP, OCO, and Coleman enabled them to proactively frame public discourse around community needs, and, potentially, to shape policy at its source by compelling candidates to focus on particular issues. As the former executive director of Coleman noted prior to its mayoral forum, because the candidates knew they would be asked to take positions on issues impacting children and youth, each was clamoring to hold the first press conference about children's policy. This political tactic enables advocates to begin to build relationships with candidates, which can then pave the way for "insider" access once the winner takes office.

While mayoral forums are examples of proactive mobilization, Books Not Bars's campaign against building a new super-jail in Alameda County is a clear example of reactive mobilization. It mounted a successful campaign to stop Alameda from building what would have been one of the largest juvenile halls in the country. Although Books Not Bars was created in response to the threat posed by the new jail, the group was successful in developing a positive alternative, redirecting funds toward education. Similarly, a coalition of organizations in our Oakland population (SOUL, Youth Alive!, and Kids First) formed to oppose Proposition 21, the "Gang Violence and Juvenile Prevention Act" that targeted young offenders. Some organizations are reactive mobilizers from the get-go: The Youth Empowerment Center was created from the merger of four organizations working against Proposition 21, and Youth Together formed as a response to Proposition 187, which denied illegal immigrants social services and public education.

Organizations that rely primarily on support from government funds are less likely to engage in reactive mobilization in the public sector. The increase in government spending on nonprofits has contributed to an understandable tension: It is much easier for organizations that do not depend on public funds to advocate with (or against) government agencies and officials than it is for organizations dependent on such funding (Duitch 2002). The executive director of Huckleberry Youth Programs, for example, comments that Huckleberry cannot be as strong an advocate as Coleman because of the funding they receive to provide city and county services: "We have a $600,000 contract with probation. so we can't advocate in the same way."

Insuring Accountability   Advocates engaged in both reactive and proactive mobilization also monitor the behavior of local officials and institutions. Acting as watchdogs, advocates can call attention to programs or activities inconsistent with existing policies or officials' promises and publicize such discrepancies to the media or to affected constituents. Advocates hold public officials accountable in ways that vary depending on organizational resources and expertise. Tactics include monitoring how public resources are allocated (budget advocacy), publicizing officials' promises and performance through the media and public forums, and, in some cases, partnering with supportive public officials to monitor governmental activities from the inside.

Of these various strategies for holding officials accountable, budget advocacy arguably requires the greatest expertise. Advocates engaged in budget advocacy must scrutinize city documents to track how money is distributed and then assess how this distribution compares with existing policies or politicians' promises. Service providers who suffer budget cuts directly often do not have the resources or impartiality to lobby effectively to preserve or increase their share of public resources. Advocates like Coleman are uniquely positioned to engage in budget advocacy because of their financial expertise and financial independence from local government. In the past, Coleman has offered itself as a clearinghouse for other programs and nonprofits affected by budget cuts, volunteering to compile their concerns, investigate the details of potential cuts, and then, if justified, mount a campaign to secure redress. Coleman's budget advocacy work on the Children's Amendment provides a clear example of a tactic traveling across geographic boundaries: Policy approaches devised by advocacy organizations in San Francisco were adopted by organizations in Oakland. Following the success of Proposition J (the Children's Amendment) in San Francisco, in November 1996, over three-fourths of Oakland voters supported an amendment to the City Charter (Measure K) that sets aside 2.5 percent of the city's general purpose funds for youth services. The measure also established the Oakland Fund for Children and Youth, the city institution that currently administers the allocated funds.

Through the use of organizing rallies and public meetings, advocacy organizations can directly pressure public officials to change their priorities.

For example, San Francisco Youth Commission's campaign for skate parks involved holding a public hearing on the issue. Because it is a government body, said the director, the Youth Commission "could mandate that the police department be there." Other city departments and about 100 residents came together and created a skateboard task force. Through the Commission's advocacy efforts, the Board of Supervisiors picked up the policy initiative, and a program was crafted and adopted. "It was a great display of city departments feeling accountable to the public," according to the Commission's director.

Similarly, Youth Alive! in Oakland launched a multiyear campaign to pressure police to trace the purchase of guns used in crime scenes, which was an attempt to hold the police accountable for the high rate of violate crime in Oakland in the 1990s. The East Bay Public Safety Corridor Partnership, a regional collaborative made up of public officials from sixteen jurisdictions in Alameda and Contra Costa Counties, came together with staff of Youth Alive! and convened a session with police to address the situation. Youth Alive! conducted research producing evidence to convince the city council in 1998 to hire a staff person specifically to trace gun sales. Subsequent police investigations found that many of the guns used in violent crimes came from illegal gun sales. Due to these efforts, the guns laws were changed.

Advocates also hold relevant nongovernment institutions accountable for actions that conflict with reformers' goals for improving conditions for youth. For example, in 2000 the *Oakland Tribune* printed an advertisement for a sporting goods store in Oakland that promoted their gun sales. A staff member from Youth Alive! pointed out that the gun advertisement was, ironically, located adjacent to the obituary of a "kid who was killed by Russian roulette." Staff also emphasized that the same advertisement was not carried in other major urban papers like the *San Francisco Chronicle* or *San Jose Mercury News,* and they concluded that it was targeting the Oakland population, particularly youth. The organization held press conferences and, in subsequent meetings with the editor of the *Oakland Tribune,* was successful in persuading the newspapers to adopt a policy against advertising guns.

In many cases the watchdog work that advocates in our populations do is collaborative rather than adversarial in relation to the organizations they seek to change. Youth Together, for example, works in schools to confront issues of social injustice that schools perpetuate: They thus partner with the members of the target organization to work together for reform. Such partnership arrangements grant advocacy groups both credibility and legitimacy and greases the wheels for reform. As their executive director put it, "you need [support] coming from within and from outside [the school]. Direct service is definitely the buy-in. It creates a safety net and they [the schools] know they need us."

First Place Fund for Youth and the Foster Youth Alliance similarly partner with foster care agencies to improve conditions for children and youth in custody. Indeed, the Foster Youth Alliance operates as a consortium of kinship providers, homeless services, intermediaries that provide services, and advocacy organizations like First Place Fund for Youth, the National Center for Youth Law, and the county itself. As such, the executive director notes, "it's a collective voice that's much more credible." Rather than blaming county agencies for failing to provide consistent and comprehensive care for children in the foster care system, the Foster Youth Alliance makes the county part of the "we," working on a common agenda. The executive director of the First Place Fund for Youth commented, "It's a lot easier than saying the County does this or that." To foster this ongoing partnership, First Place Fund holds meetings with city councils and supervisors to describe problems and propose plans to make institutions more accountable for the services they provide to youth. The partnership, however, can be difficult to maintain. The executive director said: "It's a challenge to figure out how to not undermine authority. . . . The whole key is to give them all the credit. It's like group therapy." SFCASA, similarly is able to monitor the checks and balances of the dependency system through the work of individual cases.

Regardless of the specific tactics employed, most accountability and watchdog efforts that advocacy organizations undertake are collaborative—involving partnership either with other organizations or with public institutions themselves.

Building Civic Capacity   To achieve systemic reform beyond a particular policy or program, advocates employ strategies to strengthen advocates' infrastructure and undertake efforts to build civic capacity in the communities in which they work. We take our understanding of civic capacity from Clarence Stone (2001), who defines it as "the extent to which different sectors of the community . . . act in concert around a matter of community-wide import" emphasizing that citizens must first realize that they have a common stake in the issue at hand (p. 596). The outcomes of capacity-building tactics take the longest to achieve and are the most difficult to measure: There is no clear-cut metric for assessing effectiveness here, compared to policy or budget advocacy where a measure passes or not or more funds are awarded or not.

Yet by educating and empowering citizens—especially youth—and by forging partnerships with other organizations, advocates multiply their own strength and resources.

Youth advocates build civic capacity in two distinct ways. The first requires constructing infrastructure in the trenches and relying on grassroots leadership development to carry through campaigns. The second is a more opportunistic approach: Advocates open up political opportunities at the city or county level through the strength of private and public partnerships. Local grassroots organizations that focus on strengthening ties and pushing reform at the neighborhood or school level rather than city or county level often engage in organizing tactics, relying on community residents rather than professional advocates to drive campaigns. These organizations in our population, including Youth Together, Kids First, and OCO, are primarily concentrated in Oakland.

But to varying degrees throughout Oakland and San Francisco, many of the organizations choose the first approach and aim to empower citizens to become self-advocates through leadership development training. By contrast, advocacy organizations that provide direct services tend to function more as traditional advocates working *on behalf* of constituents, using their own staff to secure resources needed by their constituents and providing less opportunity for broader public engagement. However, in recognition of the fact that their constituents' needs are rooted in such systemic social issues as poverty and discrimination, many organizations, such as EBAYC, strive to get their constituents involved to change the structures that are the source of their problems. Similarly, Huckleberry Youth Services in San Francisco provides a range of programs for youth, including health care and transitional housing; like EBAYC, Huckleberry strives to develop leadership skills in the adolescents it serves, through education and training. Though both organizations engage their citizens as more than service recipients, their primary focus on service delivery typically does not leave much room for political education aimed at organic, constituent-led advocacy campaigns.

This youth empowerment stance is also being adopted, at least in name, by more official channels in San Francisco and Oakland. The San Francisco and Oakland Youth Commissions, comprised of youth who serve as advisors to city officials, empower youth to be leaders within local government. In San Francisco, the Youth Commission members are supported by an adult director, but the youth are consulted on almost all decisions and become politically savvy advocates. As the director explained: the youth "understand the [city] budget better than 90 percent of the voting public. We give them the tools and let them go with it." If youth voice is to be effective, however, adults must be receptive to it, as evidenced by parent and adult work of Kids First and Youth Together.

Several social and demographic factors matter when youth leadership development is employed as a civic capacity-building tactic. Race and ethnicity, for instance, become salient when advocacy organizations are targeting a particular group and deciding on the issues that are important to address. When EBAYC, for example, shifted from serving Asian American youth exclusively to serving a multiethnic population, they began working on cross-cultural understandings with youth to "lower the temperature" in areas where gang violence is prevalent. Issues are often specific to other groups of youth, too. LYRIC works with lesbian, gay, bisexual, and transgender youth to help them to address their specific needs across a range of issues, which means that they are engaged in a different type of advocacy than other organizations. Larkin Street also supports youth organizing but acknowledges that homeless youth have more pressing needs, such as getting off the streets.

A second way advocates work to build civic capacity is by strategically partnering with other organizations in the field to augment their own visibility, to enhance their capacity, and to create a sense of collective purpose among advocates. First Place Fund for Youth does this in working with the Foster Youth Alliance countywide collaborative, and Coleman Advocates similarly enhances their work by convening the San Francisco Child Advocacy Network, a large coalition of children and youth service providers around the city. Youth Together and Kids First are part of a coalition of Bay Area organizations mounting a campaign called "Organize da Bay" for youth interested in organizing around school reform. These San Francisco and Oakland networks and other intermediary organizations that convene local organizations and provide training and resources for service providers work together to comprise a broader field of activity, discussed further in Chapter 8.

Youth Together has also created a different type of strategic partnership to advance its reform goals—partnerships that include youth and stakeholders at the school level. Youth affiliated with the organization leveraged funds to create a new health center on the campus of an underserved high school in East Oakland by interacting with other youth, parents, teachers, and administrators. According to Youth Together's director of programs, "The only way it could happen was with a collaborative already in place that was comprehensive." Collaborations of this sort not only facilitate a particular organization's ability to execute a particular campaign; they also contribute to the development of the youth development field itself by creating networks for sharing strategies and fostering collaborative work, increasing cohesion in this somewhat disordered and fragmented field.

Research To convince citizens and elected officials to take their campaigns seriously, advocates often attempt to demonstrate the magnitude and gravity of the issues at hand. To this end, advocates strategically conduct research to document unmet needs, to explore the merits of possible solutions, and in some cases, to support their proposed alternative. This research takes on a variety of forms and is pursued alongside the strategies already described. For example, Coleman's mayoral forum, discussed earlier as an accountability tactic, was also a research project of a sort: It pressured candidates to take a position on policy issues affecting children and youth and then publicized these "data" so that citizens could make more informed choices at the polls. Whatever its format, research conducted by advocates lends credibility to their issue campaigns by giving them facts and figures to stand on.

Research conducted by advocates may also accompany capacity-building efforts. By teaching citizens—especially youth—how to identify, document, and then publicize pressing problems, advocates empower individuals to marshal evidence present in their daily lives to press for reform. For example, Community Educational Services (CES) teaches youth how to gather data within their own schools to expose problems that should be addressed. This activity gives credibility to youth as self-advocates—especially in schools where administrators are not enthusiastic about promoting youth voice and the general school climate offers few incentives for schools to collaborate with youth organizations. The CES executive director stresses that the youth do "very careful" research and analysis to be taken seriously. Conducting research is a key part of our focal organizations' advocacy work and will be discussed in greater detail in the next chapter.

Policy Formation As they do with research activities, advocacy organizations often combine policy formulation with other tactics. Advocates in our population typically assume a reactive stance against policies proposed by others and do not frequently craft new alternatives. When advocates do propose new policies, however, they also can bring greater salience to their campaigns because elected officials are more eager to hear about solutions than problems.

Within our population—with the exception of our focal organizations—there are only a few examples of advocates successfully formulating and passing new policies and legislation. Prominent are Kids First's and Coleman's work to create a children's fund in Oakland and San Francisco; First Place Fund for Youth's legislation to set aside funds for homeless youth; and Larkin Street's success at passing legislation that allowed it to dedicate its services to a particular age group.

Other organizations become interested in passing specific local and state legislation related to their mission. In some instances, legislation is the only way to remedy the problems identified by these organizations. First Place Fund for Youth's Foster Youth Alliance helped pass AB 427 to set aside a fund for homeless foster youth. Larkin Street similarly has had legislative success at the state level with a proactive campaign to pass Assembly Bill 2982, which allowed Larkin to serve a designated age group, a practice usually prohibited by Housing and Urban Development regulations. At the local level, Youth Together and Kids First successfully passed an initiative to provide Oakland students free bus passes. In this case, working across the contexts of a school district, city, and public transportation required a ballot initiative to bring about the desired change.

The structures adopted, targets selected, and tactics employed by the populations of organizations in San Francisco and Oakland intersect to shape youth advocacy campaigns. In the next chapter, we focus our analysis more narrowly on a subset of these advocates—three focal organizations—to examine in greater detail the dynamics of effective advocacy organizations and the role they play in improving support systems for urban youth.

6 Community Organizations: Three Cases

TO UNDERSTAND HOW LOCAL CONTEXT MATTERS to the structure, strategies, and effectiveness of organizations advocating for youth, we selected three organizations from the local population for in-depth study: Coleman Advocates for Children and Youth in San Francisco, the San Francisco Organizing Project (SFOP), and Oakland Community Organizations (OCO) in Oakland. We selected these organizations for closer study based on three criteria: their reputations in their communities, their focus on citywide reform rather than state- or predominantly neighborhood-level change, and their generalist agenda, which enables them to advocate on multiple fronts in connection with a diverse network of organizations. Moreover, these three organizations have had an atypically long life and have achieved significant policy reform in their communities, including successful campaigns to improve schools and after-school programs, increase the affordable housing supply, reduce crime, and increase local spending on programs for children and youth. Coleman, SFOP, and OCO are not tinkering at the margins of public policy, nor are the results of their major campaigns fleeting. Rather, some of their reform efforts have resulted in systemic policy changes that have foundationally altered how San Francisco and Oakland respond to the needs of children and youth.

In this chapter, we offer a basic introduction to Coleman, SFOP, and OCO to give a sense of how each organization has created a distinctive niche for itself in its local context.[1] We create a brief social and administrative history of the people, processes, and events that led to each organization's "character structure," understood as a distinctive stance and value system, particular staffing patterns and modes of work, and arrangements with other community actors. We also highlight the critical decisions and events in each organization's history that give a sense of its developing and unique character. In describing each organization's central goals and strategies, we lay the groundwork for the next chapter's comparative analysis, which includes ways in which these organizations are distinct in the issues that they take on, their stance toward government, and the strategies they employ—differences that are strongly influenced by the contexts in which they work.

Oakland Community Organizations

Oakland Community Organizations (OCO), a faith-based, membership organization, has been a presence in Oakland for more than thirty years. OCO is a local affiliate of the PICO National Network (formerly the Pacific Institute for Community Organizations), which consists of faith-based community organizations throughout the United States working to unite people and communities across region, race, class, and religion. PICO includes more than 1,000 member institutions representing one million families in 150 cities and 17 states, making it one of the largest community-based reform efforts in the United States.[2] PICO's core principles distinguish it from other advocacy groups and guide its member organizations. These values include building a relational culture, holding public officials accountable, drawing power through networks, and developing leadership through faith.[3] OCO's relationship to PICO is contractual: OCO pays dues to PICO in exchange for technical assistance, a consulting director, and access to other PICO organizations across the country. PICO membership also requires OCO to adhere to an organizing model in which issue generation—an organizing process that focuses on community input—is central. As a result, OCO's advocacy agenda is not fixed; instead, the organization's goals change as the concerns of its constituency change. OCO is therefore not strictly a child advocacy organization, but the issues that OCO addresses in response to residents' concerns affect the welfare of children and youth, including education, health care, and neighborhood safety.

OCO's long history in Oakland is rooted in organizing work that Jesuit priest John Baumann started in the Oakland flatlands in the early 1970s—neighborhoods that are economically marginalized from Oakland's affluent "hill communities." Borrowing from Alinsky-style organizing tactics that he learned in Chicago,[4] Baumann expanded his initial efforts to additional flatland communities to address economic issues affecting families, including junkyards, zoning, crime, and vacant housing. A new community organizing project emerged from Baumann's efforts, which included activities through churches, merchants, and civic groups. These neighborhood projects joined forces in 1977 to create and incorporate the Oakland Community Organizations. With its early efforts focused on affordable housing, OCO slowly expanded its constituency and hired new organizers to recruit and train residents to become neighborhood leaders. Expanded local leadership helped OCO to rehabilitate 400 once-vacant homes, and the organization proved to be instrumental in developing affordable housing units for first-time homeowners. OCO also supported efforts for local and minority hiring practices, including the passage of the "Hire Oakland First" program.

Although support for OCO grew across Oakland, participation across the city was uneven, prompting the organization to look to faith institutions to cross racial, economic, and neighborhood lines to make "values and relationships the glue that holds organizations together," not just issues or neighborhoods.[5] According to OCO's executive director Ron Synder, OCO's "institution-based model of organizing," rooted in congregations, came about in part because the old model of relying on staff organizers to mobilize demands for change had stagnated.[6] By 1987 OCO launched its first citywide campaign with seven congregations.

OCO comprises forty congregations, including nondenominational, Baptist, Catholic, African Methodist Episcopal, Reformed Church, Christian Methodist, Episcopal, Presbyterian, United Methodist, and Church of God in Christ. People participate in OCO organizing meetings and rallies through schools, neighborhood organizations, and labor unions. OCO also partners with schools and community organizations that together represent 40,000 families.[7] In the late 1990s, OCO formed a partnership with the Oakland Unified School District (OUSD) and school reform affiliate Bay Area Coalition for Equitable Schools (BayCES) to form the Small Schools Initiative (SSI). The organization employs eleven staff: an executive director, eight professional community organizers, and two administrators. Its annual operating budget of over $800,000 comes primarily from foundations, several corporate sponsors, and membership dues. OCO is governed by a board that includes members from each affiliated congregation, as well as an executive board with pastors, community leaders, and former organizers.

Trained volunteers working in core leadership teams known as local organizing committees (LOCs) carry out the crux of OCO's work. Although

OCO's staff provide critical leadership to the organization's campaigns, they dedicate the majority of their time to training residents to become leaders in their own right to address community concerns through LOCs. OCO's staff and community volunteers, therefore, are often doing the same work together. One parent, OCO leader, and former board member underscores the importance of community involvement as it pertains to OCO's small schools reform: "You have to be persistent. I keep in touch with school board members, with any power player, always talking about small schools and how great our schools are, to keep them engaged." Community leadership is the means and end of OCO's work, as one staff member describes it: "Decisions are made by the leaders. It is the organizer's job to look at all the resources . . . to stretch people's imagination of what's possible."

OCO's position as a multi-issue community organization allows organizers to select issues that resonate with individual constituents' concerns. These concerns are identified by LOC leaders, who meet with residents in their communities in one-to-one conversations. LOC leaders then compile these concerns and frame them as a larger, shared agenda that can unite neighborhoods for action. As citywide advocates, however, OCO leaders recognize that a select group of organizers alone cannot carry out campaigns. OCO's executive director suggests that "third-party organizations" need to be critical partners to community leaders and public officials. Thus, in some instances, OCO partners with the institutions that it seeks to change, such as the Oakland Unified School District. Professional relations with city agencies and political leaders grant OCO legitimacy at the grassroots level, while OCO lends "street credibility" to the policy makers with whom it collaborates. PICO's organizing principles—people need power, power lies in relationships, and relationships are reciprocal—support this relational culture. Although OCO challenges officials in large actions, it does so in a constructive style, sharing questions in advance and respecting the commitment of the leaders they confront. According to executive director Ron Snyder, it is through these relationships that OCO aims to "change the whole system" as well as the processes by which change occurs.

OCO's current membership reaches beyond religious institutions to families and children without church affiliations. However, religion is infused throughout campaigns—such as incorporating religious stories and symbols into position statements—to forge a link between individual faith and political participation. OCO's work is political, not proselytizing, but faith remains a decisive motivator for staff and church leaders. For many individual participants, "it's strong faith values that drive them." Other leaders have attended church out of habit or tradition, relying on "form rather than substance," and the work of OCO transforms their faith experience.

OCO recognizes that establishing an organizing base through congregations makes available to the organization a large set of devoted supporters, something other professional advocates regularly seek. Yet it is the personally transformative nature of organizing that compels church members to act on their faith outside the church structure. The relationship between church membership and political organizing is, as OCO's executive director describes, "symbiotic in many ways." Religion helps organizers understand and justify political tension or conflict to inspire activism; faith then acts as a bridge between community members to harness their individual concerns into a united public voice. The executive director of the PICO California project said that organizers ask themselves, "How do you bring people together around hope and around a positive vision?" He thinks the context in which advocacy organizations operate plays a significant role: "When people enter the church they leave their attitudes and ugly behavior at the door."

One of OCO's most successful and systemic policy campaigns—its recent work to promote small schools in Oakland—provides a representative view of how the organization relies upon its core principles of organic issue generation and leadership development to instigate local change. OCO is able to move from one issue to the next in part because leaders and organizers recognize that the issues themselves are connected. For example, OCO's successful campaign to tear down an old abandoned Montgomery Ward store was instigated by local residents who complained that the building was an "eyesore." Later two leaders noticed a new developer seeking a permit to build over 100 units on the property. Concerned with the number of residential units, potential parking issues, and the decision to use the land for housing and not a new school (previously sought by community members to alleviate overcrowding in schools), LOC leaders met with the property owner, the developer, and the district's city council member to construct an alternative plan.

In the 1990s OCO organizers responded to members' concerns about dilapidated school facilities, overcrowded buildings, and a lack of after-school programs throughout the community. To address these issues, OCO first initiated a successful campaign to secure more money from the state for after-school programs. Yet the core problem remained: an antiquated school system that was failing to meet student demands and school overenrollment. OCO thus turned its attention to systemwide reform and began its advocacy efforts to create new small schools within the Oakland school district.

In order for OCO to shift its attention from after-school programs and dirty bathrooms to school district reform, OCO formalized relationships with parents, teachers, and the school district and strategically partnered with the Bay Area Coalition for Equitable Schools (BayCES). Together they centered on "fixing the system" by implementing a districtwide small schools campaign.[8] OCO retained its fundamental organizing model but expanded its agenda to seek more extensive and deeper reform. In partnership with BayCES, OCO was able to secure a state commitment of $8.2 billion for new school construction. OCO and BayCES were later joined by OUSD to form the Small Schools Initiative (SSI), which worked to create the New Small Autonomous Schools Policy.

OCO did not foresee that acting upon its members' initial concerns would lead to such a policy. Rather, it proceeded incrementally to address growing concerns as they arose; as the executive director of People Acting in Community Together (PACT), formerly an OCO staffer, put it, "It started with a focus on dirty bathrooms . . . And we were all learning how complicated the problem was." The small schools policy resulted in the opening of six new autonomous schools at the beginning of the 2001 school year. OUSD, through requests for proposals and oversight from SSI sponsors, has continued to invite new school designs and conversions or subdivisions of large comprehensive high schools. With the help of OCO's citywide campaign, Cesar Chavez Elementary School, the first school built in Oakland in thirty years, is now operating on the disputed Montgomery Ward site, and OCO is nationally known for its successful community-driven school reform effort—an effort that began by listening to residents' concerns and grew into a major policy triumph that has changed the public school system in Oakland.

In addition to its strategic relationships with organizations like BayCES and its emphasis on local leadership development, OCO uses research and presents its findings at large political actions to advance its campaigns. Organizers use data to expose social inequalities that are of concern to residents; these data then help OCO pressure policy makers to address issues, propose alternatives, and monitor outcomes. As a former OCO organizer and California PICO executive director explains: "It's definitely policy research that enables us to put forward proposals . . . The classic protest model is [that] you react to government and it's negative, whereas if you walk in the door and say this is what we want to do and this is how you can fund it, you become a proactive player."

OCO's large public rallies are also the most visible aspect of its work. The organization's political events take place in churches, community recreation centers, and schools and have attracted thousands of residents. With the help of media publicity, the actions provoke public promises from officials. For example, in 2004, OCO launched a campaign in support of a city crime prevention initiative, Measure Y, to secure funding for positive youth programs and more police enforcement. As part of this effort, OCO hosted research actions that helped to register thousands of voters; direct involvement of city and county agencies and public officials also helped OCO to insert specific language in the legislation. Although the city's previous attempts to pass similar prevention measures were unsuccessful, OCO's community recruitment efforts helped secure a victory.[9] Such meetings not only provide residents opportunities to interact with policy makers but also help to fuel a campaign and broaden constituency support. As one OCO organizer explained, "People get excited when they meet the chief of police, mayor, and education board. They feel they have the power to give their testimony . . . and spread the word to others."

San Francisco Organizing Project

The San Francisco Organizing Project (SFOP), like OCO, belongs to the PICO National Network. SFOP is a faith-based, grassroots, membership organization comprising thirty-seven congregations as well as two schools and a youth organization, all in San Francisco. Together, these parts of SFOP represent over 40,000 families—a constituency that far exceeds the organization's paid staff of six and that gives SFOP significant political influence because of the large crowds it can rally for public events. SFOP's work centers on making San Francisco a livable city for its diverse population—particularly low- and moderate-income families. Although SFOP is not explicitly a child advocacy organization, its focus on families commits it to many issues affecting the welfare of children and youth, including public education, recreation, housing, and health care. Following the PICO model, SFOP makes leadership development its first priority, and it tackles social justice issues by empowering its members to become advocates through the context of their faith.

SFOP was founded in 1982 and has been a member of the PICO National Network since 1992. In its decade as an independent organization before joining PICO, SFOP was a coalition of faith-based organizations and unions that grew out of local Catholic community organizing efforts; SFOP focused on safety and health care during this period. Increasing dissatisfaction with its labor union partnerships, however, prompted the organization to join PICO to clarify its identity and strategy. Like OCO, SFOP receives technical assistance, a consulting director, and access to PICO's national network of organizations in exchange for membership dues. SFOP's professional staff includes an executive director and five community organizers; SFOP is governed by a board made up of up to five members from each active member congregation, as well as an executive board with one member from each congregation. SFOP, like OCO, has local organizing committees (LOCs) based in its member congregations as well as issue-based committees for its citywide campaign areas, including education, housing, and health care. Although SFOP staff coordinate LOCs, local leaders are responsible for directing and executing the committees' work. SFOP staff manage citywide campaigns, but SFOP's work largely falls to local leaders to develop their leadership capacity, in line with a central PICO organizing principle, "organizers teach leaders, leaders organize." SFOP staff, therefore, are best understood as facilitators rather than managers of the organization's work. SFOP has an annual budget of about $730,000, most of which comes from foundations, with additional support from corporations, individual donors, congregation dues, event proceeds, and contracts with other nonprofits.

Although SFOP's advocacy work follows residents' concerns rather than a fixed agenda that focuses on children and youth, SFOP has a history of successful youth-related campaigns in San Francisco. In the mid 1990s, SFOP's neighborhood revitalization work included a $7 million initiative to establish a youth center in the city, which opened in 1998 and is now part of the San Francisco Boys and Girls Club. Several years later, SFOP helped to secure $7 million to install cameras on city buses in response to students who felt unsafe riding to school; in one trial, these cameras reduced violence on buses by 80 percent. And in 2000, SFOP worked with the California PICO Network to secure $50 million from the state for after-school programs, thirty-six of which are located in San Francisco.

SFOP organizers perceive members' faith to be a significant advantage for the organization because faith gives its members a common framework within which to work. SFOP believes community members' religious commitments can promote and support civic engagement and activism. As one SFOP partner said, "The church is a natural built community." Faith is woven throughout the activities of the organization. Prayers or passages of scripture are read at the opening of meetings, and members often refer to their faith when discussing issues that concern them. SFOP also gains moral legitimacy among city actors from the faith of its members, according to its executive director, Kim Grose. Different LOCs, however, invoke faith to different degrees depending on the nature of their work and members' background; scripture, for example, has permeated a church-based LOC, while the education committee takes a more secular stance. This variety allows SFOP to incorporate residents of many faiths as well as those who have questioned how they might fit into the faith culture of the organization, including an atheist board member and a staff organizer who was initially hesitant about faith-based organizing.

SFOP's emphasis on helping community members become their own advocates commits the organization to making leadership development its top priority. Staff organizers identify potential leaders in one-to-one meetings with community members and then provide abundant opportunities for residents to get involved in campaigns so that they can learn, by experience, how to advocate for policy change. As one SFOP organizer describes it, the "world view of organizing is that people learn through experiences so you are constantly creating experiences." Because SFOP aims to give as many residents as possible opportunities to learn and practice advocacy strategies, the organization does not have one spokesperson, as many typical advocacy groups do. As Grose notes, San Francisco public officials would probably acknowledge that they deal with many different SFOP-affiliated residents because the organization is "cycling through a lot of different people." Although this lack of continuity could have drawbacks for SFOP, the organization mitigates this risk with its well-defined procedures and scripts for meetings with public officials, which allow residents to manage events. Leadership development, in spite of its limitations, takes precedence over outcomes.

SFOP's emphasis on process over outcomes deeply shapes the way in which the organization selects and frames the issues it pursues. SFOP organizers say that the concerns that members want to address arise from the pain that they feel in their daily lives, which they share in one-to-one meetings or at other SFOP events. As a result of this organic issue-generation process, an organizer believes that residents involved with SFOP tend to feel the work that they do is "from the heart rather than the head." SFOP's training helps new leaders translate personal concerns into broader, actionable campaigns; this training often centers on assisting individuals turn a problem (which SFOP views as an unmanageable task) into an issue (viewed as a manageable task) that can result in concrete changes. In many ways, SFOP's campaigns are therefore more opportunistic and pragmatic than they are expert. The majority of SFOP's work involves helping residents identify and seize opportunities to improve their daily lives by developing their leadership skills to address policy issues. SFOP's members identify problems, research and analyze current and proposed policies, and then hold meetings with public officials to win their support. As one close partner said of SFOP's process, "they know how to make grassroots work and policy work come together, and that's probably the most powerful thing that they do."

This reliance on leadership development does limit SFOP's potential impact, however. The solutions that leaders devise may not be what experts would consider the best response to policy problems. Moreover, leadership training is time consuming. It prevents SFOP from doing in-depth policy research, and the organization must endure a slower process than professional advocacy organizations as it attends to individuals' needs and skills. SFOP maintains, however, that the people closest to the problems know what solutions are best for them. PICO principles also suggest that when community members collectively identify and resolve community issues, they are more likely to assume ownership of policy solutions in a way that increases the probability that solutions are successful.

Before 2001, SFOP had done only piecemeal organizing work related to education. Yet as word of OCO's success with small schools reform in Oakland spread across the bay, educators in San Francisco were inspired to attempt similar reforms.[10] Although SFOP typically proceeds from members' concerns, SFOP's small schools campaign began when a group of teachers from a troubled San Francisco high school approached the organization about initiating a reform effort. SFOP formed a relationship with the teachers' new organization, Small Schools for Equity, and consulted its members about their interest in pursuing a small schools campaign. Once they determined that members were interested in school reform, SFOP leaders traveled to New York City to visit small schools there and then organized an action with about 250 parents to raise awareness in San Francisco about small schools. A school board resolution for the creation of small schools failed to pass in January 2002, but SFOP leaders persisted with their campaign and held another action in June 2002 to hold district officials accountable to their intention of starting small schools through a High School Task Force. In the end, Small Schools for

Equity won a district grant to start a small school; the new school opened in September 2003 with 100 ninth graders and was to expand each year until it is a full high school with about 320 to 400 students.

In its campaign for small schools, SFOP recognized the necessity of taking on more systemic policy problems. While SFOP had initially begun organizing around an individual school, it quickly found that lasting education change would come only from organizing around the entire school system. The new school superintendent formed a working group to write a small schools policy, and SFOP was involved in that process, meeting with the new superintendent in early 2006, monitoring the work, and ensuring broad participation. They were also "organizing money" for the infrastructure. As the executive director observes, their organizing efforts and leadership development are in large part helping the organization to be prepared for the time "when the window opens" for a political opportunity.

SFOP continued its work with youth in other ways too. In November 2005, SFOP also launched Avenues of Hope, a campaign to provide positive opportunities for youth, particularly older youth, as a way to stem violence in the city, using money from the city's $100 million surplus. As part of this effort, SFOP secured hundreds of summer jobs for youth in the justice system. It has also worked for job training programs and promoting small autonomous schools as an alternative for many youth.

Although SFOP was able to have an impact on the small schools movement in San Francisco, the movement itself had not yet had a significant impact in the city in large part because it has not achieved the same level of institutional or financial support as it has in Oakland and elsewhere. The lack of district support has been a struggle; a large grant from the Gates Foundation for the redesign effort, for example, was cut significantly because the district did not have a comprehensive policy for small schools (Blitstein 2006; Knight 2005b). But while their small schools campaign went through fits and starts over four years, SFOP's persistence began to pay off.

Coleman Advocates for Children and Youth

Coleman Advocates for Children and Youth in San Francisco, in contrast to SFOP and OCO, is an independent, secular advocacy organization that focuses exclusively on issues related to children and youth. Like SFOP and OCO, Coleman has enjoyed an unusually long life for an advocacy organization, with its origin extending back to the 1960s. Coleman aims to secure support for child-friendly policies and programs by exerting pressure on public officials to be accountable to their constituents—particularly low-income children and families often neglected in interest group politics. Through vigilant monitoring of public officials and its willingness to be strategically confrontational with local government, Coleman generates political pressure in San Francisco to keep children's needs at the top of the public agenda. Coleman traditionally has been particularly attentive to the development of the city budget as a political process, and it carefully follows the allocation of public resources. This strategy distinguishes it from other advocacy organizations because it enables Coleman to proactively influence the allocation of public funds at their source, rather than taking a reactive stance to budget decisions.

Coleman began as an organization dedicated to juvenile justice reform; it was created from a predecessor group, Citizens for Juvenile Justice in San Francisco, started by San Francisco resident Jean Jacobs. Jacobs was concerned about conditions for children in the juvenile justice system and became instrumental in securing funds to start another nonprofit to advocate for children more generally. In 1975, members of Citizens for Juvenile Justice incorporated Coleman Advocates to be this new voice for children in San Francisco. Coleman began advocating for the rights of children in the juvenile justice and foster care systems. Yet Coleman gradually decided that it needed to focus on a broader children's agenda to address the enduring problems of urban poverty that children face. In 1978, Coleman expanded its agenda beyond the juvenile justice system and later adopted a more general mission: "Making San Francisco a better place for children." During our data collection period, Coleman's agenda included child care, public education, affordable housing, parks and recreation, and health care, in addition to its founding commitment to juvenile justice reform.

In contrast to SFOP and OCO, with their heavy reliance on grassroots volunteers, Coleman has historically been a staff-run advocacy organization with about seven full-time professional staff who have been responsible for developing and executing the organization's campaigns. Coleman does convene service providers and community activists across sectors to support its campaigns, but it does not have official members like OCO and SFOP's congregations. Coleman has about twenty board members representing a variety of professions and interests, including medicine, law, education, and community organizing. Coleman also has a National Advisory Board, chaired by Peter Edelman of Georgetown University Law Center. Coleman's annual budget is approximately $760,000, the majority of which comes from foundations.

Coleman is also home to a youth organizing group, Youth Making a Change (YMAC), and, during our data collection period, a parent organizing group, called Parent Activists for Youth (PAY). YMAC and PAY are largely autonomous groups within Coleman's structure; they have their own budgets and select their own campaign issues, though they do coordinate with Coleman as a strategic partner that can offer critical aid to their efforts. Coleman started YMAC in 1991; it operates as a member-based organization in which youth members select and pursue issues of concern to them, including the condition of school bathrooms, creating school-based health centers, and creating a policy to regulate police on school campuses. According to a former Coleman staff member, YMAC reflects Coleman's belief that community members—particularly young people—can and should become advocates for themselves. Building on its commitment to empower residents to become advocates, Coleman founded PAY in 1994. Issues that PAY has taken on include improving city recreation programs, public parks, school governance, affordable child care, and programs for children with special needs. The director of PAY emphasizes that the group is more diverse than typical parent groups such as the PTA, and it is this diversity that gives the group greater legitimacy when advocating for issues that affect a cross-section of the public, such as education. The youth and parents that YMAC and PAY bring to Coleman help gain the organization legitimacy in many neighborhoods and make Coleman more than a group of professionals advocating on behalf of communities. As a former associate director of Coleman said, this inclusion of parents and youth within the structure of Coleman ensure that "the issues are real issues coming from real people."

Although Coleman's campaign issues may not explicitly reflect a commitment to a particular conception of children's rights, Coleman's ethos as a child advocacy organization is deeply rooted in a belief about the role of the polity in providing for children's welfare. Coleman is unequivocal about its belief that it is the duty of government to provide for children by ensuring their basic needs. Yet Coleman also asserts that "policies and programs for children, youth and their families should be determined by the *community,* particularly those directly impacted by those policies and programs."[11] Coleman's work is thus twofold and implicates both the private and public sectors: Basic rights and needs should be defined locally, but resources to realize these rights and needs should be ensured by public institutions. Coleman's work first involves helping residents prioritize their needs—a process that occurs most directly through YMAC and PAY. With this input, Coleman proceeds to construct a campaign around these dominant issues to marshal support from elected officials for reforms. Coleman then positions itself as a "watchdog" to ensure that government institutions fulfill their responsibilities to children.

As Coleman's advocacy agenda for children and youth has expanded over the years, its advocacy tactics have also evolved. Coleman initially concentrated its efforts on city departments that were service providers, such as juvenile probation, but budget cuts and impasses with public officials and agencies led Coleman to shift its focus to City Hall and the political process.[12] As Coleman became increasingly involved in politics in San Francisco to advocate for children, it learned to use the media to get public officials' attention instead of meeting with officials directly. A longtime Coleman board member noted this shift in strategy: "We were at a point of diminishing returns of sitting down and being really nice with people in city government." Coleman has been particularly attentive to the San Francisco city budget and carefully monitors the allocation of public funds to fight against what it views as gratuitous spending that siphons resources from children's programs. In addition to monitoring the distribution of existing funds, Coleman has also worked to create new sources of funding for children, most notably in its successful and nationally recognized Children's Amendment campaign, which dedicates a percentage of city tax revenue to children's services.

Coleman's work to pass the Children's Amendment illustrates how Coleman has historically prioritized outcomes over process, in contrast to SFOP and OCO. In 1991, Coleman had reached an impasse with the mayor of San Francisco, who refused to continue discussions with Coleman regarding the share of public funds spent on children and youth. Intent on increasing the city's budget for children and youth services, Coleman circumvented this roadblock by collecting signatures for a ballot measure to establish a Children's Fund, which dedicates .025 percent of local property tax revenue to children's services. The measure passed and has been reauthorized, indicating that Coleman's efforts have been institutionalized in local government and affirming Coleman's foundational belief that it is the responsibility of government to meet children's basic needs. Coleman's efforts to pass the Children's Amendment undoubtedly gave involved parents and youth an opportunity to develop their leadership skills and witness firsthand the potential of civic activism. However, these lessons were by-products; Coleman's clear priority was passing the measure.

Coleman also closely monitors elected officials and reports back to the community on whether officials' or candidates' statements and actions are "child friendly." The localness of Coleman's advocacy makes this sort of watchdog activity possible because Coleman can communicate directly with voters and elected officials in San Francisco. Coleman circulates a weekly "Advocate Alert" by email and fax to communicate politicians' promises and to distribute information about its concerns and campaigns to residents; it also issues "report cards" on officials' performance. A former Coleman staff member highlighted the content and efficacy of these forms of communication: "Even if no one reads the fax alert, the fact that the politician knows that information is in the hands of thousands of people matters." Like SFOP and OCO, Coleman also holds large public rallies in strategically visible locations to compel public officials to respond to its campaigns.

Coleman's focus on institutional reform means that its successful campaigns often culminate in the creation of new advisory committees to public officials, new policies, and new laws to support children and youth. Examples include the passage of the Children's Fund (Proposition J), creation of the San Francisco Youth Commission, the creation of the Juvenile Probation Commission, and the creation of the Mayor's Department of Children, Youth and Families (which its former executive director presently heads). These successes mark the moments at which Coleman hands off its campaigns to local government entities, entrusting them to carry forward policies supportive of children and youth. They signal a shift from dependence on the mobilization of community members—a process requiring much time and continuing effort—to the harnessing of the interests and energy of full-time officials who are authorized to make decisions and to take actions on the public's behalf. There are drawbacks to this outcome of advocacy; once Coleman hands off its efforts to government bodies, it largely loses control of the implementation process. But according to Coleman's former executive director, this limitation is perhaps what naturally separates advocates from direct-service providers and evaluators. Advocates can secure resources, but others have to make effective use of them. Coleman may have to relinquish implementation control of policies passed to realize its goals; but, nonetheless, its efforts gain stability and the official sanction of local government. A former staff member emphasized Coleman's unique ability to embed its reform goals in government, saying that Coleman leaves in its wake "a trail of institutions." In addition to this historic focus on institutionalizing its reform efforts, Coleman's new leadership also seems to be moving the organization more toward a community organizing and empowerment model.

Dimensions of Organizational Design and Repertoires of Action

As these case descriptions imply, OCO, SFOP, and Coleman have similarities and differences in their organizational design and in the strategies and tactics they employ in their work. Comparisons of these dimensions help illustrate different ways to address advocacy for children and youth and suggest different frameworks and logics for this work, which we will address in the next chapter.

Organizational Structure

Organizational structures refer to the archetype adopted for organizational features such as governance systems, staffing arrangements, and the extent and stability of interdependence with other organizations.[13] Despite historical differences in the ways in which Coleman, OCO, and SFOP have involved residents in their advocacy efforts, cursory inspection suggests that their organizational structures are similar in many ways. The organizations are approximately the same size, with roughly similar staffs and budgets; all have governance boards, all collaborate with other organizations in pursuing their goals, and all have involved citizens in their advocacy efforts. However, closer inspection suggests quite fundamental differences, particularly between Coleman's structure on the one hand and OCO's and SFOP's on the other, with respect to professional staff and community members, relationships with other organizations, governance boards, and funding.

Professional and Community Staff Coleman's structure during our data collection period may be characterized as a *professionally directed advocacy structure:* a type of organization that places primary responsibility for the design and implementation of advocacy efforts on its professional staff. Coleman's greater reliance on its professional staff to select and pursue campaign issues allows it to seize on political opportunities as well as to employ strategies most likely to realize policy reform. For example, Coleman's decision to draft the Children's Amendment after reaching an impasse with the mayor about the city budget was not contingent on constituents' consensus. As a professionally run organization, it had the flexibility to quickly turn to the ballot initiative process to meet its policy goal of increasing city spending on children and youth.

By contrast, both OCO and SFOP embody *professionally enabled, volunteer-staffed advocacy structures* that emphasize the education and empowerment of laypersons, whether youth or adult, to assume a leading role in defining and achieving policy objectives. Their commitment to leadership development puts residents in charge of executing campaigns. Although the policy solutions that members propose are often not "expert" and might not have as much traction as "professional solutions," said SFOP's executive director, they do reflect both the interests and actions of those most affected by the policy outcomes.[14]

Organizations that are devoted to improving or altering social arrangements are generally cognizant and intentional about their internal makeup so that the composition of the organization reflects the type of social order for which the organization is advocating. The role and relationship of staff to local community members and officials, for example, is closely linked to the organizations' management scheme. OCO, SFOP, and Coleman each illustrate this relationship by striving to include community members in central, substantive ways. The participation of a critical mass of local residents not only gives the organizations more leverage with elected officials but may also help advocacy organizations achieve legitimacy in the neighborhoods in which they work so as not to appear as just a group of professional advocates or policy wonks. Although OCO, SFOP, and Coleman share this goal of incorporating residents into the structure of their organizations, they do so in distinct ways that bear on the nature of the advocacy work that they undertake.

SFOP and OCO, unlike Coleman, are coalitions with membership made up mostly of congregations and several small schools created by their advocacy efforts. Staff train volunteer leaders and coordinate local organizing committees (LOCs) responsible for carrying out organizing work. Involved community members are therefore fully incorporated into the structure of SFOP and OCO, and there is less separation between staff and residents. As one OCO staff member explained, most of the time, staff and community leaders are "doing the same things, reading and thinking, and all in response to what's happening locally." SFOP and OCO's staffs represent a small fraction of each organization's available workers.

Because SFOP and OCO are dedicated first and foremost to fostering democratic participation through local leadership development, they do not have one widely recognized person to represent their organization as do many advocacy organizations, including Coleman. This structure allows a changing cadre of residents to serve as leaders of campaigns, while at the same time allowing the organizations to maintain relationships with officials because their meetings had a standard format that public officials came to recognize and respect. An SFOP board member called the organization a "well-oiled machine" because of its internal procedures and scripted meetings with public officials that enable residents unfamiliar with conventional political protocols to become effectively engaged.

Coleman's central mission—improving San Francisco for families—has not much constrained the organization in the past with respect to internal processes.[15] Coleman has been able to shift quickly from one campaign to another as called for by changing opportunities. Their staff has functioned as "experts" capable of assessing conditions and devising responses without having to consult with constituents at length before pursuing a course of action. By contrast, SFOP and OCO's central commitment to engaging local residents restricts their ability to rapidly shift targets or tactics.

Because SFOP and OCO are focused on leadership development, the organizations have a wider range of individuals involved in their structure and emphasize civic engagement more so than particular policy issues. This commitment to empowering citizens is demonstrated by the autonomy members have within LOCs to define and execute advocacy campaigns, from start to finish: Members decide what social issues to pursue, what specifically to advocate for, and how to go about achieving desired reforms. This stance makes SFOP and OCO sites for widespread democratic participation and mobilization and ensures that their advocacy campaigns are not executed *on behalf* of families and youth, but rather with them leading the way.

This membership-driven organizational structure has benefits and drawbacks. OCO's structure as a network of faith-based organizations, as discussed further below, helps their ability to turn out large crowds for their events and, by extension, augments their legitimacy with elected officials. This structure, though, in a different context, can have limitations. At the end of SFOP's initial small schools campaign, it turned its attention to other issues, as prioritized by its members, and education mobilizing waned. Because SFOP and OCO's campaigns are driven by residents' concerns, they face the possibility that their goals may be viewed as inconsistent or short-term; the organizations do not have the capacity to manage multiple large issues at once.

Coleman also seeks to involve residents in its organizational structure but has historically done so in ways that do not permeate the organization as thoroughly. Instead of relying on residents to define and execute all of its campaigns, during our data collection period Coleman enabled parents and youth to direct a subset of the organization's activities through its parent (PAY) and youth (YMAC) organizing groups. These groups are encouraged to choose their own issue campaigns, which have historically been separate from staff-defined programs and campaigns. For example, the youth in YMAC are taught to think of Coleman as a critical ally. The structure of YMAC is also different from Coleman's, as are its core beliefs. YMAC is a membership group, and its philosophy centers on the "self-determination for young people and communities of color," said the director of youth policy and development, while Coleman's advocacy orientation has represented more of a fiduciary model for change. Coleman's former executive director comments that it is difficult to have YMAC youth more involved in the decision-making processes of the organization, such as sitting on the Board: "The kinds of things boards do, [youth] tend to get bored with. You work so hard to engage them and support them, and then they really want to just be in YMAC." Tensions also sometimes exist between Coleman and PAY due to their different perspectives. According to PAY's director, parents involved in PAY may feed a greater sense of urgency for reform than do professional advocates, who recognize that change comes slowly.

Because Coleman has involved parents and youth through separate entities within its organization, there has been a greater distinction between the role of its staff and that of involved citizens. Outside PAY and YMAC, Coleman staff largely directed the organization's campaigns during our data collection period; although they seek input from residents, they have historically pursued the organization's policy goals and enlisted residents for support. This structure, therefore, is less integrated than that of OCO or SFOP. Because Coleman has involved parents and youth in semi-independent organizational entities, it faced the additional task of holding its constitutive parts together—a challenge that OCO and SFOP do not confront because resident involvement is built into the organizations' structure more systemically.

In both instances, however, leadership, whether from staff "experts" or community members, requires a series of compromises and negotiation among diverse stakeholders—city and school officials, educational or other employee groups, or other residents with differing interests. Effective leaders in this environment, as Philip Selznick (1957) reminds us, are those who are able to transform relationships that are often overly bureaucratic or impersonal into connections that people value. In addition to forging relationships with public officials, advocacy groups have distinct ways of working with each other; we next turn to these interorganizational relationships.

Relationships with Other Organizations   Perhaps the greatest point of structural contrast between our focal organizations is the nature of their relationship with other organizations: stable versus shifting networks. SFOP and OCO are members of the PICO National Network, while Coleman operates as an independent organization. Permanent network structures like PICO can both inhibit and greatly enhance the work of their member organizations. On the one hand, PICO provides SFOP and OCO with a family of like-minded organizations with which to network and share strategies, as well as technical assistance from the national organization. The relational characteristics of networks like this can boost organizations' ability to learn and transfer new knowledge and skills (Powell, 1990). On the other hand, it binds SFOP and OCO to the PICO model. Coleman's independence from fixed networks similarly has its advantages and disadvantages; this flexibility allows Coleman to enter and exit strategic, issue-based partnerships as needed, but it does not provide the stable network of support that structures such as PICO can supply.

OCO's executive director believes the stronger and more permanent the network, the better. The PICO network provides a large and stable base from which to operate and enables organizers and community leaders to share expertise and coalesce around common goals to strengthen particular campaigns. The national staff of PICO also provides training assistance for and organizational oversight of OCO and SFOP, supporting these local affiliates' administration as well as adding a layer of accountability for organizational outcomes.

Becoming a member of PICO requires mutual interest on the part of PICO leaders and an established community advocacy organization, and according to the executive director of PICO's California Project, PICO historically has added between one and three affiliates a year. OCO's executive director commented that existing community organizations hoping to affiliate with the network set up a series of meetings with PICO staff and become familiar with the "consistent model that allows leaders to communicate across organizations." Although leaders representing different organizations gather for annual national training to share ideas, to reflect on the year's campaigns, and to provide guidance and advice for organizing, PICO affiliates retain their individual character and local identity. OCO and SFOP therefore remain dependent on local community leadership, and decisions are made locally in organizing committees. As SFOP's executive director underscored, despite the strength of the PICO network, each PICO organization is different according to "local taste" and "director's style."

Being based in a network of established, ongoing organizations, such as church congregations or unions, enables organizations to have access to an existing store of social capital—a collection of organized individuals who know and trust one another and can provide a ready body of prospective conscripts for ongoing reform efforts. The faith-based aspects of such organizations provide many participants with a common frame of reference and common core values. As Warren (2001, p. 21) notes, "religion can offer a moral vision for political action."

Nevertheless, some limitations and drawbacks are associated with OCO's and SFOP's membership with PICO. The goal-setting procedures, which emphasize participation and consensus, reduce organizational flexibility and ability to respond rapidly to changing circumstances. In addition, embedding all issues in a faith-based framework means that more controversial or divisive issues, such as abortion, are simply "off the table" for such organizations. Sometimes these controversial issues also tend to be more about individual choices; according to OCO's executive director, they are consequently not issues of concern for their community organizing.

It is because of such constraints that many advocacy organizations prefer to operate more independently. Thus, Coleman deliberately refuses to join permanent networks or coalitions at the city, state, or national level. In contrast to OCO and SFOP, Coleman's former executive director firmly believes that coalitions should be created or joined only on an as-needed basis: "Coalitions work best around specific issues and people. We prefer to go in and out of coalitions depending on what the issue is." Such fluid, issue-based partnerships allow Coleman to accomplish discrete goals without the extra effort required to maintain ongoing relationships. Coleman avoids the tension that OCO faces between moving forward with advocacy activity and returning to the cycle of leadership development to sustain the PICO network and increase its own member base.[16] Moreover, forming permanent coalitions within the child advocacy arena—a narrower focus than PICO's work—is particularly challenging given the field's instability. Brodkin said: "I guess the whole advocacy community is so unstable you can't talk about 'permanent.' There are only a certain number of permanent structures."

Still, Coleman's independence from a network like PICO does not mean that it works in isolation. It has "stable" partnerships with "allies"—those organizations that are likely to agree with Coleman's position on most issues, such as the child-serving organizations in the San Francisco Child Advocacy

Network (SFCAN). Such partnerships may take on a variety of forms, depending on Coleman's needs. Coleman has very strong partners ("almost permanent") with the Youth Commission and the Student Advisory Council (both units operating within the city government) around youth organizing issues. The maintenance of other partnerships might amount to little more than a Coleman staff member attending a meeting once a year to lend symbolic support to a like-minded organization. Coalitions and partnerships also shift, depending on the issue and leadership. For example, Coleman's former executive director acknowledged that San Francisco's Parent Teacher Association, though usually "very weak on advocacy," can be a helpful ally on a particular issue or when its leadership is strong. Labor unions are also "on and off" allies, including the controversial teachers' union. Brodkin said, "Most of my colleagues in the child advocacy world hate the teachers' union. I believe in developing real partnerships with the teachers' union." Other strong partnerships are rooted in specific relationships staff members have with other groups or service providers, like Coleman's lead in organizing SFCAN.

Despite this basic difference regarding network membership, these organizations share beliefs about the importance of forming local coalitions and having fluid rather than fixed partnerships. Although Coleman has reservations about permanent coalitions, it recognizes the importance of forming coalitions around children's issues so that organizations can come to see themselves as part of a larger field with common goals and to move agencies beyond their basic concerns for securing funding to a sense of a larger, shared purpose.

Coalitions also compensate for the limited capacity of an organization's staff. As Coleman's former executive director observes, "When you have four staff people or two staff people or even six people, you have to work through other organizations as much as individuals." And although Coleman is not a membership organization, as OCO or SFOP are, a former Coleman assistant director noted a similarity: Just as SFOP [and OCO] are dependent on congregations, Coleman is dependent on service providers for access to families. On the flip side, even though SFOP and OCO are permanent members of a national network, one of PICO's central tenets is: No permanent allies, no permanent enemies. This principle does not endorse long-lasting partnerships with those organizations outside of PICO's membership but rather encourages relationships that shift as issues and leadership change. For example, when OCO actively recruited teachers, administrators, and parents to support school reform, for the first time non–faith institutional actors became active participants in

Table 6.1 Case Organization Funding[a]

	Coleman ('04–'05)	SFOP ('04–'05)	OCO ('04–'05)
Annual budget	$763,000	$732,000	$839,000
Total assets	$3,500,000	$642,000	$830,000
Gifts received	$932,000	$970,000	$666,000
Membership dues	None	$ 28,000	$ 6,700
Program/Consulting revenue	$58,000	$66,000	None
Lobbying expenses	$3,015	None	None

[a]Numbers are rounded; OCO and Coleman budgets taken from IRS Form 990 2004–2005; SFOP budget is from its financial statement.

the PICO model. Thus, in spite of their basic structural differences regarding network membership, SFOP, OCO, and Coleman converge on the necessity of building local coalitions to advance broad goals and agree that such coalitions can and should shift over time as issues and contexts change.

Funding   Although each of our focal advocacy organizations receives support from local foundations and other philanthropic sources, their different organizational forms and goals generate differences in the source and stability of funding for the organizations. (See Table 6.1.) SFOP and OCO, for example, receive membership dues from congregations and other organizations participating in their networks, while historically Coleman has not, though these dues are not a large percentage of SFOP's or OCO's income. Coleman, on the other hand, generates some revenue from programs in the form of rental services, while SFOP and OCO do not.[17]

While the organizations' annual budgets vary somewhat, with OCO's the largest, their total assets are quite different, with Coleman's assets over four times that of OCO and over five times that of SFOP, likely due to Coleman's ownership of its building. These organizations rely heavily on foundations, however, with SFOP getting 60 percent of its funding from foundations and OCO 98 percent. This funding reality means that they all are subject to the programmatic changes that occur regularly at foundations and must contend with a lack of long-term support for general expenses.[18]

Organizational design alone cannot tell the story of advocacy organizations' work. Structures interact with sets of tactics and strategies, known as repertoires of action, in efforts to achieve social change, and it is these repertoires that we consider next.

Repertoires of Action

The ways in which organizations carry out their work—their repertoires of action—follow from the frames and logics that shape the problems they identify and tackle. Repertoires of action consist of the activities or tactics that organizations employ to achieve their goals. All types of organizations embrace a set of distinctive forms of action. As Tilly observes: "Collective action usually takes well-defined forms already familiar to participants" (1978, p. 143). This is true of social movements; it is even truer of organizations. For advocacy organizations, frequent actions include holding rallies, conducting research, sponsoring forums for political candidates, canvassing, and leadership training.

Political influence is not necessarily a resource contest: Those with the most money or people do not always win (Clemens, 1997). This observation bodes well for advocates for children and youth, who are unlikely to have deep pockets and may be hard-pressed to mobilize a massive body of supporters. Contest models of political influence do not tell the full story; the strategic use of resources—and a willingness to alter tactics in response to changed conditions—can be just as critical to an organization's success as its budget or size (Clemens 1997). Flexibility is critical: Tactics that work in an affordable housing campaign, for example, may not be effective in public school reform efforts. Moreover, the choices that organizations make regarding what strategies to use to advance their cause can either heighten their impact or push them outside the sphere of influence. We explore these choices here, particularly how the use of familiar organizational forms and a recognized repertoire of action in political contexts may enhance the prospects for success, making institutional change more likely.

The larger population of organizations advocating for youth in San Francisco and Oakland employs a wide range of tactics (see Chapter 5). We have depicted the various approaches utilized by organizations—including carrying out political campaigns, measuring accountability, attempting to build civic capacity, conducting research, and formulating policies. Here, we emphasize that specific organizations are defined by the particular repertoire of tactics they use. SFOP and OCO, on the one hand, and Coleman, on the other, select from a limited range of action repertoires as they attempt to meet the changing demands of specific issues and political climates.

Coleman's Repertoire   Coleman's major actions during our study were directed at challenging and changing the political agenda of the city of San Francisco so as to increase resources available for the positive development of youth. Rather than focusing exclusively on a specific issue—such as job training, juvenile justice, or education—Coleman elected to devote its energies to increasing the overall resources devoted to youth programs and fostering the extent to which young voices are incorporated within the forums of city government. Their actions principally targeted City Hall and its political processes. They have drawn their tactics from the palate of other "special interest" lobbying organizations, which have learned how to move from attempts to influence elections to intervene in later phases: monitoring the legislative process, helping to draft position statements and ballot initiatives, holding officials accountable for their choices, and generally practicing the art of shaping the political decision-making environment.

Coleman has mastered the full spectrum of actions designed to influence and monitor the political process. Their tactics, as described above, include: educating candidates about the conditions confronting youth in San Francisco, convening and directing forums, conducting independent analyses of city budgets, canvassing voters, sponsoring rallies, and using direct democratic processes. A few of these are considered below.

In its independent analyses of the city's budget, Coleman notes where the city's fiscal priorities differ from those espoused by its officials and calls them to account. Coleman recognizes that the budget process is a uniquely open process and one that meaningfully connects rhetoric and resources (see Wildavsky, 1988). It views city resources as collective entitlements that should be distributed to children as a priority. Even more important, it identifies questionable expenditures that could be redeployed to better serve the needs of their constituents. Coleman's research enables it to be an informed critic and to propose promising alternatives. As Coleman's former executive director emphasizes: "Of course we're critics—I'm a wonderful critic—but we also really propose a lot of positive ways to do things differently and be part of the solution."

In its budget analyses and elsewhere, Coleman engages in direct canvassing of voters, circulating information supporting its position. For example, Coleman targeted the Fire Department as the recipient of excessive funding— excess that it viewed as a drain on resources for the city's children. After this department had placed flyers on the door handles of homes in San Francisco defending its position, Coleman prepared its own flyers, supported by the slogan, "Who's for Kids and Who's Just Kidding?"

Throughout all of its tactics, Coleman's persistence pays off. For much of the public, interest in politics heightens during elections but then quickly recedes into inattention. Through the use of both public and private pressures and by following issues from initiation to resolution, Coleman demonstrates the importance of "just being there ... and being there ... and being there." In many respects, Coleman's staff has mastered the "nuts and bolts" of city decision making, identifying the intricacies of the city's budgeting process, the strengths and weaknesses of the political actors, and the local district politics affecting each supervisor, to a greater extent than have the political pros. Their repertoire of advocacy tools provides an instructive guide about how to be a serious force in the determination of public policy at the local level.

OCO and SFOP's Repertoire   Whereas Coleman borrowed many of its tactics from special interest and lobbying organizations, in selecting their repertoires OCO and SFOP have drawn primarily from the PICO community organizing model, which includes identification of issues based on one-to-ones, research on problems in the community, collective action to influence decision makers, and reflection on the effectiveness of strategies and actions. A critical thread running throughout SFOP's and OCO's portfolios of activities is the priority placed on the importance of actions being driven by and occurring in ways consistent with a shared Judeo-Christian faith. Organizations such as PICO are built on the possibilities offered by religion "to provide a set of value commitments to combine with practical self-interest" (Warren, 2001, p. 58). Most SFOP and OCO meetings begin with prayer and the reading of scripture. Biblical language and imagery permeate the rhetoric of their meetings. For these groups, faith—as a set of common values—acts as a bridge between traditionally divided bodies within the urban community, most importantly between racial and ethnic groups, but also between classes and more conventional interest-based groups.

Tactics also grow out of their commitment to building communities: the cultivation of "values and relationships that hold organizations together"[19] and support the pursuit of common objectives. Specific tactics, as indicated in the case descriptions, include conducting one-to-ones, establishing local organizing committees, promoting leadership development, mobilizing for political attention (turning out large crowds), and conducting research on local needs.

Different Targets, Tactics, and Indicators of Success

Each organization's beliefs about community change are reflected in the way it frames problems, the targets it identifies, and the tactics it employs to execute its campaigns. Whether through large public rallies, budget proposals, or private meetings with public officials, organizations' repertoires of action distinguish their work from that of other advocates and determine the type and depth of impact that they have in communities. As we have emphasized, organizations choose targets based on their mission and ideology, as well as the political opportunities available to them. They then tailor their tactics to effectively push against these targets to compel reform.

Organizational beliefs not only inform what work advocates take on but what they consider to be an indicator of success. For example, Coleman's focus on concrete policy reform and budget advocacy has prompted it to measure its impact by public dollars or number of children served by new programs—numbers it has treated as a proxy for a positive impact on its constituents. By contrast, because SFOP and OCO focus primarily on the process of organizing to develop residents' leadership skills, they are more attentive to the number of community members involved in their campaigns and members' sense of effectiveness when assessing their organizational impact. In the next chapter, we look across these three organizations to understand how their ideas about community reform and their chosen strategies define the work that they do and its impact on their communities. We will highlight the differences between process- and outcome-oriented advocacy and trace how these different orientations influence organizations' goals, their strategies, and their community impact.

7 Diverse Ways of Making a Difference

THE THREE FOCAL ORGANIZATIONS have each attempted to improve the quality of life and opportunities afforded to the youth of their communities, endeavored to realize positive change through public policy reform, and helped community members participate in the democratic process in their cities. And each experienced successes in their efforts on behalf of youth, but they did so in diverse ways. These organizations advocating for youth differ in the structures and social logics that defined them and in the organizational, political, and historical contexts within and through which they operated. Distinctions in organizational design affected the mission, capacity, and accomplishments of our focal organizations. Context differences posed different challenges and opportunities for each organization.

In this chapter, we probe the implications of the organizational and contextual differences highlighted in Chapter 6 to understand the impact these differences have had on advocates' efforts to instigate social reform to benefit youth. We consider how context differences interact with organizational design and repertoire to privilege some tactics, render others less effective, and chart a course for change. Our focus in this chapter on *how* organizational and contextual factors shape advocates' efforts necessarily centers our analysis on the specific features of our three focal organizations and their environment. As we emphasize, advocacy efforts do not occur in a vacuum but are situated in a particular time, place, and political context. Yet this approach has implications beyond our case studies for understanding how third sector advocates shape and are shaped by the landscape in which they work and also helps to explicate the types of social reform that advocates may achieve on behalf of urban youth.

Cultural Frames and Social Logics

Cultural frames refer to the beliefs, assumptions, and definitions that shape participants' conceptions of the phenomena with which they deal. Social logics refer to an organization's beliefs about what it wants to do, its goals, and how to achieve them—its strategies (see Chapter 2). Focusing on cultural framing and the logics of action has fruitfully turned the attention of organization scholars from their relentless concentration on structure to a renewed interest in the role of ideas in social life. Indeed, a rediscovery of the central role played by symbolic systems in social structure and social order is a pervasive theme associated with the "new institutionalism" in economic and social analysis. Attention to the power of ideas is especially relevant to the study of organizations attempting to foster public policies to promote reform because ideas are the "stuff" of policy (Stone 2002). Policies reflect particular ideas about the problem to be addressed, about promising solutions and conceptions of the "causal story" that motivates public attention and political action. Policy constructions enact ideas through decisions about priorities and choices of policy goals, instruments, and resources. Ideas thus describe the context for action, constraining what policy can and cannot address and how. Policy change of the type pursued by our focal organizations typically requires change in what Mark Moore (1988) calls the "public ideas" that underlie existing policies (or lack thereof)—conceptions about appropriate targets for public policy and framing of the problem to address the role of government. We begin our examination of the ideas that shape our focal organizations by considering the "cultural frames" that they employ.

Cultural Frames

John Campbell (2004, p. 94), like Moore, considers targets for change in terms of public ideas about what currently exists, what is possible to change, and the assumptions and beliefs that reinforce the status quo. He provides a useful representation of types of ideas—*cultural frames*—and their implications for policy making. His typology draws on Scott's (2008a) distinction between cognitive and normative elements—the former emphasizing shared understandings and constitutive schema, the latter stressing the "prescriptive, evaluative and obligatory dimension in social life" (p. 54). These elements are cross classified by "depth" of penetration, with some norms and beliefs being taken for granted, residing in the deep background of consciousness; whereas others are located in the foreground of discussion, being explicitly debated and contested.

Our case organizations share common assumptions but work with them differently in their particular contexts. At the *paradigm* level, all three organizations act on the assumption that it is the state's responsibility to meet the basic welfare needs of children and youth; and at the *public sentiment* level, their work is rooted in the belief that programs for youth should not single out "problem" kids and be primarily punitive but should emphasize the need to expand resources and opportunities for all young people—a youth development perspective. Although all our case organizations base their work on these assumptions, for Coleman these principles provide their primary raison d'étre, whereas for OCO and SFOP, they are embedded in a broader matrix of concerns for expanding opportunities for marginalized neighborhoods and their families.

It is at the foreground level that differences in goals and approaches for realizing them appear most clearly among our case organizations. In particular, the foreground is heavily influenced by the sector targeted by the organization. In the early years of Coleman, when their primary concern was with reforming juvenile justice and foster care programs, the frames it selected highlighted the rights of juveniles within the system, and its programs were led by lawyers and heavily laced with legal approaches to defending or advancing the rights of youth. In its later phase of attempting to increase the proportion of resources devoted to youth programs and creating structures to support their participation in policy decisions at the citywide level, Coleman faces the challenge of securing political backing in a city with the lowest child population of any major city in the country. To achieve its goals, Coleman framed its campaign for the Children's Amendment at the normative level stressing moral purpose and civic responsibility. Organizational leaders emphasize meeting the needs of *all* of San Francisco's youth in ways that carry weight with San Francisco's traditionally progressive, liberal electorate. The relative marginalization of children and youth in San Francisco played a key role in Coleman's ability to achieve its goals because it was able to capitalize on voters' ideas about taking responsibility for the politically disenfranchised, underrepresented youth residents of the city. Passing the Children's Amendment and creating the youth commission were depicted as the "right thing to do."

"San Francisco is better with children," proclaimed Coleman's advocacy materials. This moral rhetoric can be especially critical given the invisibility of youth in policy making and distinctions that are sometimes made between the deserving and undeserving poor. Coleman's historic use of race-neutral moral rhetoric—framing campaigns around children, generally speaking (as opposed to black or Latino children)—has also enabled the organization to sidestep potentially divisive racial politics.

Whatever its focus, moral rhetoric must be heard positively if it is to motivate action. A thought experiment that moves Coleman Advocates to Oakland raises questions about how effective its campaign message would be in a different political and organizational context. For one, the youth development gestalt differs in San Francisco and Oakland. Coleman's message and campaigns around youth policy are firmly rooted in youth development principles—integrated, strength-based supports for youth and attention to their positive development—ideas that have resonance with San Franciscans. Oakland's higher percentage of poor youth (almost twice that of San Francisco) and higher concentrations of poverty, as well as its high crime rates among youth, make young people a high-profile but more divisive issue in that city. Numerous leaders in Oakland call for a "get tough" stance rather than a youth development one—calling for aggressive crackdowns on gangs and zero tolerance policies. As one Oakland advocate put it, a culture of "more rigid control and containment" of minority youth has developed in Oakland. Former Mayor Jerry Brown's military-style charter school embodied this perspective. Historically high rates of crime and truancy in Oakland have kept violence prevention and neighborhood safety at the top of OCO's organizing agenda.

By contrast to Coleman's broader budget advocacy, OCO's and SFOP's signature efforts have concentrated on educational reform. In "majority minority" Oakland, families of color were successful in pushing for school reform because of the strongly normative appeals made to the broader community. Documentation provided by OCO highlighted undeniable inequities between the educational opportunities available to white students in the hills versus those available to low-income students of color in the flatlands. OCO's tactics aimed to change influentials' ideas about appropriate educational programs and the paradigms that shape educational policy and resource allocation in Oakland through pressures generated by grassroots organizing. OCO turned out hundreds of stakeholders who demanded change in the demonstrably unequal allocation of educational resources and who pushed for the adoption of a clear alternative to existing practices: new small schools. OCO's effective mobilization of existing voters, and enfranchisement of new ones, compelled elected officials' attention to school reform, especially the school board.

SFOP, like OCO, pursued education reform under a banner of redressing inequities. SFOP followed a grassroots leadership development logic to garner support for small schools, an approach that was less effective in the San Francisco demographic and institutional context. Grassroots pressure for implementing small schools reform achieved little traction among voters, most of whom had not much interest in or knowledge about San Francisco's schools. Nor did the campaign grab the interest of school officials, who were wrestling with significant system dysfunctions. San Francisco's lack of strong commitment to the reform may have contributed to the Gates Foundation's withdrawal of money for a small schools initiative in the district. Though SFOP was trying to convince the district to be more aggressive in its push for funding, its efforts were not sufficient to overcome the district's lack of support, and small schools supporters expressed concerned that the reform has "fizzled" (Knight 2005b). Pursuing an effort to change policy elite's ideas about or concerns for San Francisco schools, then, proved a problematic strategy in this community context, at least in the near term.

Social Logics

Corresponding to the structural archetypes selected, Coleman differs greatly from OCO and SFOP in their *social logics:* their mode of working, the means–ends connections they make, and their greater willingness to be confrontational with public officials. As discussed, Coleman has relied primarily on *professional advocacy* to carry on its work; OCO and SFOP on *grassroots leadership development and democratic participation.* In the former logic, professional staff members decide which issues to pursue and which actions to take to achieve their policy goals. In the latter, staff members facilitate the involvement of those whose interests are not well served by current policies, meeting frequently with individuals or small groups of community members, eliciting from them their primary concerns, and then working to train and empower them to exercise leadership in pursuing solutions.

Coleman has historically employed the first logic and uses policy entrepreneurship to focus on system change and to reform policy to improve conditions for youth. Its leaders identify a few major priorities to guide its campaigns and then design programs—meetings, campaigns, coalitions—to achieve them. OCO and SFOP, on the other hand, enact the second logic, empowering individuals to be their own advocates. Different scripts accompany these different emphases and shape the work of the organization. SFOP and OCO organizers, for example, will not tell their lay leaders what issues to pursue and will not provide solutions to the problems they identify. Instead, they help leaders break problems down into manageable "slices" and assist them in considering alternative courses of action.

Each logic has its strengths and weaknesses. The professional advocacy approach is able to concentrate on issues of salience to the organization. Much less time and energy are consumed in making choices of targets, and the model affords much flexibility to respond to changing circumstances. On the other hand, the approach confronts the challenge of mobilizing new combinations of diverse parties for each issue pursued: Every campaign requires a new organizing effort to locate and bring on board supporters and allies.

The grassroots leadership development approach presents almost a mirror image of strengths and weaknesses. Although OCO and SFOP certainly seek to make policies in Oakland and San Francisco more supportive of children and youth, their emphasis on democratic participation impedes their ability to single-mindedly pursue a series of specific policy reforms to achieve this objective. The PICO model's focus on the *process* of advocacy—organic issue generation and training residents to frame and execute campaigns—not only constrains what issues SFOP and OCO take on but limits the way they conduct their campaigns. Constituents' concerns come first, and means often matter more than ends. As a consequence, SFOP and OCO will not become involved in issues that would be conducive to a policy impact but are not salient to the organizations' members. Conversely, issues that are most important to constituents may not lend themselves to a broader policy campaign. As an OCO member put it, an OCO campaign might be as small and targeted as getting a new stoplight on a street or a crosswalk in a neighborhood—types of campaigns that do not connect to broader, city-wide reforms. But if you are the affected resident, a new stoplight on a busy street is likely to be a valued policy achievement.

As faith-based organizations, OCO and SFOP believe residents' religious commitments can promote and support civic engagement and activism. The director of PICO California and former OCO staff member further explains:

> I think we're really different from other organizations in that our primary focus is leadership development and that we have the capacity to develop regular people in the community to create change in the communities . . . It's not

staff saying, hey, you guys really need to organize for a school! But it's really tapping into people's pain and interests and passions and using that as a motivating factor to get people involved.

Coleman is also committed to leadership development and empowering residents to become advocates in their own right. However, these process-oriented goals have typically been subordinated to outcome-oriented goals, such as policy reform. As Coleman makes clear in one of its guiding principles, the welfare of children is ultimately the responsibility of the government: "All children and families deserve to have their basic needs met, and it is the role of government to ensure that this happens."[1]

This different level of emphasis on process and outcome goals distinguishes SFOP, OCO, and Coleman; however, these organizational orientations are not mutually exclusive. The distinctions one can draw between these organizations based on their process or outcome-focused goals are not hard and fast categories but rather are ongoing, internal tensions that are continuously reevaluated and rebalanced by the organizations, influencing the design of each campaign. In some cases, constituent members who feel a level of discomfort with the process of advocacy proactively push for organizational change. Indeed, one possible pressure for an organization's internal reform derives from the extent to which groups are dissatisfied with an organization's ability to accommodate their interests (Greenwood & Hinings 1996). As OCO's executive director emphasized, there is a "healthy tension" between maintaining a group of leaders dedicated to a particular campaign and the time and effort required to find and train new leaders. OCO must continually confront the question, "At what point do social issues take precedence over maintaining organizing coalitions?"[2]

Diverse Ways of Making a Difference

Organizations working between movement and establishment to affect change consider a variety of indicators of their effectiveness. Some indicators are immediate and clear, while others implicate process concerns such as community involvement, individual empowerment, or developing political will around particular policy issues. Still other outcomes of advocacy work are evident in the ways in which a new program or policy is implemented. The eventual assessment of advocates' accomplishments awaits history's verdict about the extent and type of change associated with policy victories. Did policy wins or new capacity result in significant change in resources and opportunities, or did advocates' short-term successes eventually fade away? Our focal organizations aimed to and did make a difference in diverse ways. In this section, we detail the different ways of making a difference that fall within organizations' shared goal of reforming policy to improve conditions for youth in local communities.

In the Near Term

Policy Victories   Virtually all advocacy organizations have as one of their primary objectives exerting influence on the policies and practices of other organizations and public agencies. Most youth advocacy organizations focus their attention on the public sector, attempting to persuade voters, politicians, or civil servants to act in ways consistent with the interests they advocate. For these organizations policy "victories"—elections won, legislation passed, initiatives approved—represent relatively rare and highly important outcomes. In the political process, there is no more significant moment than when your candidate has been elected to office or legislation you back has been passed. Such results are often the most clear-cut outcomes that advocates can secure. As Coleman's former director said: "It either got passed, or it didn't." Coleman has an impressive list of policy successes: the creation of the Juvenile Probation Commission; passage of the Children's Amendment (Proposition J); creation of the San Francisco Youth Commission; and the creation of the Department of Children, Youth and Families housed in the San Francisco's mayor's office. OCO scored an important victory in Oakland with the passage of its small, autonomous school reform. The verdict on the success of SFOP's small school strategy was still to come, but with change in the district leadership, the organization's reform initiative appeared to be making positive gains.

Building Civic Capacity   Each focal organization invested in developing grassroots capacity for change but assigned different priority to it. Coleman attended to building civic capacity as it trained youth and parents to define and pursue issues of interest to them through its two empowerment groups, Youth Making a Change (YMAC) and Parent Advocates for Youth (PAY). But Coleman's historic focus on policy outcomes rendered empowering residents a subset of its work rather than its primary objective. In contrast, the primary goal of OCO and SFOP is to build capacity within communities and to increase civic engagement, focusing on empowering economically marginalized residents of San Francisco and Oakland to participate in decisions that affect them. As SFOP's executive director put it, their work is about "how many people have been activated to read the local paper or know who their supervisor is or understand how local elections work or care about local issues and feel some degree of power to do something about it." OCO members report how their involvement with the organization has made them more effective in different parts of their lives. One community member underscores how OCO has transformed her life: "Now I am a more valuable person in church, in my family, in my community . . . It changed the way people at work look at me . . . It transfers in all facets of our life." These testimonies signal the effectiveness of grassroots capacity-building organizations such as OCO and SFOP. As Daniel Patrick Moynihan, a master of public policy, observed, "Anecdote is the singular of data."

In the Longer Term

Advocacy and organizing groups' particular institutional and political contexts shape the longer-term policy consequences of their work in two important ways: what happens when the "establishment" takes over the cause and what happens over time as contexts shift and successes are counted—or not.

The Handoff   Policy victories signal the turning point when an advocate's cause has been embraced by the wider public and issues are to be addressed by public officers backed by public funds. This is the moment we term the "handoff": Advocacy staff and their movement allies hand off responsibility for the goals they have advocated for public officials who are both obligated and empowered to implement them. The impact of organizations advocating for youth on their institutional context ultimately turns on the handoff—when action and responsibilities for outcomes move from advocates to implementers—to the establishment. Handoffs signify the transition from street-level actions, protests, and meetings to city agencies and officials: The action moves from the streets to the suites.

The extent to which our focal organizations hand off their advocacy campaigns reflects their organizational structure, mission, and ideas about social change. Coleman, given its historic focus on staff-driven advocacy to yield policy reform, has traditionally handed off its policy triumphs to local officials so it could direct its limited resources and staff toward the next campaign issue. By contrast, SFOP and OCO, given their central focus on empowerment and relationship building, may be more likely to have what OCO Executive Director Ron Snyder called a "spinoff" than handoff—meaning they remain more engaged in how policies are implemented as a matter of maintaining partnerships with local officials and other organizations.

Although moving, in the form of a handoff or spin-off, out of "streets"—dependence on the actions of those working from the outside with modest and unpredictable levels of support and a heavy reliance on volunteer participants—into the "suites"—the corridors of institutionalized power, with seasoned politicians and experienced civil servants taking control—sounds like a clear victory, it can come at a cost and is always unpredictable. A very large literature contrasts the operations of informal, marginalized, spontaneous social actors and movements with formalized, mainstream, highly routinized institutions (Davis et al. 2005). Part of this literature describes the shift that occurs from those actors involved in the policy decision-making process to those who manage the policy-implementation process. We should know by this time that when different organizational actors enter with their distinctive structures, contrasting cultural frames and social logics and peculiar repertoires of action, that such handoffs may not be a neutral process. Recall the case of the U.S. civil rights movement that culminated with street protests transmigrating into actions within legislatures, courts, agencies, and firms. No one would claim that the major reforms demanded by civil rights activists have been achieved by those establishment structures that took up the action. Viewing such transitions, McAdam and Scott conclude:

> It becomes clear that no movement ever manages to "succeed"—to fulfill all the hopes of those who labored to instigate institutional change. Goals are transformed as they are translated, and today's "victories" give rise to tomorrow's disappointments, provocations, and—eventually to new reform efforts. (2005, p. 40)

All three of our case organizations are aware of this dilemma, as well as the fact that San Francisco and Oakland represent very different contexts for action and prospects for a successful handoff. San Francisco, despite its occasional political dramas, has a relatively stable, high-capacity government bureaucracy. The coexistence of county and city offices and resources also adds to the coherence of its governance structures. Oakland, on the other hand, is famously in perpetual upheaval, and public policies move through an extremely contentious bureaucratic and political setting. Coleman's policy triumphs are often rooted in its long-standing relationships with city officials and agencies—relationships it persistently cultivates and then draws on to achieve its reform goals by calling on its "kid-friendly" allies and by challenging its detractors.

The relative instability of Oakland's public institutions and political bodies provides sharp contrast and casts uncertainty on the district's implementation of OCO's small schools reform. Shortly after the initiative successfully garnered board approval, OUSD's superintendent was dismissed, and the district was consigned to state receivership, meaning that the state administrator rather than district officials had the ultimate say. Thus, prior deals negotiated and agreements made were off as OCO handed off the small schools initiative to a weakened district operating under temporary arrangements.

Close monitoring of handoff and implementation matters to the eventual outcome of advocates' work, and all organizations have continued to work alongside the public organizations and officials to support an effective handoff and implementation. OCO and SFOP continue to collaborate with district and school officials to support and monitor the progress of small school reform. Coleman has regularly partnered with the Youth Commission to assist its studies and advance its agenda. And in an interesting "reverse cooptation" process, in 2004, Mayor Gavin Newsom named the former executive director of Coleman, Margaret Brodkin, to head the Department of Children, Youth and their Families (DCYF). Just as former politicians and civil servants can move from the "inside" to serve as advisors for think tanks and policy advocates, occasionally "outside" advocates are invited into the halls of power to direct the programs of the agencies their efforts helped to create.

What Was Achieved, Finally?

The ultimate impact of advocates' work depends on more than a successful handoff and the near-term support of bureaucrats and politicians. Only time will tell whether change resulting from advocates' victories was merely a blip on the policy screen or resulted in fundamental change. Did it represent a substantive addition or amendment to existing practices? Or was the change achieved by merely "tinkering," albeit moving in the right direction from advocates' perspective? Did small wins lead to significant downstream change?

Institutional theorists distinguish between *radical* or *revolutionary change* and *evolutionary* or *incremental change*. The former represents a significant rupture or dislocation in established patterns; the latter, smaller modifications or adjustments in existing arrangements (see Campbell 2004; Greenwood & Hinings 1996). Other theorists, such as Pierson (2004) caution that those attempting to assess the extent of institutional impact of a change need to take a longer view—that what might seem revolutionary in the near term may fade in significance over time, and what might seem merely incremental in the short term may over time add up to extremely consequential change. In a related argument that questions the appropriateness of dichotomous evolutionary/revolutionary assessments, Djelic and Quack (2004) propose what they call the "stalactite" model of change to represent the possibility that small, incremental changes "may lead in time and progressively to a profound and qualitative transformation of those institutional order or at least some of its key dimensions" (p. 22). They advance a more nuanced assessment of change that allows for intermediate developments that are neither revolutionary nor evolutionary and that call attention to the significance of pathways for change as well as to time frames.

Our focal organizations differed in the type of change they worked for in their community. With respect to direct effects on public policy, probably the most radical change effected by our case organizations was Coleman's successful attempt to influence San Francisco's budgetary and decision-making processes. As a result of Coleman's efforts, San Francisco became the first urban center in the country to have a designated percentage of its budget set aside for child and youth programs. Several years later, in 1995, Coleman led a community effort to increase youth voice in city politics by drafting and passing a ballot initiative to establish the San Francisco Youth Commission. This advocacy effort represents the introduction of new logics—positive conceptions of youth and the contributions they can make to the public good—as well as structures to support such participation.

Located between revolutionary and evolutionary change are the small, autonomous school's programs advanced by OCO and SFOP, which represent significant intermediate policy changes that have revolutionized school structures in some places but amounted to little in others. Small schools represent a bundle of reforms, including a reduction in the numbers of students and teachers at a given site, greater decentralization of decision making to the school level, and the use of more student-centered teaching methods. Such changes can alter ways of thinking about classrooms and district structures, but the basic structural vocabulary of district-school-teacher-student organizing schema remain in place.

Viewed through a more macro and longer-term lens, OCO's and SFOP's efforts to revitalize local political systems by engaging and empowering disaffected, marginalized, and suppressed individuals and groups may well become an instance of revolutionary political change, though it appears limited in the short term. Observing the development of similar political groups in Texas, Warren celebrates their potential for political renewal:

> A key to renewing American politics is to rebuild its foundations in the values and institutions that sustain community. . . . I see the possibilities and rewards of value-based politics, of multiracial collaboration, of patient relationship building in local communities. . . . The key to reinvigorating democracy in the United States can be found in efforts to engage people in politics through their participation in the stable institutions of community life. (2001, pp. x, 15)

In the long run, the organization and the empowerment of the ethnic and working-class communities of urban America may well become the most significant—and revolutionary—development of our time.

The differences and similarities in our focal organizations, as well as the work they have carried out, have implications for the development of a field around youth services and a youth development stance. In the domain of youth development, both the success of the handoff and the type of change accomplished by advocacy and community organizations signal the consequences of their work for youth. These local accomplishments, or lack thereof, also shape the emerging field of youth development though the prominence and resources they afford young people and a youth development perspective. We turn next to the field level, how these organizations and their populations look through this lens, and what some early signs of field development are.

8 Community- and National-Level Processes

PREVIOUS CHAPTERS HAVE DESCRIBED wider social structures and forces shaping youth organizations at the turn of the twenty-first century. We have considered changes over time in national and state political and policy contexts affecting youth programs and have detailed changes in the sociodemographic and political environments of two urban communities—Oakland and San Francisco. Such factors, we assert, have shaped the fate of the population of advocacy organizations that have operated in these locations over recent years. The number and characteristics of organizations in the two populations—their diversity, size, and influence—reflects the imagination and energy of their participants and also the opportunities and constraints at work in each city.

To this point, the trajectory of our arguments has progressed from a description of macro forces to an examination of more micro structures and behaviors. In this chapter we climb back up the ladder of abstraction to consider the connection between local community organizing and field-level structures and processes at the local and the national level. Can we begin to connect the threads across these various levels to construct a broader tapestry that reveals the origins, development processes, and early stages of a youth development field? To be sure, our focal advocacy organizations have played a role in these processes, but field forces have a life of their own.

We begin by reviewing the activities of organizations advocating for youth in San Francisco and Oakland, with attention to their implications for field building. Just as in the private sector, where the actions of firms, intentionally or not, contribute to market building—the "invisible hand"—and field structuration, so in the nonprofit world the actions of nonprofit organizations contribute to (and are affected by) the construction of a broader field of organized, meaningful behavior. We then shift attention to the national level for a brief consideration of indicators of and evidence for field formation at this level. In this discussion, we venture beyond the boundaries of our own empirical project to incorporate more fugitive, anecdotal, secondary data on evidence of field building at the national level. We do so in order to call attention to the dynamics of field structuration processes, which link local and nonlocal organizing activities in complex, reciprocal causal patterns.

In Chapter 2, we differentiated between levels of units and levels of analysis, the former referring to the level at which individual organizations operate (for example, local or national), the latter to the type of explanation employed (for example, whether we concentrate on the actions of individuals, organizations, populations, or wider fields). In this chapter, we concentrate on the field-level structures and processes but emphasize that fields (treated as units) themselves operate at differing levels. That is, analysts can somewhat arbitrarily decide to concentrate attention on a given field, such as youth development, as it operates within a single community, a region, a state, or a nation. In each case, it is necessary to take into account the openness of a given level to wider forces, but, with this proviso, fields can be arbitrarily bounded. In the current discussion, we concentrate our efforts at two levels: (1) the local community level (San Francisco or Oakland); and (2) the national level (the United States). We omit consideration of the state level because we have already commented on structures and policies relevant to youth development in California (Chapter 3), noting that most of the action in this state is at the local level.

Field Structuration at the Local Level

We employ the term *structuration* to characterize the manner and extent to which a collective conception arises among a set of organizations that they are mutually interdependent—whether as allies or enemies—and are involved in interdependent relations to advance or oppose a given agenda. As a field becomes more highly structured, organizations interact more frequently, share more information, develop patterns of coalition and clearer status and power structures, and develop more broadly shared beliefs and logics of action (see DiMaggio 1983; DiMaggio & Powell 1983; Scott et al. 2000). By contrast, in their early stages of construction, before any broad institutional settlement has been reached, fields are likely to exhibit much more controversy, disorder, and conflict (DiMaggio 1991).

Within the local community, field building goes on at two levels: (1) within participating organizations and (2) among organizations, including the population of advocacy organizations, their supporters, and their targets.

Field-Building Processes at the Organizational Level

Up to this point, our analysis has focused primarily on work at the organization level as, for example, participants endeavor to align their organization with appropriate social norms and logics or as they adopt and adapt their modes of acting to contest or imitate the actions of organizations with which they compete or that they admire. Even in our discussion of the population of advocacy organizations, our focus remained primarily on the similarities and differences among individual organizations comprising the population. Such interorganizational efforts inform and constrain activities and shape the development of structures and strategies at the level of the individual organization. But many of them also contribute, at least indirectly, to field building in several ways.

Consider, for example, the field-level effects of organizations that increase their *awareness and attention*. Organizations that attend to others in their environment—by, first, casual observation and, subsequently, by systematic monitoring of the other's structure and behavior—contribute to the creation of more systematic comparison sets and information flows at the field level. Organizations also contribute to field building through *imitation* and *learning*. By making comparisons or seeking out organizations that will enhance their own learning, organizations not only stimulate changes in themselves but contribute to the crafting of a larger field. Indeed, such comparison and imitation processes lead, over time, to increased sharing of logics and structural isomorphism among the interacting organizations.

Field building is also promoted by organizations' *susceptibility to joint action*. Organizations that see themselves as sharing ideological commitments or modes of acting are more likely over time to engage in joint activities to achieve specified objectives. Finally, organizations' *responses to reactive mobilization* also contribute to field development. Organizations attend to the behavior of others whom they seek to challenge and change. These "target" organizations, as detailed in Chapter 5, importantly shape the strategies and tactics of advocacy organizations. But such adversarial relations can themselves become more regularized over time—with change agents and targets developing routines and wider structures for managing and accommodating their different interests and agendas. Examples of such processes include

Coleman's relation to San Francisco's city government and OCO's work with the Oakland school district.

Although all of these and related types of actions by organizations were taken to improve each organization's situation or stance within its environment, all of them create ripple effects that work to shape the contours of the wider, field-level structure.

Field-Building Processes at the Community Level

Participants within organizations can also work more directly and overtly at the field level to construct shared meanings and structures supporting not only their own but also the work of other organizations. We consider four types of actions operating primarily at the field level: field-level framing processes, coalition building, constructing community infrastructure, and linking local and wider initiatives and programs.

Field-Level Framing Processes   We have described in previous chapters the important role played by framing processes: the conceptualization and packaging of issues and solutions to motivate and mobilize action. Of interest here is the nature, in particular, of the *level of generality,* at which the frame is constructed.

All actors, both individual and collective, construct conceptual frames to guide, and to justify, their acts. Organizations seek to construct frames that will appeal to their constituents and clients and, perhaps, attract new participants and allies. Actors seeking to construct field-level frames must identify issues or approaches that will appeal to a wider range of field participants. Sometimes, as Snow and colleagues (Snow & Benford 1988; Snow et al. 1986) describe, this can involve *frame alignment.* In their earlier work, Snow and his associates defined frame alignment as "the linkage or conjunction of individual and SMO [social movement organization] interpretative frameworks" (Snow et al., 1986, p. 467), but they subsequently extended the concept to include the ways in which frameworks can be employed to align the work of two or more organizations. Through such mechanisms as *frame bridging, frame amplification,* and *frame extension,* organizations seek to define problems or solutions that will attract partners or create coalitions with other organizations. We have seen, for example, how OCO members' concerns with filthy bathrooms in schools generalized to other types of school problems and how SFOP's attempts to deal with the problems in one school were broadened into a concern with the reform of the entire school system.

Another widely used mechanism for fostering relational connections among organizations is to adopt a *multi-issue* organizing frame (Smith 2005, p. 234). Because they simultaneously organize their work around more than one issue, organizations like Coleman, OCO, and SFOP are in a better position to enter into alliances with other organizations on one or another activity or campaign. As the former executive director of Coleman reported, "There are coalitions we're convening and coalitions we're active participants on. They constantly shift. And some of them are issue oriented and some are geographically oriented, and they shift as issues shift."[1] Because they relate to multiple rather than single issues, these organizations can flexibly adapt their agendas and targets to changing circumstances—both constraints and opportunities.

Frames can also be constructed to define broader and more *generalized* problems or goals. For example, when Coleman decided to focus attention on the proportion of the city's budget devoted to children and youth, this device cut across specialized service sectors, departments, and agencies to highlight citywide priorities—spotlighting which groups and interests were being served and which were not. Money is a generalized medium of exchange. Budgets are often regarded as dull and esoteric, but as Wildavsky (1988) has taught us, they provide both a metric for comparing how various interests are faring in competition for public funds as well as a clear indicator of the operational goals of a political system.

Also, from the standpoint of organizations concerned with youth development, a focus on public education represents a much more general and inclusive focus than does attention to juvenile justice, foster care, or homeless youth. Public education affects the lives of a broad cross-section of young people in our society over a substantial portion of their development. It attends not only to the marginal and disadvantaged, but to mainstream youth who exhibit a wide range of aptitudes and capacities for learning as well as those confronting special challenges. And a concern with the improvement of education is not a controversial or divisive issue but one garnering widespread public support. Thus, it is not surprising that all of our focal organizations chose to devote a substantial proportion of their time and energy to educational or school-related issues.

Constructing Coalitions   Neil Fligstein (2001b) asserts that a key ingredient in field building resides in the ability of some social actors to motivate collective action within the field. When fields are in the early stages of construction, some actors have the social skill to skillfully use rules and resources not only to frame a new vision but to motivate others to join with them in working to bring it about. Such is the art of constructing coalitions or longer-lasting alliances. We discussed in Chapter 7 the advantages falling to individual advocacy organizations to joining or building a coalition. Here we focus attention on field-level effects of these processes.

Coalitions contribute to field building insofar as they motivate organizations and their leaders to *engage in issue blending*—acknowledging that the issues being pursued by one's own organization are connected to others being addressed by different organizations. As one community leader in Oakland said: "You can't talk about crime without talking about truancy and prostitution and education—lack of educational opportunities—and lack of employment opportunities. You know, I mean it's all one; it's a bundle; they're all interconnected." Recognition of this reality makes it both easier and more necessary to forge coalitions.

Organizations also contribute to field building through their *function as intermediaries*—serving to link organizations and persons across specialized sectors and levels. Advocacy organizations can connect to organizations that do not themselves engage in advocacy but whose interests are strongly affected by particular policies or issues. For example, the former executive director of Coleman regarded the set of service organizations working with children and youth as "the core of our network." Coleman endeavors to help each of these agencies "see their work as part of sometime bigger—as partners in a broader thing." Needless to say, advocacy organizations that lack a membership base must rely heavily on coalitions to advance their agendas. But, more generally, by functioning as intermediaries, advocacy organizations can help to build the capacity of other organizations to work with youth, identify best practices, help to set standards, and broker opportunities for technical assistant and staff training (Wynn 2000).

Advocacy organizations also connect organizations across levels, serving as mechanisms to inform and mobilize grassroots neighborhood groups on the one hand but also reaching up to relate to staff and officers of targeted sectoral organizations and to city officials on the other. Simply making the connections across levels can provide incentives to member units. As a staff member of OCO reports, "People get excited when they meet the chief of police, mayor, and education board member. They feel they have the power to approach them and give their testimony, and they not only get excited themselves but also spread the word to others." In their work advocating school reform, SFOP and OCO staff report working with students, parents, teachers, teacher unions, principals, the PTA, the school district office, and board members. In this sense, as a staff member explained, "OCO is very far into the system."

Leaders in Coleman recognize the tensions involved in building networks and coalitions. For example, as Coleman was seeking to work within "a whole citywide coalition on the budget," it struggled to find a role for its own board in this approach. The former executive director commented: "On the one hand, we have got a governing structure that thinks it's in charge; on the other hand, we have this community organizing structure that we feel we've facilitated and have an obligation to follow through on the things that group decides." Collaboration reduces autonomy of action; structures empower, but they also constrain.

Linkages can also go beyond city boundaries as organizations connect to their counterparts or targets at the regional, state, and national level. The flows across levels can involve, variously, individuals, resources, influence, and ideas. Among the national-level networks of importance to local advocacy organizations are the Children's Defense Fund, the National Association of Child Advocates, and PICO. A leader of a local advocacy organization noted that when they became a part of the National Association of Child Advocates, "the first thing that happened was to sort of name what it was we did and begin to realize that there are other people out there who actually conceptualize what they do in somewhat similar ways." Identifying and connecting to distant and supportive organizations can power the development and structuration of a local field.

Coalitions also enable organizations to *fashion and sustain their infrastructure,* which provides some continuity of leadership and direction over time. Although most coalitions are short lived, constructed around particular problems or issues, some become more permanent, providing an ongoing network to support collective learning and action. Among these more stable coalitions among advocacy organizations in the Bay Area are

- The Bay Area Partnership for Children and Youth, dedicated to building the capacity for local schools and communities serving youth in the Bay Area's low-income communities
- The Community Network for Youth Development (CNYD), whose goal is to improve the quality of programs for youth by supporting and strengthening the people and agencies who work with them
- The Youth Development Peer Network, an initiative of the CNYD, designed to bring together youth development practitioners to investigate ways to influence the field of youth development

Although advocacy organizations specialize in initiating issues and mobilizing actions, some of their most important work involves not initiating but *sustaining* interest, attention, and effort around ongoing problems and programs. As a leader of OCO notes, OCO's role is "not necessarily in terms of initiating, because I think that efforts can get initiated from a lot of places; rather our focus is on sustainability—through political change and turmoil, leadership change and turmoil, and financial change and turmoil."

Coalition and networks also help generate *new organizations*—serving as midwives to the birth of new organizations working for reform. A well-kept secret in the world of entrepreneurship is that a substantial number—about 25 percent—of the new organizations founded every year in the United States are founded not by an individual but by an organization (Ruef, Aldrich, & Carter 2003). Advocacy organizations are particularly likely to participate in this process because they see their role as helping individuals find ways to mobilize to better address their problems.

In addition to their work in crafting less and more permanent coalitions or network organizations, the organizations we studied also helped to spawn other types of organizations. Some of these organizations operate as semi-independent subsidiaries, for example Coleman's YMAC and PAY. Others are fully independent. For example, SFOP was instrumental in helping a group of teachers start Small Schools for Equity. And other organizations are more loosely connected to their mother organization, such as the San Francisco Child Advocacy Network (SFCAN) started by Coleman. Although Coleman convenes SFCAN, it is a coalition of child-serving community agencies the collective interests of which guide the group's activities. The coalition chose not to have formal membership or leaders so they could maximize flexibility in their work, which is focused on budget advocacy and electoral politics to protect and augment programs for children.

Finally, coalitions and networks are able to *convert proposed policies into publicly funded programs*—thus ensuring a greater degree of stability, continuity, and legitimacy than an advocacy group acting on its own might be able to achieve. Pierson (2004) correctly emphasizes that public policies should be included in any discussion of formal institutions. He argues

> While policies are generally more easily altered than the constitutive roles of formal institutions, they are nevertheless extremely prominent constraining features of the political environment. Policies, grounded in law and backed by the coercive power of the state, signal to actors what has to be done, what can-

not be done, and establish many of the rewards and penalties associated with particular activities. Most policies are extremely durable. (2004, pp. 34–35)

While it is important to recognize the dangers and liabilities of turning one's favorite program over to others to administer and implement, as already discussed, there are also significant advantages. The programs are much more likely to garner regular funding, to receive sustained attention from officials whose roles specify what activities or goals they are to pursue, and to be accorded the legitimacy that attends any function that is legally mandated. For example, San Francisco's Department of Children, Youth, and Their Families, a product of Coleman's successful Children's Amendment ballot initiative, has been engaged in surveying after-school programs to assess existing resources, develop common definitions and identify core principles to govern their operation, and formulate standards for their operation. These field-building activities are being conducted not by nonprofit advocacy groups but by public employees using taxpayer dollars.

It is also the case that, like all institutions, political policies enshrined in legislation and administrative bodies can set up a multitude of positive feedback processes—including learning effects, coordination supports as other programs and activities adjust to create and connect into an interlinked structure, and adaptive expectations, as individuals come to use and rely on the program (see Arthur 1994; Pierson 2004). Such processes foster rapid structuration of a field.

The Role of Local Foundations   The nine-county San Francisco Bay Area is characterized by a large and active philanthropic sector. A recent survey reports 754 "public charity supporting organizations," including community and family foundations (Gammal et al. 2005). Of these, 46 percent supported a single organization, most concentrated in the field of education. The remaining 44 percent "provide general fundraising, grantmaking, or other support activities for the public benefit" (p. 46). Such organizations provide much of the fiscal infrastructure for the nonprofits in our communities, and the Bay Area has a higher density of supporting organizations for its operating charities than either the Los Angeles area or California as a whole" (p. 46). The Northern California Grantmakers' Association also provides support to these philanthropic organizations by creating networks of funders, providing information on the community, and holding workshops and other educational events.

Local foundations provide critical support for community advocacy efforts; they typically fall into three categories: independent family foundations focusing on a specific area; community foundations, which pull together funds from a variety of local donors; and local corporate foundations. Though these community-focused foundations have long played a significant role in supporting local nonprofit organizations and engaging in local reform, there has been little systematic analysis of their role (McKersie 1999). These community-focused funders tend to have a different philanthropic role than larger national foundations because of their closer ties to local leaders and other local institutions, knowledge of local needs and issues, and concern for the community's health (McKersie 1999; Wolpert 1999). They also vary by the affluence of their communities. Local foundations in well-off suburbs have different concerns than do local foundations in larger cities with distressed neighborhoods. In San Francisco and Oakland, local foundations have been tackling some of the most entrenched urban problems of poverty, education, health care, and community revitalization.

Although the first community foundation, the Cleveland Foundation, was created in 1914, their numbers have grown rapidly, especially during the 1980s and 1990s, to the point where there are now more than 650 community foundations in the United States. Since 1995, their numbers have grown more rapidly than independent or corporate foundations. They differ from these forms in their focus on a specific geographic area and their pooling of assets from multiple types of donors; they are also unusual in that they are considered both public charitable organizations and nonprofits. (Hammack 1989; Wolfe 2006). Whereas, in the early stages of their life cycle, community foundations tend to focus attention primarily on donor services, over time their interest usually shifts to performing an intermediary role between donors and nonprofit organizations, becoming "responsive grantmakers." Many retain this more passive strategic posture; but some assume the more forward-leaning stance of serving as catalysts for change in the community (Graddy & Morgan 2005; Wolfe 2006).

The San Francisco Foundation and East Bay Community Foundation are the only two community foundations in the cities in which our case study organizations operate. Some of the local family foundations that have been prominent in our study are the Haas family foundations, including the Evelyn and Walter Haas Jr. Fund, Walter and Elise Haas Fund, the Miriam and Peter Haas Fund, the Zellerbach Family Foundation, and the Mary A. Crocker

Trust. These foundations range in size and funding interests, but they are all concerned to some extent with the well-being of the Bay Area. They also differ in that some accept unsolicited proposal though others do not. And some, such as the Haas and Zellerbach foundations, have deep roots in the community, with long family histories there and with their sources of income having been generated in the area.

Corporations donate to charitable organizations both as corporate entities and through separate foundations that are often connected to their community relations efforts. Companies, such as Clorox, that have headquarters in the Bay Area have been instrumental in funding local initiatives. Much like other corporate foundations, the Clorox Foundation was established to "improve the quality of life in which Clorox employees live and work." It is now administered through the East Bay Community Foundation. Additionally, several local banks have supported the housing initiatives of the San Francisco Organizing Project.

There are, of course, many levels of funding that support community-based work. Regional, state-level, and national foundations, including Charles Stewart Mott Foundation, S. H. Cowell Foundation, James Irvine Foundation, and the California Endowment, have also supported the local work of our case study organizations and population organizations.

Local foundations, more than any other type of organization, are in a position to guide and support field-building activities at the community level. Because they are locally based, they can become expert on the people, problems, and politics of a given community. They can serve as catalyst to foster change in many ways—by convening interested parties, holding conferences and workshops, gathering information and funding data collection, providing technical support to nonprofit agencies, and, most importantly, providing funds to support projects and initiatives and to build organizational capacity (see Hammack 1989; Mayer 1994; Wolfe 2006). Leaders of youth development advocacy organizations in our two communities were fully aware of the influence and importance to their work of local foundations. The former executive director of Coleman declared, "I credit the wonderful foundation community of the Bay Area that has sustained this effort over time. If it weren't for the Bay Area foundations, I don't think this organization would be alive."

In his study of federal funding for arts organizations, DiMaggio (1983) reminds us that nothing concentrates the mind of nonprofit professionals like an announcement of the availability of funding. Because the National

Endowment for the Arts was a national body created to make grants to organizations in the performing arts, this source of federal funds led to increased structuration of the arts field at the national level: Interaction among arts organizations increased, the amount of information exchanged increased, more regularized coalition structures developed, social logics became more similar, and organizations became more structurally isomorphic or similar. An identical process would be expected to take place at the local level with the availability of competitive funding from community foundations.

Local foundation support is particularly critical for organizations, such as our case organizations, that do not use government funds to support their advocacy efforts. It is not surprising that advocates might not want the government's helping hand: It is much easier to advocate with government agencies and officials who do not directly fund the organization advocating (Duitch 2002). Whether a sign of successful organizational fund development or a supportive and progressive local foundation community, our case study organizations have survived for over two decades without having to rely on public money to support their efforts; this in a funding climate in which more and more nonprofits are sustaining themselves with government grants, including some advocacy organizations.[2] The need for developing new platforms, short-term strategies, and the ability to respond to an issue in a timely way, however, requires a degree of freedom not typically allowed by government contracts or some foundations. Coleman is uniquely situated to do budget advocacy because it does not accept government funds; particular organizations and programs whose budgets have been cut cannot impartially represent a general children's platform, whereas Coleman's financial independence from local government gives it the credibility to be the general voice and offer more objective financial analysis.[3]

Field-Building Processes at the National Level[4]

As we have discussed throughout all the chapters of this volume, the youth development field is, at best, at an early stage in its evolution. Consider the hallmarks of a mature organizational field: We would expect to see

- High consensus on the mission or goals of core organizations
- High levels of information sharing among field participants
- Stable systems of service providers
- Clear standards of service effectiveness

- Standardized modes of training and certification
- Coherent and effective field governance mechanisms
- Stable funding patterns (see DiMaggio 1983; Scott et al. 2000)

By these criteria, youth development is clearly in its infancy as a field. Think about these criteria in relation to a reasonably mature field such as higher education or major league baseball. Across all of these dimensions, youth development lags far behind.

But perhaps it is inappropriate to expect to find much evidence of the type we would use to evaluate a highly structured field. Rather than looking for indications of a mature garden, we might be better advised to search our young field for early signs of spring. We obtain valuable help from other scholars who have examined the emergence of new organizational fields, including Hoffman (1997), who examined the appearance of corporate environmentalism, Lounsbury and colleagues (Lounsbury 2005; Lounsbury, Ventresca, & Hirsch 2003), who report on the development of the recycling industry, and Lee and Lounsbury (2004), who studied the emergence of the organic food industry. Following these and related leads, we propose a few indicators for detecting and assessing early stages of new fields, together with evidence regarding the progress of youth development.

First is the presence of visible, notable individuals who champion the cause. Environmentalists point to the 1962 publication of Rachel Carson's *Silent Spring* as a critical event raising public consciousness about the dangers of chemical pesticides, thus launching the environmental movement in the United States (Hoffman 1997, pp. 50–57). In a parallel fashion, J. I. Rodale is credited as inspiring the U.S. organic movement through his books and magazine, *Organic Farming and Gardening*, launched in 1942 (Lee & Lounsbury 2004).

Those reviewing the history of youth development suggest that a more "coherent, holistic framework that would help orient thinking about youth and inform policies to address those needs" began to come together during the late 1980s (Costello et al. 2000, p. 190). Influential leaders in this movement include Karen Pittman and James Connell (see, for example, Connell, Gambone, & Smith 1998; Pittman & Wright 1991); but without question the most well-known and influential advocate for children's rights on the national scene is Marian Wright Edelman, founder, in 1973, and first president of the Children's Defense Fund.

A second telling indicator is the number and impact of national (or international) conferences designed to clarify and advance the agenda. Conferences and major publications highlighting problems that children and youth face can lead to increasing visibility of the needs and issues and help to mobilize attention and support for a developing field.

National foundations have often played a leading role in the structuration of professional fields in the United States. Their conferences and attendant publications garnered influential attention for the youth development perspective, especially the Carnegie Corporation's *Turning Points: Preparing American Youth for the 21st Century* (1989) and *A Matter of Time: Risk and Opportunity in the Nonschool Hours* (1992); and the W. T. Grant Foundation's *The Forgotten Half: Pathways to Success for America's Youth and Young Families* (1988).

Governmental bodies in this country have also sponsored conferences devoted to youth. Beginning in 1960, several White House Conferences on Children and Youth have been convened. In 2003, the White House Task Force on Disadvantaged Youth issued its report noting problems attending the breakdown of family units. At the international level, 1995 witnessed the signing of the United Nation's Convention on the Rights of the Child, and the World Youth Forum of the United Nations System has advocated the more effective participation of youth in every aspect of society. The International Youth Leadership Conference has met annually since 1998 to provide a forum enabling the next generation of world leaders to showcase their leadership skills.

A third indicator of field development at the national level is the creation of national and regional centers to distribute information, promulgate standards, and foster networking among disparate organizations and groups. Today's centers are less likely to be the outcome of lengthy organizing processes building up from local and state efforts, more often taking the form of professionally crafted and managed units that base their operations on the new communication and information technologies. They build websites on which they post large amounts of information, and they do much of their work by e-newsletters and email.

Among such centers working in the youth development arena is the National Collaboration for Youth, a thirty-year-old organization that is a coalition of youth-serving agencies that collectively serve more than 40 million youth. Other nationally active centers include Connect for Kids, the Forum for Youth Investment, Youth Policy Action Center, and Every Child Matters. These organizations provide voice for youth development at the national level and resources for advocates working at state and local levels.

A fourth indicator of field development is the creation of metrics and data-gathering mechanisms for assessing current conditions and progress in achieving field-level objectives. Another important indicator is the extent to which metrics have been developed to enable the routine evaluation of existing needs and to assess the effects of programs designed to advance field goals. What gets counted and how increasingly matters in societies organized around intentionally rational principles and policy setting (Ventresca 2002).

Since the 1990s, a growing number of published reports about youth outcomes—some issued annually—attest to substantial progress in this arena. Influential reports include *Youth Risk Behavior Surveillance,* administered by the U.S. Centers for Disease Control and Prevention, 1998; *America's Children: Key National Indicators of Well-Being,* compiled from federal data sources by the Federal Intra-agency Forum on Child and Family Statistics, 1998; *Trends in the Well-Being of America's Children and Youth,* compiled from federal data sources by Child Trends, Inc., 1997; and *Kids Count Data Book,* compiled from various data sources by the Annie E. Casey Foundation and published annually (MacDonald & Valdivieso 2000). Although considerable data exist for tracking the well-being of children, only in recent years have there been concerned efforts to identify and measure more positive evidence of development, including self-worth, sense of mastery, sense of belonging and responsibility, and various physical, intellectual, civic, and social abilities (Hair et al. 2002).

Finally, a fifth indicator includes efforts to promulgate the development of a professional culture, including the formation of associations, educational and training opportunities, certification programs, and journals. Professionals play key roles in the design and development of most fields in modern society. More so than other groups, they operate at the field level, moving among and between organizations and helping to found and nourish field-level structures (see DiMaggio 1991; Scott 2008b).

Modest evidence exists of progress at this level in the youth development area. In his introduction to the 2002 debut of the new Jossey-Bass journal, *New Directions for Youth Development,* editor Gil Noam wrote, "we have for too long viewed adolescence as a time of crisis and danger, and we need to understand the positive and productive aspects of this important time in life. This journal is dedicated to this shift in thinking. It is unique, created for an amazingly innovative time and an emerging field." (Noam 2002, p. 1.) And professional development opportunities are gradually increasing at community colleges, four-year colleges, and universities for the training of front-line workers and managers as well as policy analysts and designers of youth development programs. Programs range from a Youth Development Leadership Master of Education degree offered by the University of Minnesota or a Master of Science in Youth Development program at Clemson University to an Indiana Youth Development Credential available through Ivy Tech Community College. A widely accepted certificate or credential has yet to be developed.

An important dilemma confronting all service fields attempting to professionalize at this time is that they confront the tensions that currently exist between two models of professional expertise—the mastery of knowledge of a particular substantive area, such as youth development, versus knowledge of management, particularly management of nonprofit organizations. Professionalization is currently proceeding along both axes, which represent alternative modes emphasizing attention to related but distinct values. Directors and leaders of a variety of nonprofit organizations, including those engaged in youth development, have opted for MBAs or degrees in public administration rather than in education, social work, or youth development (Hwang 2006; Scott 2008b).

Embracing the field level of analysis, this chapter has examined developments underway at both the local—San Francisco Bay Area—and the national level, as we review the types of processes underway and evidence of progress to date in field structuration. Clearly, the field of youth development is in its infancy, and it is still too early to conclude whether it will prove to be a viable basis for the reframing and reorganization of services for children and youth in this country.

Field-building processes can be assessed at the local level both within participating organizations and at the wider community level. Within local organizations we have observed signs of their increased attention to and awareness of other organizations with similar interests, increased learning from their allies and competitors, and increased levels of cooperation and collaboration in projects that advance mutual interests. At the community level, we report evidence of the development of more general and encompassing frames to support collaboration, coalition formation around specific initiatives, the construction of more durable community-level infrastructure, and the development of linkages between local and regional, state, and national initiatives. The presence and increased vitality of community foundations, which have provided funding, help with agenda setting, and incentives for collaboration among advocacy organizations, have been vital in fostering these advances.

At the national level, evidence of progress is less obvious. There is some awareness of a few recognized champions for youth development, some evidence of attempts to clarify the policy agenda at this level, and modest progress in the creation of an infrastructure to collect and distribute relevant data, devise relevant training and certification programs, and coordinate efforts across national, state, and local jurisdictions.

Clearly, the youth development field is a work in progress. Whether, and how quickly, it progresses will depend not only on the imagination and energy of its leaders but also on the changing economic and political opportunities afforded by national, state, and local environments.

9 Youth Advocacy on the Ground

AS WE HAVE EMPHASIZED THROUGHOUT, organizations advocating for urban youth confront barriers rooted in established ideas, society's institutions, and existing privilege. In urban America, the policy contexts surrounding youth range from benign acceptance to indifference to antagonism. Advocates working in these settings often find it difficult to arouse passion and mobilize action around youth because most urban voters have little direct interest in youth issues—either they have no children using public resources or have no children at all. Consequently, urban youth, most especially impoverished youth, often are politically marginalized and of little account in city halls when priorities are set and power resides across town in the wealthier, mainstream neighborhoods.

Advocacy organizations are not "mainstream" players but a distinctive population unto themselves. They do not comport themselves as conventional producers or consumers but rather as advocates or social reformers who are attempting to redefine the rules of the game that guide and control the behavior of mainstream players. For our case study organizations, youth development is the alternative idea they are promoting from the margins. Coleman Advocates, SFOP, and OCO are trying to redefine the rules of the game for youth in San Francisco and Oakland through a youth development stance. By promoting new frames for thinking about youth, new types of relationships among stakeholders, and new ways to use resources for youth, they are advancing innovation in the diverse institutions within and through which youth move. Because of their flexibility and their deep local knowledge, among other things, these advocacy organizations have successfully worked to change policy in their communities and create structures that support youth in mainstream institutions, despite all the political and economic hurdles evident in their urban contexts.

Our title, *Between Movement and Establishment,* indicates the defining feature of the space occupied by advocacy organizations. To be effective in their mission, advocacy organizations must find ways to work with both established sectors of the community—schools, juvenile justice and welfare systems, governmental systems—on the one hand and disadvantaged, subordinated, disempowered subgroups and interests within the community on the other. On both sides of this divide the types of participants are multiple and varied—schools are not organized like juvenile justice systems, and disadvantaged groups vary in their interests and degree of organization—so that there is not one but many ways of connecting these groups and orchestrating their interchange. Our focal advocacy groups have aligned themselves both with differing subsystems and actors within the establishment as well as with differing subgroups of the community, positioning themselves to be both challenger of and collaborator with status quo interests.

Establishment or "no-change" interests characterize youth-serving institutions themselves. Youth development goals expressed in terms of integrated services and comprehensive supports implicate "silos" of diverse youth institutions and threaten both professional autonomy and dedicated budgets. Some institutions, like public schools, are notoriously insular and reluctant to collaborate with others working in the youth sector. Others, such as child protective services and community law enforcement, operate according to somewhat different logics of action, social purpose, or regulatory arrangements. At the community or county level, youth-serving institutions compete for scarce resources and tend to see budget deliberations in zero-sum terms, where one agency's gain could mean loss to another's programs and resources. Collaboration or integration among youth-serving agencies, public and private, thus can represent risk and not opportunity for any or all of these reasons.

All of these value-based, contextual, and institutional issues present tough challenges to youth advocates—because in urban areas neither the direct self-interest of powerful organizational players nor warrant for public investments consistent with a youth development perspective is particularly obvious or especially compelling. These tensions and challenges generated the questions that motivated our study: *What are the structures and strategies that enable organizations advocating for youth to mediate the quicksand of social reform—to operate between movement and establishment? What are the opportunities and challenges particular to advocacy for youth at the local level?*

As we have seen, when advocacy organizations operate effectively between movement and establishment, they are able to connect citizens and local government in new ways, providing alternative methods for political expression to voices often unheard in corridors of the establishment. Their intermediary status enables connections between marginalized members of the community and local decision makers. To be effective, however, advocacy groups must attend to and nurture both sides of the divide. To be of interest and use to disadvantaged groups, they must have knowledge of and access to the community's established structures and empowered leaders; to be regarded as legitimate by the establishment, they must be regarded as credible spokespeople for these underrepresented interests. To stray too far in either direction is to endanger their strategic competence—their utility as conduit, interpreter, and broker. How advocates frame problems and promising solutions and how they manage local discourse thus matter fundamentally to their success in engaging consequential community players in their cause.

In this concluding chapter, we return to the local level to underscore the distinctive niche that advocates for youth occupy there—which is where needs are most deeply felt and oppositional rhetoric most prevalent but also where meaningful change has proven to be within the reach of savvy advocates. We review the successes of Coleman, SFOP, and OCO to emphasize how these organizations have effectively countered obstacles with rhetoric and strategies tailored to advance the concrete needs of local youth. Although our contextualized analysis necessarily highlights how these organizations managed the specific challenges they faced as politically, historically, and organizationally situated actors, their strategies have broader lessons by illuminating how advocates must align their reform goals and tactics with local norms and conditions.

Managing Community Discourse

Organizations advocating for youth almost always assume a challenger's stance—they are outsiders pushing for change in existing policies, practices, and institutional arrangements. On just about all counts, the resources and opportunities available to urban youth are insufficient or lacking. Engaging these challenges on behalf of this population necessarily embroils advocacy organizations in the age-old dialectic between advocates for change and supporters of the status quo—debates between movement and establishment. Political actors, be they stand-patters or challengers, try to manage the discourse around a policy issue by means of rhetoric, symbols, and analysis (Baumgartner & Jones 1991). As we saw, much of advocates' work involves just that.

Advocates for change confront predictable and reactive push-backs to progressive agendas such as those advanced by organizations advocating for youth.[1] One oppositional argument holds that advocates' proposals are wrongheaded and will in fact produce outcomes contrary to intended results. In Oakland, for instance, OCO heard from prominent members of the community that the youth development perspective they advocated was "soft," and its pursuit would just exacerbate already high levels of crime and violence in the community.

Defenders of the status quo also advance the argument that advocates' proposals for change are pointless—that they cannot make a dent in the situation of concern, either because the problem is too big or because advocates have identified the wrong problem. The proposed reforms thus inevitably will be a waste of time and money. Advocates working to promote school reform in both San Francisco and Oakland contended with this contrarian view. Some community leaders suggested that expanded or new investments in public education focused on youth at risk of failure could not amount to much because the problems of school failure are rooted intractably in society's fabric and in the youth themselves. Advocates' school reform proposals, critics alleged, therefore were futile because these kids would not succeed in school despite new educational arrangements or resources.

And probably the most difficult status quo argument for advocates to confront, especially in a time of tight resources, asserts that a proposed reform involves unacceptable costs because it will imperil earlier, hard-won accomplishments or threaten existing privilege—for example, worries that new youth-focused expenditures would imperil resources valued by and available to the mainstream community such as tracked academic opportunities.

For advocacy organizations to be successful they must provide persuasive counters to these claims and conserving positions. And these rebuttals or reassurances must be offered in a form of discourse that resonates with the local setting; their narrative must have fidelity in local terms (Benford & Snow 2000). Our focal organizations generally prevailed in managing the discourse surrounding youth issues in their communities; they defined effective counter frames to status quo defenders' concerns and did so in concrete, contextually specific terms.

Perverse outcomes, Oakland's OCO argued in response to critics, would follow not from the youth development stance they advanced but instead from the existing "get tough" policies that pushed youth out of school, onto the streets, and into the juvenile justice system. Advocates presented data to show that once in "the system," few youth reconnect with positive pathways but instead return to crime and eventually to adult prison. Advocates argued that the most promising strategies for connecting troubled urban youth to positive futures lay in approaches that focus on ways youth can stay connected to schools, families, and the workforce. In a setting where more capacious prison facilities, strict antigang policies, and other uncompromising youth policies were being pushed by a powerful segment of the Oakland community and Alameda County, OCO countered these sentiments with research evidence of successful youth outcomes associated with the small schools model they advocated and with youth discussing in public hearings their hopes for the future and what they needed to achieve them.

Advocates countered futility arguments with concrete counterexamples based in local realities. OCO drew on student experience in their successful small schools to feature research-based instances where the different school environment students encountered there enabled at-risk or delinquent youth to reimagine their futures and begin to succeed in school. In Oakland, school officials risked additional public embarrassment if they ignored the stark evidence of educational inequalities OCO presented in public forum. OCO turned threat into opportunity by providing a clear, well-thought-out course of action grounded in research. The organization translated its constituents' unhappiness with the Oakland Unified School District's response to failing schools into a cogent course of policy action.

Youth in both Oakland and San Francisco were marshaled to give expression to their desires for change. For example, youth involved with SFOP led research meetings with city officials in both the small schools and local parks campaigns, demonstrating their knowledge of the issues and offering articulate accounts of why and how these initiatives were important to San Francisco youth. Youth's message of hope and support for a small schools strategy provided compelling counter to naysayers critiquing it as a pointless, expensive response to school failure.

Youth advocates also upended concerns about damage to existing institutional and political investments. They turned politicians' concerns about political peril from "damned if you do" to "damned if you don't." The political pressure advocacy organizations brought to bear in both San Francisco and Oakland constituted clear risks to city hall and elected officials should they neglect or obstruct their youth agenda. Coleman used politicians' public statements of commitment to youth—delivered while campaigning—to hold them accountable. What politician wants to be portrayed as breaking promises to the city's children and youth? In this way, Coleman recast the inherent political liability of urban youth (they and their parents don't vote) into a political asset congruent with San Francisco's progressive values and culture (our community has a moral obligation to its most vulnerable citizens).

OCO's executive director pointed to the payoff of collective action by its constituents: "I think what made us successful is that we were able to mobilize and we were able to organize hundreds of parents who had not been accessed before and if anything is going to move the school district, it's going to be large numbers of parents."[2] OCO and SFOP made sure that community members were a significant vocal presence at all relevant hearings and relied on the strength of grassroots connections to wait out the opposition.

Each of our focal organizations managed community discourse about youth in astute and skillful ways. They framed issues in ways that connected with their community's cultural base; they acted quickly and strategically to seize local political opportunities for their proposals. And, as we take up next, these strategies were distinctly local in their focus, appeal, content, and warrant—and unlike advocacy at other levels of the government.

Localness: The Home Advantage

These examples of advocates' responses to potential opposition highlight the ways in which the discourse of youth advocacy at the local level—the rhetoric, symbols, and actions employed—differs from that operating at other levels of the policy system. To be sure, local contexts are vulnerable to political shifts and policies originating at state and national levels. Embedded within larger systems of government and broader social environments, local actors are influenced by forces outside their community boundaries. The high-stakes accountability measures contained in the current federal education act, No Child Left Behind, for instance, have led to an exclusive focus on student achievement outcomes and fostered an environment inhospitable to significant attention to youth development outcomes, more broadly conceived. This contemporary climate was preceded by an earlier example of significant federal influence on local policy contexts for youth: Local advocates for children and youth were hamstrung by the deep cuts made by the Reagan administration in domestic programs focused on children and youth. "Everything was shut down by the Reagan people," said Margaret Brodkin as she recalled the evolution of advocacy for youth in San Francisco. "You no longer had confidence that there was *any* impetus for reform within [the federal] government and I don't think we [local youth advocates] have had any confidence since then [the early 1980s]." The state's influence has been felt heavily in Oakland. OCO's work on education reform has been deeply affected by the state's takeover of the Oakland Unified School District. The district's single-minded focus on student test scores and the district's academic ranking have muted the youth development stance that characterized OCO's small schools initiative.

Although they are affected by influences from outside their communities, local advocacy organizations operate in an institutional and political environment distinctly different from the settings advocates at state and national levels work in; these differences present both particular opportunities and constraints for local advocacy and action (see Stone, Orr, & Worgs 2006). At a fundamental level, the discourse of advocacy at the local level is unlike that at other levels of government in its structure and content—its linguistic rules. At the national level, politics are deeply partisan and debates are structured in highly charged ideational terms; ideas often serve as "weapons of mass persuasion" (Béland 2005, p. 12; see also Rutherford 2004). Advocacy language in federal and state arenas features general, notional claims about the benefits or costs of a particular policy move. For example, the prominent 1983 report on American education from the National Commission on Excellence in Education, *A Nation at Risk* (National Commission on Excellence in Education 1983), famously mobilized Congress and state policy makers to increase education spending under the threat that a "rising tide of mediocrity" would cost the United States dearly in the global economic race and consign the country to second-rate status. The report intoned: "If an unfriendly foreign power had attempted to impose on America the mediocre educational performance that exists today, we might well have viewed it as an act of war."

Mobilizing support at the local level relies less on ideological, partisan persuasion and more on specific appeals to concrete action. What *should* the community do for its youth? What *can* the community do for its youth? What do our youth *need?* OCO's concrete details on resource differentials between hill and flatland schools stirred support for school reform across the community. Coleman's straightforward budget reviews showed where more money for youth could come from with no reduction in service—the fire department's budget. Debates about educational equity at the national level, by contrast, often are waged in ideological absolutes that allow, at least in public, little middle ground and force contestants to a higher level of abstraction. In several ways, then, local advocates' rhetoric and relationships differ from that found at higher levels of government. Here we explore some of them.

Specific Proposals and Concrete Actions

Advocates at the local level can reference details of past bargains, specific contexts, and consequences. Problems beset specific people in particular spatial and temporal locations; disembodied policies and specialized services converge on particular citizens and clients. Armed with local knowledge about who is hurting and who may be able to help, local advocacy organizations are in a superior position to observe problems, diagnose causes, and seek redress. "Institutional memory of how to effectively move the system," said Margaret Brodkin, "is what has helped sustain [Coleman's] effectiveness." Known personalities, familiar positions, and concrete tasks shape the discourse and argumentation of local advocacy organizations. And local youth have names, faces, and connections to community institutions; they are not hypothetical "American youth" failing to "meet standards." Coleman, OCO, and SFOP successfully assembled scores of community youth to march in front of city hall, to attend school board meetings, to meet with the media. OCO, SFOP, and Coleman rallied hundreds of parents to let elected officials know where they stood on issues such as school reform and community-based resources for youth. Both small schools campaigns involved a lot of local knowledge and embedded relationships. Local advocates' rhetoric and symbols represented political pressure officials could not ignore and enabled reformers to shift the terms of the discourse. The fact that in many instances these shifts required status quo defenders to act more like challengers underscores the effectiveness of advocates' tactics.

Our cases also show how local reformers can mobilize support when they speak in more than abstractions and are able to point to specific action and local consequences. In so doing, local advocates offset the "uncertainty advantage" used by status quo defenders to erode support for change (Hojnacki et al. 2006). They ask: What would it look like? What would it cost? Who would benefit? Best to stick to the known, defenders' argument goes. John Campbell (2004), considering the sources of institutional change, offers the following proposition: "Problems are more likely to be perceived as requiring institutional changes if there are institutional entrepreneurs on hand who can articulate and frame them as such in clear and simple terms" (pp. 177–78). We find strong support for this suggestion. Each focal organization constructed compelling arguments designed to change public ideas about youth and community responsibilities for them. They compiled data that detailed youth's needs and the shortfalls or inequitable resources currently available to them and then crafted well-supported proposals for change in clear evidence-based terms.

Our focal organizations intentionally positioned themselves as part of a solution. They minimized their position as challengers and mainstream threats by advocating *for* something consonant with existing policies, rather than merely pushing *against* the status quo—an effective response to detractors' jeopardy argument. "We propose a lot of positive ways to do things differently and be part of the solution," reflected Coleman Advocate's Brodkin. Similarly, OCO's Snyder said: "We don't want to get in an adversarial kind of situation where we become another protest. We want to find a way in which a positive agenda can get advanced." OCO's response was an especially attractive one in a community torn by racial contestations and negative, finger-pointing politics. None of our focal organization resembled 1960s tie-dyed activists, storming buildings, vowing to overthrow an existing regime, and threatening influentials. Instead, our case organizations engaged power in ways that connected with elites' own self-interests and rhetoric. Their strategy of being part of the solution contributes significantly to the unusually long life they have enjoyed. Single-issue groups founded in protest usually dissolve once their issue is resolved or loses salience.

Advocates highlight the "local advantage" to their work and effectiveness. As Brodkin put it: "The localness of it is one of the things that has kept us innovative and me interested all of these years . . . it is very easy to translate [goals into action], to have both contact with the people that you're trying to see things changed *for* as well as the systems you're trying to change." In this way, localness can shift the discourse from the ideologically based contentions heard at state and national levels to alternative proposals for immediate action. "Rising tides of mediocrity" or other similarly abstract slogans are unlikely to move local voters or influentials unless they are detailed, pictured, and positioned in local terms.

Logic of Appropriateness

Deep social and political knowledge of their context enables local advocates to build situationally persuasive cases. Advocates we studied articulated what James March and Johan Olsen (1989, p. 23) term a "logic of appropriateness," or arguments that individuals consider appropriate in a particular social, political, and institutional context. In San Francisco, the logic of appropriateness associated with Coleman's strategies existed in their symbolic resonance with the city's populist values and progressive voters; for example, the Children's Fund offered a clear way for voters to express their support for the city's youth. Coleman acted to defuse potential voter concern about how a Children's Fund might negatively affect or jeopardize the city services available to them by providing evidence of waste in San Francisco's municipal budget. Coleman's research showed how new resources for youth could come from more efficient government spending. Coleman developed a specific, appropriate course of action for liberal voters and the politicians who wanted to retain their favor. This strategy changed many voters' assumptions about what was necessary support for the fire protection and enabled them to do "the right thing" by San Francisco's children and youth.

SFOP, in a similar vein, featured the moral legitimacy of their work, organizing the faith community around doing the right thing for children and families in San Francisco and presenting their proposals to civic leaders and officials in terms of what was just and honorable for them to do. As an SFOP organizer put it, "We believe people are precious and should be treated that way . . . society should be organized . . . to reflect that." This appeal connected with the city's long-standing commitment to human development (as opposed to economic development) and social justice. SFOP's express moral stance may be one reason why, according to the organization's executive director Kim Grose, the former mayor Willie Brown once said that SFOP "scared the heck out of him."

Our focal organizations strategically crafted their campaigns to provide an "overlap between the organizational repertoire of the challenging groups and the organizational forms embedded in existing institutions and recognized by those in power." (Clemens 1997, p. 44.) The social logics and repertoires at work in these instances were institutionally derived and establishment sanctioned but used in service of the movement.

Relationships and Coalitions

Local advocacy organizations' dexterity and political power draw heavily on the coalitions they can assemble, often on short notice, to lobby for an issue. Coleman Advocates acted as a broker and convener, creating new coalitions and relationships to press for a youth agenda and policy change. "It is about grooming and building coalitions," said Brodkin. Coleman made connections and used information strategically, constructing each campaign's "army of advocates" with specific attention to the community and agency power relationships surrounding a particular issue. This strategy proved especially effective in a community context where majorities are made not found (De-Leon 1992). Coleman exploited relational mechanisms to bring pressure on policy makers and elected officials. The organization's brokering of coalitions in support of youth policies created an effective voice for change and action, relationships that changed depending on specific issues and key people. Coleman's extensive contact list of influentials enabled flexible assembly of politically consequential supporters. These relationships built on the executive director's broad acceptance and credibility in the community. Coleman's robust social capital made the organization both a threat and a positive collaborator in the youth policy arena. Archon Fung (2003) describes this tension: "The association that best presses [values of participation, deliberation, political accountability, and effective administration] may require the strength to protest local autocrats even as it retains the flexibility to cooperate with officials who are disposed to fair engagement" (p. 536).

SFOP and OCO acted primarily as community organizers, enlisting and enabling member congregations to speak to power through their political presence. As organizers, these organizations built local grassroots capacity for political change and alternative mechanisms for political expression, creating constituents through relationships of trust. By empowering citizens to become self-advocates through leadership development and political education, SFOP and OCO opened up the policy-making process to otherwise marginalized voices and worked to make public officials accountable to all of their constituents. SFOP's Grose put her organization's mission this way: "It's about reclaiming and revitalizing democracy . . . building a strong democracy . . . where ordinary people are really engaged in running the country." SFOP and OCO's capacity to quickly mobilize [and register] voters through their member churches confronted elected officials and community elites with the collective voice of citizens. In so doing, these organizations did much to amplify values of pluralism and participation in their communities.

These effective relationships are local relationships, ties that feature multiple connections and interlocking loyalties. Our focal advocacy organizations' social, political, and institutional location at the intersection of several networks enhanced their message and base of support. This kind of social and political capital supporting youth advocacy efforts has distinctly local character and roots. "You can only do it at the local level," said Coleman's

Brodkin. "You just have the proximity of people . . . when you're shut out of the mayor's office or someplace, you make connections with someone who isn't shut out. It's all about being good politicians." SFOP and OCO, operating according to PICO's organizing principle of "no permanent enemies, no permanent allies," likewise mobilized coalitions around supports for specific issues rather than ideological affiliation or former position. SFOP's executive director Kim Grose said: "We have that niche and that credibility of representing a very wide base and being nonpartisan, being a more moderate voice. I think one of our greatest strengths is that we really are not seen as sort of one side or the other." SFOP's successful creation of consensus support for a housing bond turned on that nonpartisan credibility and ability to mobilize support from across the city—homeowners, renters, the wealthy, and the poor—and, as Grose put it, "help them see common values . . . and the common ground we all share around our families and children."

Range of Action

Advocates for youth at state and national levels typically specialize in a particular policy area or institution—health, juvenile justice, special education, school finance, for example. Rarely do these advocates venture outside their domain of expertise to consider youth issues, or a youth development agenda, more broadly. However, for individuals involved with youth advocacy at the local level, opportunities exist to work across youth-serving sectors to address youth issues and resources more comprehensively. This local capacity to pursue cross-agency and sector range of action fosters innovative solutions. The Department of Children, Youth and Their Families in San Francisco, for instance, is a product of Coleman's efforts to integrate and coordinate the city's health and human services for youth, consistent with core youth development principles. The wide range of youth advocacy effort possible at the local level is what keeps policy entrepreneurs like Margaret Brodkin energized and focused on the broader picture for youth. In the course of a week, for example, she meets with an array of individuals affecting youth policies—pediatricians, school officials, neighborhood parent groups, the local media, foundation program officers, the heads of various city departments. And, if one agency or official is not receptive, local advocates can approach another for support. The narrower scope of advocacy work in Sacramento or Washington, D.C., she says, "isn't anywhere near as interesting" as what she can tackle and potentially accomplish for youth in San Francisco.

Local advocates also are able to adjust the scope of action to suit the local "comfort zone," build support for their cause one step at a time, and seize a window of political opportunity when it opens. We have considered the extent to which some advocacy organizations are willing to work slowly and incrementally, taking small steps forward as opportunities allow, while others are less patient and more ambitious, seeking ways to redefine the debate or move the goalposts. Most of the population of service organizations in our study that engaged in advocacy was observed to settle for small, achievable improvements, working within the current contours of prevailing modes of service delivery within existing definitions and striving for small increases in budgetary limits. However, our focal advocacy organizations, while by no means revolutionary in their tactics, routinely sought to redefine the prevailing discourse, to forward more radical models of programs objectives—for example, the small schools agenda—and to mobilize and empower new constituencies' entry to the arena.

The local context allows a "take a bite" approach to social change and permits advocates to address their goals through successive approximation rather than major legislation or policy change. SFOP deliberately pursued this strategy with their small schools campaign, starting with one school and educating district officials along the way, activities that finally resulted in passage of a board resolution supporting small schools. Small wins can add up to significant change in policy and practice at the local level both because they can demonstrate to naysayers that the proposed change did not result in the anticipated negative consequences and because proximity to practice permits midcourse corrections and adaptations.

Advocates as Educators, Conduits, and Translators

Local youth advocates also can be educators in ways difficult to accomplish at national and state levels—teaching local influentials and politicians about the needs of youth and promising practices through direct experience and contacts. Leaders of our case organizations see coalition building as a fundamental educational task, teaching community members and others about the nature of an issue and possible responses. And that education can be hands-on, locally meaningful in both warrant and consequence. OCO's Ron Snyder and others in the organization spent countless hours briefing school board members and other public officials about their plans—getting them on board before crucial votes were taken on the small schools project. SFOP staff likewise had numerous meetings with the superintendent of schools, the mayor, school board members, county supervisors and others, and they show up regularly at gatherings where issues of interest are discussed. Coleman Advocates met with Mayor Newsom just as he was coming into office and drove him around the city to see schools, parks, and other youth resources, providing him an up-close, thorough education on youth issues.

Coleman Advocates also sees its educator role in terms of "growing up" politicians headed for the state level about youth issues and policy opportunities. For example, Coleman worked closely with CA Assemblyman Mark Leno when he was a member of the San Francisco County Board of Supervisors, encouraging him to support youth-friendly measures in areas such as universal health care for children and attention to childhood obesity. Leno took those interests with him when he went to Sacramento in 2002 and provided effective backing for policies benefiting youth. Leno successfully sponsored a bill that provided more than $14 million for college readiness and assistance for foster youth in the 2006–2007 state budget.[3]

Advocates as Guardian Angels

Advocates' inability to participate very deeply in the process of policy implementation represents both a frustration and a practical fact. Once a measure is passed, a budget is approved, an initiative is rolled out, and the action moves to the agency or organization responsible for the next steps. In large measure, advocacy organizations have little influence once that handoff has taken place. Coleman, SFOP, and OCO may engage in implementation oversight to different degrees that reflect their organizational culture, structure, and resources. Yet none of these three organizations typically makes the implementation of their reform goals, once they are handed off or spun off, a central feature of their work at the local level. Nor are they involved much with implementation of policies from the federal or state level.

Though local advocates cannot be implementers, they nonetheless have greater opportunity to influence the course of implementation than do their counterparts at other levels of the policy system. Advocates working at the local level are on the ground, close to the action and knowledgeable about consequences. They have the opportunity to monitor implementation and call attention to problems or failed promises. OCO's army of parents, for instance, provided motivated and articulate witness to Oakland's level of attention to and resources for the small schools their children attend. Coleman Advocates keeps an eye on the extent to which promised resources show up in the Department of Children Youth and Family budgets or in parks and community centers. An OCO organizer likens this oversight role to that of a guardian angel: "Early on we were looking for somebody in the district to be a guardian [for the small schools]. So it became the Office of School Reform—somebody that would protect us. Well, then that disappeared. We've discovered *we* have to be the guardian angel." Guardian angels of this sort are a distinctly local presence.

Local Mechanisms:
Precipitating Events and Enabling Factors

Coleman, SFOP, and OCO are not unique in adopting roles as urban educators, brokers, or organizers to push a youth agenda and neutralize rhetoric harmful to their cause. Nor are they unique in crafting specific proposals keyed to local contexts. But they have been arguably more successful than many similar organizations working between movement and establishment for youth in urban settings. Factors operating in their larger political context influenced their ability to succeed where advocates using similar tactics in other environments have come up short. Mechanisms operating in their immediate environment shaped both the opportunities for and the contributions of our focal organizations.

Ideas and concrete plans of action matter most in conditions of crisis and upheaval. Oakland schools were in crisis and heading for state takeover as OCO was mounting its campaign for small, autonomous schools. OCO proposed a clear, well-substantiated alternative in the context of state pressure for the district to do something about its failing schools. OCO's campaign had a major impact in Oakland and earned the organization a national reputation for spearheading one of the few community-based school reform initiatives to take hold in a large, urban area.

No such precipitating event animated change in education policies in San Francisco; and, as a consequence, SFOP and OCO have not been equally successful with their very similar small schools campaigns. SFOP's small schools campaign in San Francisco had just begun to make progress after more than five years. Although the campaign resulted in the opening of one new small school, the city has not adopted a small schools policy, though the school board has passed a resolution to create a small schools policy. The Oakland context of school crisis enabled OCO's pursuit of equity to override the district's commitment to professional authority and bureaucratic efficiencies.

SFOP faced a more stable and entrenched school bureaucracy in San Francisco, which made its reform goals harder to pursue; moreover, SFOP was sometimes perceived as confrontational—perhaps because of its tactics, but perhaps because the city and district were not as open to school reform as Oakland had to be.

A more broad-based environmental factor facilitated Coleman Advocates' work: concern over the flight of families from San Francisco (Blash et al. 2005). Coleman's slogan, "San Francisco is better with children," struck a cord with the electorate and received public endorsement from Mayor Gavin Newsom and other influentials. Youth-focused policies aimed at health care, recreation, and other social supports garnered voter support not only because of Coleman's moral message about social obligation but also because of the alarming decline of the number of youth in the city. Not just white, advantaged families have left San Francisco; the city has experienced the steepest drop in black population of any major American city (Yogis 2006). Coleman leveraged this community population decline into an issue requiring attention and promoted proposals to make the city more attractive to families.

Both SFOP and Coleman exploited another particular San Francisco feature to their advantage. The unusual number of commissions in San Francisco combined with the transparency required by the city's especially strict Sunshine Ordinance makes policy change slow in the city.[4] According to one observer, these factors are "effective largely in stopping things . . . It tends to be easier to advocate to stop something than to get something going because then you get the next group who is saying, no, no, no! We shouldn't do this! So if you think about it, commissioners feel safer by doing nothing." Yet the upside of having many commissions is that advocacy organizations have more opportunities to voice their concerns in official public forums. SFOP aggressively used this feature to achieve its goals. As one participant put it: "The city is unusual in having an extraordinary number of commissions . . . And so if you have an organization like SFOP who can get the troops out, you can say we need 100 people to show up at 6 o'clock on next Tuesday at the health commission to protest this. It's very effective in the city."

Local foundations also figure significantly in youth advocates' effectiveness in San Francisco and Oakland. Bay Area youth benefit materially and politically from philanthropies knowledgeable about and invested in the communities and youth development, as well as in advocacy for them. Foundations established by the Haas family, the East Bay Community Foundation, the San

Francisco Foundation, and others take an active role in holding advocacy organizations accountable for their work, and in celebrating their successes (Yee 2008). As Brodkin said, "They live here; they know what's going on, and they get excited when they see change."

Precipitating events and enabling factors in both communities provide explanation for the outcomes achieved by our focal advocacy organization and suggest reasons why our focal organizations could accomplish what they did for youth. Ideas take hold close to the ground. Local advocates can keep a weather eye out for shifts in the institutional setting or political context—new actors or agencies sympathetic to their message. SFOP's Kim Grose told us: "We as organizers are always looking for what are the political windows of opportunity, and that's in part why we are doing some of our own reconnaissance and meeting with people and reading and trying to figure out what those might be." Local advocacy organizations are able to move quickly and effectively in their local contexts, generating a pace of change difficult to achieve at state and national levels where ideologically based deliberations can slow down policy response and policy decisions are of greater magnitude.

These environmental mechanisms underscore the influence of local political and cultural contexts as additional sources of complexity in understanding the work of advocacy organizations. They also point up a barrier to generalizing across settings about the implications of particular organizational designs and strategies, because community contexts can differ in important ways. But the significance of these elements also suggests ways in which the local context can present the most meaningful opportunities for organizations advocating for youth. Local level politics, institutions, and relationships afford youth advocates opportunities for action that are unlike those at other levels in terms of their immediacy and concreteness. They call for discourse and symbols directly resonant in their community context—a locally defined and accepted logic of appropriateness. Conceptions and expressions of "effective advocacy," then, vary not only across local settings but also across levels of government.

Implications

Our study highlights the distinctive and essential role advocacy organizations play for young people who grow up in big cities such as San Francisco and Oakland. It deepens our appreciation of how youth advocates work in urban settings and moves our understanding of their activities beyond lists of "best practices" and decontextualized anecdotes. Further, our study suggests that any examination of the character and consequences of youth policy at the local level would be both incomplete and potentially misleading were these nonsystem actors excluded. We saw that advocacy organizations made a substantive and significant difference for Bay Area youth, whether those differences are counted in the new dollars provided by the children's budgets, tallied in terms of policy changes such as the educational reforms represented by small schools, or seen in the visibility afforded youth commissions in both cities. Arguably, the persistent and smart work of our focal organizations was essential to these positive outcomes for Bay Area youth.

Although we have aimed to understand our case organizations in their localized contexts, our study has implications that extend beyond the San Francisco Bay Area to organizations advocating for youth in other big-city contexts—and suggests promising directions for future research on local advocacy efforts. Our case examples underscore the uniqueness of advocacy organizations as nonsystem actors and the essential contribution they make to the lives of urban youth. Their organizational nimbleness and intermediary location allows them to push for change and advance the cause of youth in ways other local actors usually could not. Establishment actors, constrained by their institutional and political settings, typically have difficulty moving too far from status quo majority interests. Individuals at the grassroots, most especially young people, lack the authority or opportunity to speak to power. We saw how organizations advocating for youth, when attentive to political opportunity and in tune with the community's ways of working, could push ideas and proposals from the margins to the mainstream in ways that insiders likely could not. Advocacy organizations thus constitute a critical source of social change and innovation for their community's youth. However, we also saw how potentially fragile were advocates' wins and how little understood was the handoff from streets to suites. These observations suggest a number of implications.

Philanthropic Investment in Advocacy for Youth

As nonsystem, third-sector actors, advocacy organizations have limited sources of financial support, and foundation investments contribute critically to their ability to be effective and indeed to survive. Yet many foundations' policies restrict support to start-up or time-limited funding—a reality that has pushed many community organizations to cut back or stop advocacy work altogether in order to take up fee-carrying service provision. Given the distinctive and crucial ways that local advocacy organizations support youth, philanthropies committed to the well-being of their community's youth can strategically augment their returns by investing in the stability and vitality of those advocacy organizations making a difference for them.

Links across the Policy System

Our study shows how advocacy at the community level differs in tone, tools, and tempo from advocacy at other levels. And, consistent with decades of implementation research, we see that local actions and responses matter fundamentally and particularly to the resources and opportunities afforded a community's youth. Advocates working at the local level are advantaged by their local knowledge, contacts, and reputation. Yet these special resources are woefully underused by the broader policy system. Some national youth advocacy groups, such as the Forum for Youth Investment, do connect with local groups to advance their goals. But, for the most part, these connections across levels of the policy system are seldom made. Local advocates such as those we studied generally are absent as agendas are set and policies affecting youth are made at state and national levels. Likewise, their potential as policy partners is little considered. As a result, reformers external to the community fail to benefit from local advocates' special relationships, knowledge, and perspective about what would or would not work in their communities and for whom. An analytical and thus a policy problem highlighted by our study is one of linkage between macro and micro levels of action. What structural, procedural, or institutional conditions enable and frustrate such linkage?

Questions about the Handoff

Our research on youth advocacy organizations in the San Francisco Bay Area raises many issues for future research and theorizing. Few questions are of greater interest, in our view, than those surrounding the process and consequences of the handoff from advocacy organizations to the establishment.

The handoff or the spin-off from what we have called the "streets to the suites" ranks as a necessary but insufficient condition for the organizational or institutional change sought by advocates. Advocates' formal work may be done with the handoff, but their mission is hardly finished. Advocacy groups are in the business of formulating new policies and demonstrating the feasibility of new programs for their constituents. But for a public policy to succeed, it must be turned into formal agreements and supported by the allocation of public moneys: Handoffs are not choices but necessities. Unless the program is to remain highly localized and circumscribed, not even the Rockefeller or the Gates Foundations have sufficiently deep pockets to long sustain new programs at urban community, state, or national levels.

Handoffs are fraught with danger. New agencies and organizations and personnel take charge, and their structures, training, and commitment will alter the intended policies and programs in multiple ways impossible to foresee. Because all successful policies undergo this transformation as a consequence of being handed off, this appears to us among the most important (and most neglected) topics to be pursued in the continuing study of advocacy organizations. The handoff takes place in a dynamic political context and usually is managed by a bureaucracy. Lynn Zucker (quoted in Clemens & Cook 1999, p. 446) sees the process of institutionalization as one in which the "moral becomes factual." The same might be said for the handoff process. Advocates' principled vision moves to procedural corridors of the establishment. This transfer raises challenges, of course, when policies on the ground depart from the moral visions of advocates.

A handoff can take different forms. It can be a mandate for government action, as was the Children's Amendment advanced by Coleman Advocates. Or it can consist of authoritative action as was the case with OCO's small autonomous schools initiative. The handoff could be located in construction of a constituency sufficiently powerful to sway a vote, as was the case with Books not Bars' efforts to stop the building of a megaprison in Alameda County.

Regardless of the nature of the handoff, once advocates' wins move to the domain of a maintenance organization, to "the system," advocacy organizations lose significant control of how the change they sought is rolled out and sustained. Coleman Advocates had many opinions, for instance, but little say in how funds resulting from the Children's Amendment were allocated. OCO gained approval to start small, autonomous schools in Oakland but had scant power to influence the many aspects of the district environment that affected the schools' establishment and operation. Although all three organizations attempted to ensure that their reform goals were faithfully implemented by "establishment" officials, their organizational structure and limited resources precluded them from having deep and sustained oversight.

OCO, Coleman, and SFOP may act as watchdogs or guardian angels once their reform campaigns have been institutionalized, but they are necessarily once removed from the implementation process—a distance that is both the marker of their success, and also a potential source of frustration when policies on the ground depart from their intentions. Two important questions associated with the handoff require attention from both reformers and scholars: What factors influence establishment responses to an advocate's initiative and the character of implementation? What aspects of the institutional setting influence an initiative's stability and sustainability?

Factors Affecting Implementation   Implementation is a people-dependent process. Factors affecting the reception given advocates' goals at handoff could be many. Do the core assumptions or beliefs underlying advocates' efforts align with those of key actors in the implementing agency? For example, early gains made by SFOP to introduce small schools to the San Francisco Unified School District initially were short circuited because they found little support among important SFUSD decision makers.

These normative and cognitive aspects of establishment reception highlight the critical role that advocates must play to educate key decision makers about issues fundamental to their advocacy efforts. Change in policy learning generally starts with change in an individual—the education of San Francisco Mayor Newsom offers a prime example of how education paid off with key support from the system. The extent to which the handoff is accompanied by educational efforts to support learning within the implementing system—and what those efforts look like—pose promising questions for social movement theorists.

Institutional capacity comprises another feature of the implementing system over which advocates have little control. The school reforms imagined by OCO advocates confronted limited ability within OUSD to staff and support the new schools. Or legal wins may award remedies beyond the resources of the responsible systems. What happens when advocates' successes outreach system ability to respond? Are adjustments made institutionally? politically? organizationally?

Handoffs may assume substantive interagency collaboration around youth resources and policies, a famously difficult feat to accomplish. San Francisco's Department of Children, Youth and Their Families, a creation of Coleman Advocates, struggles with this challenge, even in the city's progressive context. Such interagency collaboration has been much harder to come by across the bay in Oakland where advocates hoped that the city's own children's budget would prompt cross-agency work.

Factors Affecting Stability   Even with key insider support and sufficient capacity to carry out advocates' intent, handoffs remain vulnerable. Change over time in the distribution of beliefs or authority within the system can create an inhospitable climate for advocates' intent. Inside supporters may move on, be reassigned, or lose their ability to influence implementation. Turnover of powerful individuals could marginalize advocates' objectives. Or, while top officials may have signed on to advocates' mission, individuals further down in the system may not be supportive, and their actions or inactions can stymie implementation. As one midlevel school district administrator commented regarding the uncertain future of a superintendent-supported initiative he personally did not favor: "Never underestimate the power of a dragged foot."

External forces can also derail advocates' gains once the handoff is made. The dynamic local political context can impact the longer-term prospects of advocates' work, for better or worse. Changed constituencies or sources of political power might shift institutional responses and acceptance of advocates' social movement agenda. State takeover of the Oakland Unified School District transferred power from the OUSD school board to a state administrator, for instance. This shift voided previous agreements between OCO and OUSD concerning small schools and largely shut down advocates' access to the district's administration. Conversely, the election of a new San Francisco mayor favorable to a youth development perspective boosted Coleman's agenda, access, and influence.

Developments external to the local system also can affect the focus and priority associated with advocates' goals. For instance, the federal No Child Left Behind education measure has trumped efforts to assume a broader youth development stance in many school and after-school settings. Academic indicators rule in this context of high-stakes test-based accountability. Shifts in federal funding priorities associated with NCLB have pulled financial supports from the after-school programs for which nonprofits successfully advocated in major cities around the country.

Exogenous forces such as these join internal normative, cognitive, and structural factors to make the handoff from the streets to the suites problematic in both near and longer terms. The handoff from movement to establishment raises important questions that sit at the intersection of social movement and organizational theory. To our knowledge, little empirical or theoretical work exists on patterns, mechanisms. or conditions associated with handoffs from advocates to implementers, work that could distinguish between those that are successful and those that are not. Existing literature places most stress on external and internal forces producing change. Much less attention has been afforded the organizational and institutional conditions that make those efforts more or less likely to be effective or endure once the "change agent," in this instance the local advocacy organization, moves from center stage to the sidelines. Research on this broad topic would further our understanding of institutional change as well as knowledge about the types of circumstances that enable or constrain advocates' social movement mission. In particular, research on the handoff from the streets to the suites is central to comprehending the different short- and long-term consequences of wins achieved by organizations advocating for youth at the local level.

Appendix: Respondent List

Respondent	Organizational affiliation & title[1]	Interview date(s)
Kimberly Aceves	Youth Together, Executive Director	July 17, 2003
Renato Almanzor	Bay Area Coalition for Equitable Schools, Manager, Community Partnerships Development	April 9, 2004
Deborah Alvarez-Rodriguez	Omidyar Foundation, Vice President	January 6, 2004
Jen Berman	San Francisco Organizing Project, Organizer	November 23, 2003
Richard Bernard	Oakland Community Organizations, Organizer	March 18, 2004
Bea Bernstine	Oakland Community Organizations, Member	November 19, 2003
Margaret Brodkin	Coleman Advocates for Children and Youth Executive Director	January 31, 2003; March 7, 2003; May 6, 2004; August 5, 2003
Peter Bull	Coleman Advocates, Board Member	May 21, 2003
Dana Bunnett	Kids in Common, Executive Director	February 11, 2004
Rebecca Cherin	Larkin Street Youth Services, Director of Education and Training	September 24, 2003
Libby Coleman	SFCASA, Program Director	July 14, 2003
Kathy Emery	San Francisco Organizing Project, Board Member	November 19, 2003
Rona Fernandez	Youth Empowerment Center, Executive Director	July 8, 2003
Sandra Fewer	Coleman Advocates for Children and Youth Director of P.A.Y.	April 2, 2004
Bruce Fisher	Huckleberry Youth Programs, Executive Director	September 10, 2003
Amy Fitzgerald	Oakland Community Organizations, Volunteer	July 20, 2004
Jen Franchot	Larkin Street Youth Services, Staff	September 24, 2003
Jean Fraser	San Francisco Health Plan, C.E.O.	November 19, 2003
Shawn Ginwright	Santa Clara University, Assistant Professor	April 14, 2003

[1]Affiliation at time of data collection.

Respondent	Organizational affiliation & title[1]	Interview date(s)
Kim Grose	San Francisco Organizing Project Executive Director	July 18, 2003; December 5, 2003; May 30, 2006
Matt Hammer	People Acting in Community Together Executive Director	February 10, 2004
Taj James	Urban Strategies Institute, Executive Director	February 20, 2004
Claudia Jasin	Jamestown Community Center, Co-Director	November 20, 2003
Raquel Jimenez	Youth Together, Director of Programs	July 17, 2003
David Kakishiba	East Bay Asian Youth Center Executive Director	August 22, 2003
Jim Keddy	PICO California Project, Executive Director	January 23, 2004
Janet Knipe	California Youth Connection Executive Director	September 10, 2003
Adam Kruggel	San Francisco Organizing Project, Organizer	October 23, 2003; May 7, 2004
Krishen A. Laetsch	Oakland Cross City Campaign, Director	December 8, 2003
N'Tanya Lee	Coleman Advocates for Children and Youth Director of Youth Policy & Development	November 21, 2003
Amy Lemley	First Place Fund for Youth, Executive Director	June 25, 2003
Michael Lombardo	San Francisco Organizing Project, Board Member	November 20, 2003
Jonathan London	Youth in Focus, Executive Director	July 10, 2003
Lilian Lopez	Oakland Community Organizations Board Member	June 23, 2004
Dan Macallair	Coleman Advocates, Board Member & Executive Director, Center on Juvenile & Justice	November 18, 2003
Rachel Metz	Safe Passages, Fiscal Policy Director	July 29, 2003
Colleen Montoya	San Francisco Youth Commission, Director	August 6, 2003
Kim Myoshi	Kids First, Executive Director	October 9, 2003
Stephanie Ong	San Francisco Child Care Providers Association, Coordinator	June 3, 2003
Darin Ow-wing	Community Educational Services Executive Director	June 16, 2003
Emma Paulino	Oakland Community Organizations, Organizer	December 15, 2003
Macheo Payne	Youth Advisory Commission, Coordinator	August 20, 2003
Dawn Phillips	People United for a Better Life in Oakland Executive Director	August 19, 2003
Kathy Phillips	St. John's Educational Threshold Center, Executive Director	April 16, 2003
Alecia Sanchez	Children's Advocacy Institute, Senior Policy Advocate	January 22, 2004
Mark Sanchez	San Francisco Unified School District School Board Member	January 20, 2004

Respondent	Organizational affiliation & title[1]	Interview date(s)
Jonathan Schorr	Knowledge is Power Program (KIPP) Director of New Initiatives	August 25, 2003
Teresa Shartel	Youth Alive! Program Coordinator	October 3, 2003
Ron Snyder	Oakland Community Organizations Executive Director	January 31, 2003; May 16, 2003; March 12, 2004; November 10, 2004
Anne Stanton	Larkin Street Youth Services, Executive Director	September 24, 2003
Liz Sullivan	Oakland Community Organizations, Organizer	October 19, 2003
Gary Thompson	Interagency Children's Policy Council, Director	March 11, 2004
Maria Luz Torres	Parent Voices, Organizer	July 28, 2003
Michael Wald	Stanford University Law School, Professor	May 5, 2003
Marybeth Wallace	Coleman Advocates, Board Member	April 1, 2004
Joe Wilson	Coleman Advocates for Children and Youth, Associate Director	December 3, 2003

[1]Affiliation at time of data collection.

Reference Matter

Notes

Notes to Introduction

1. Among the thirty countries in the Organization for Economic Cooperation and Development (OECD), for example, the child poverty rate in the United States is topped only by that of Mexico (United Nations Children's Fund, 2004, p. 28). Similarly, this country's social expenditures for children and youth are the lowest among OECD countries, excepting Mexico (United Nations Children's Fund, 2004, p. 35).

2. www.kidsource.com

3. Research shows that children exposed to neighborhood violence typically are significantly disadvantaged in other ways: They are more likely to have ill-educated parents, to live in poverty, and to do poorly in school (Aizer 2008, for example).

Notes to Chapter 1

1. While we examine both advocacy organizations and organizations helping community members engage in advocacy themselves, or community organizing groups, we sometimes refer to both types of organizations as organizations advocating for youth because they both engage in advocacy at different levels of the political system. We recognize their differences but also note many similarities in their strategies and tactics throughout our analysis.

2. An accurate assessment of the number and focus of advocacy organizations operating in a given time or place is difficult to achieve because advocacy happens across nonprofit, for-profit, and public sectors and not just in organizations explicitly labeled

as advocacy organizations (McCarthy & Castelli 2002; Reid 2000). Federal tax status distinguishes the mission and focus of advocacy organizations and service organizations. Federal tax code reserves the "nonprofit" form—501(c)(3)—for charitable, social welfare, educational, and other civic activities that benefit the general public *without* explicit advocacy activities; 501(c)(4) designates social welfare advocacy groups the purpose of which is to lobby for change in government programs or policies.

Groups designated 501(c)(4) lobby at all levels for programs, policies, and legislation favorable to their group's mission. Politically active advocacy organizations aim to change policy by setting the agenda, shifting resources and political support, and making sure that favorable decisions are implemented (see Jenkins 2006). Broad purpose and clientele distinguish among advocacy organizations engaged in political action and lobbying 501(c)(4)s (see Berry 2001). One category supports legislation and policies that benefit their members politically or financially; typically they represent business or professional interests, and examples include the American Medical Association or the American Petroleum Institute. A second category of politically active advocacy organizations are rights oriented and focus on improvements in civic liberties and similar issues for their members—for example, the National Rifle Association or the National Gay and Lesbian Task Force. These groups lobby political leaders and civic elites and also use the courts and related venues to protect their clients' rights under the Constitution. A third category of politically active advocacy organizations, in contrast, advocate on behalf of broader public interests or in support of rights for groups other than their own members, for example, underprivileged or marginalized groups. Rights-oriented advocacy groups have successfully pursued major policy changes regarding treatment of racial and ethnic minorities and women. The ACLU, for example, effectively used the courts *(Williams v. State of California)* to demand equitable resources for California public school children.

In practice, IRS categories are slippery and do not convey an accurate picture of advocacy in the United States because some charitable nonprofits, such as (c)(3), set up an advocacy arm, i.e., (c)(4), so as to facilitate political action without jeopardizing their charitable tax status; some advocacy organizations create a loosely affiliated, exempt social welfare nonprofit to produce tax advantages (see Jenkins 2006 and Reid 2001, for elaboration of tax status details). As Elisabeth Boris and Rachel Mosher-Williams (1998) detail, it is virtually impossible to obtain valid information on the numbers and types of nonprofit organizations engaged in advocacy activities because existing codes used in the National Taxonomy of Exempt Entities classify nonprofits by purpose, not by activity. Because no cross-cutting codes exist, organizations engaged in both service delivery and allowable advocacy are likely to be overlooked.

3. Recent studies of institutional entrepreneurship and institutional change report that individuals and organizations that are not mainstream, but marginal to the existing regime, may be more likely to develop and advance alternative ideas and pro-

grams. For example, the women's movement in the United States adopted organizing tactics from disreputable groups but then adapted them for use in mainstream political arenas (Clemens 1997). Network theorists (Granovetter 1973) have stressed that individuals and groups linked by "weak" ties to entities different from themselves are in a better position to introduce new ideas and practices into an existing field than are units connected only by "strong" ties to those similar to themselves. Aldrich and Ruef (2006, ch. 4) review a number of studies linking variety of linkages with individuals or organizations to the ability of such units to create new kinds of organizations. As Campbell (2004: 74–75) concludes:

> The key is to recognize that being located at the border and interstices of several social networks, organizational fields, or institutions can enhance the probabilities for relatively revolutionary change. Why? Because if leaders have extensive ties to people beyond their immediate social, organizational, or institutional locations, they are more like to have a broad repertoire with which to work and they are more likely to receive ideas about how to combine elements in their repertoire, all of which increase the possibility for creative and revolutionary thinking, innovation, and bricolage.

4. www.childrensdefense.org

5. Some philanthropic support is explicitly political. Covington (2002) details the strategic role of conservative foundations in funding nonprofits engaged in developing ideological briefs to undergird political action.

6. Corporate giving provides another source of financial support for nonprofit advocacy organizations and also tends to go to the politically "safer" 501(c)(3) public welfare groups. Advocacy groups pushing for social change in various quarters, such as the Sierra Club, Move On, or People for the American Way, 501(c)(4) political action organizations, rely heavily on individual contributions because government cannot support such groups and foundations or because business interests often are leery of partisan political identification. (It is increasingly common, however, for wealthy individuals to channel their contributions through a privately funded foundation, such as the Hewlett or Gates foundations, through small family foundations, or through community foundations' donor-advised funds.)

7. Advocacy organizations have long wrestled with the tension between providing direct services or organizing for social action, debating whether hybrid organizations lose their confrontational edge and become little more than social service agencies. Historically, many advocacy organizations have moved from organizing to services for financial reasons. See Brooks (2005) for a review of that debate and evidence from ACORN (Association of Community Organizations for Reform Now), whose services include advocacy for welfare recipients having a dispute with the welfare department, that a single organization can pursue both goals effectively. Minkoff (2002) likewise

finds that hybrid advocacy organizations attract more resources than do single-purpose organizations.

8. See www.childadvocacy.com/legislation.php.

9. Some of the nation's most prominent foundations have taken up the youth development banner and provided leadership for reframing conventional paradigms of youth development as well as the programs and policies associated with them. Influential reports issued by the Carnegie Corporation, *Turning Points: Preparing American youth for the 21st century* (1989) and *A matter of time: Risk and opportunity in the nonschool hours* (1992), and the W. T. Grant Foundation, *The Forgotten Half: Pathways to success for America's youth and young families* (1988), assembled evidence and analysis that provided authoritative support for complaints from youth practitioners about the ineffectiveness of the dominant categorical, reactive policy model and advanced a youth development perspective. They highlighted the need to consider a young person's day in its totality, not just school hours, and demonstrated that nonschool hours are as significant to development as school hours, for better or worse. They featured the special needs of adolescents, pointing out that, for the greater part of the twentieth century, public and private programs directed at young people focused primarily on children. Adolescents received little attention except where policy aimed to fix problems or punish youthful offenders. These reports pointed to society's moral obligations to adolescents and underscored the critical shortfall in programs and resources available for youth, most especially the nation's most vulnerable. The nascent youth development movement can trace its roots to these foundation initiatives. More recently, the National Research Council and Institute of Medicine (2002) issued its influential volume, *Community programs to promote youth development,* which lent the cachet and imprimatur of the scientific community to youth development principles and programmatic assumptions.

10. See especially Iowa's Collaboration for Youth Development (www.icyd.org/). This Collaboration sponsors statewide data collection of youth development indicators to provide county report cards and partners with communities across the state to provide services and opportunities supportive of positive youth development.

11. Important exceptions to this general statement exist in research on community organizing—see, for example, Deschenes, McLaughlin, & Newman 2008; Ginwright & James 2002; Oakes & Rogers 2006; Shirley 1997; Warren 2001; Wood 2002.

12. Note, however, that this is an instance of the general problem defined by Michels (1949/1915) in his classic discussion of the ways in which the processes of established organizations operate to redefine and tame more revolutionary agendas.

Notes to Chapter 2

1. Coleman Advocates for Children and Youth, "2004 Rally for Kids," April 15, 2004.

2. "Open Letter to Mayor-Elect Newsom," by Coleman Advocates for Children and Youth, December 23, 2003.

3. There exists a prejudice in contemporary social and political science to utilize cross-sectional data and to focus on both short-term causes and short-term effects (Pierson 2004, p. 81). This tendency causes analysts to overlook or to misspecify important long-term processes affecting current outcomes. Similarly, consequences that develop over longer time periods are less likely to receive attention. While we have not carried out an extensive historical study of the emergence and development of the youth development field, we endeavor to place our own study in this larger historical context.

4. Note also that, like women early in the twentieth century, children and youth today lack the right to vote. If they are to be political actors, other avenues of self-expression and of exerting influence must be contrived.

5. Twenty-three organizations were surveyed, many of them having been founded in the nineteenth century. All but three were founded prior to the twentieth century.

6. Associations gaining members were the Veterans of Foreign Wars, American Farm Bureau Federation, YMCA, and the American Automobile Association.

7. It is significant that the members of Alcoholics Anonymous introduce themselves at meetings with the statement: "My name is John, and I am an alcoholic." Nevertheless, we recognize that the role-identity distinction is complex. For example, a number of women's organizations emphasize the role aspects of female behavior, focusing for example on the issue of unpaid work for the "homemaker." And some gay and lesbian groups organize around (worker) role issues such as job and pay discrimination rather than identity issues.

8. As previously discussed, such groups exhibit some of the features associated with "identity" groups, cultivating not only general skills but more specific attributes recognizing the distinctive strengths of their subgroup: not simply excellence, but authenticity.

Notes to Chapter 3

1. State Senator Dede Alpert, for example, attempted to pass legislation from 1990 to 2002 to create various state commissions for children and youth. In 2001, she introduced the Youth Development Act to coordinate policies regarding youth, but the legislation was vetoed by the governor because of fiscal concerns. In 2004, under a new banner and broader endorsement, Alpert's "Youth Policy Act" (SB 215) was vetoed once again.

2. In 2003, the Senate passed a resolution to establish March 28 as an annual day to recognize youth for their involvement in the creation of youth programs. The reso-

lution recommended that "the Legislature encourage individual members of the Legislature to include local youth in their policymaking efforts" (Foster et al. 2005).

3. Oakland gave birth to the Black Panther party. It was founded in the 1960s by Merritt College students Huey Newton and Bobby Seale when the killing of black youth by a predominately white police force fueled racial militancy (Self 2003).

4. California counties are central actors in passing and implementing youth policy. State–local realignment policies early in the 1990s shifted responsibility for many social services from the state to counties and cities. As a result, responsibility for most mental health, public health, and social services was transferred to local governments in 1992. Counties administer most of the essential services for children except for schools, while state departments play a relatively smaller role in implementing programs and operating services. Counties share law enforcement and fire protection services with cities but counties alone have the responsibility to "lock them up," conducting legal proceedings and housing prisoners who are not in state penitentiaries. Cities, by contrast, have a more limited role in government for children, though advocacy often targets the city level.

5. Brookings Institution 2003.

6. Alameda and San Francisco counties are the first and third most diverse in the region, based on the relative proportions of ethnic and racial groups. The diversity index rates the distribution of racial and ethnic groups from 0.0 (only one racial or ethnic group in the population) to 1.0 (equal distribution of all racial and ethnic groups). Alameda's diversity index was 0.889 in 2000, and San Francisco's was 0.818. See the Association of Bay Area Governments' website: census.abag.ca.gov.

7. The national average is 11.1 percent (U.S. Bureau of the Census 2000).

8. Kids Count 2000 census data, available at www.aecf.org/kidscount/census.

9. The child population has dropped from 24.5 percent in 1960 to just 14.5 percent in 2000 (Coleman Advocates 2001).

10. Interview with Margaret Brodkin, May 6, 2004.

11. U.S. Bureau of the Census 2000.

12. This is compared to 52 percent of U.S. households with children under age 18.

13. Kids Count 2000 census data, available at www.aecf.org/kidscount/census.

14. Interview with Director of Alameda County's Interagency Children's Policy Council (ICPC), March 11, 2004.

15. Oakland Profile www.edab.org, accessed September 25, 2005.

16. Data from FC Search database, retrieved from the San Francisco Foundation Center, September 2004.

17. Foundation funding in the Bay Area for both youth services and youth advocacy organizations typically comes from a set of foundations with a program area dedicated to children and youth. Many of these foundations are well known and fund projects and programs throughout the Bay Area, as well as in other parts of California

and the United States, including the Robert Wood Johnson, Annie E. Casey, Evelyn and Walter Haas Jr., Hewlett, Ford, Packard, James Irvine, Mott, and Stuart Foundations.

18. www.ci.sf.ca.us/site/mainpages_index.asp?id=7695#agencies

19. Kids Count, Measures of Child Well-Being in the Nation's Largest Cities, Annie E. Casey Foundation, 2004.

20. www.cnn.com/2007/US/11/18/dangerous.cities.ap/index

21. Coleman Advocates, Take Action Now! Available at www.colemanadvocates .org/take_action/strategies/childrens_amendment.html

22. Interview with the Director of the Interagency Children's Policy Council (ICPC), March 11, 2004.

23. Community Crime Prevention Associates 2001.

24. Knight 2005a.

25. The percentage of English learners rose from 26.3 percent to 34.7 percent during this time.

26. Buchanan 2004.

27. http://orb.sfusd.edu/profile/prfl-100.htm;   http://webportal.ousd.k12.ca.us/docs/7302.pdf. Both sites accessed August 4, 2008.

28. www.greatschools.net. Accessed July 15, 2008.

29. www.ed-data.k12.ca.us. Accessed July 15, 2008.

30. www.ed-data.k12.ca.us. Accessed July 15, 2008.

31. Information on health services from the San Francisco Department of Public Health website: www.sfdph.org/.

32. See Siler 2005.

Notes to Chapter 4

1. We used the term *youth advocacy* as a keyword, which yielded sixty-four organizations in San Francisco and twenty-seven in Oakland. The Bay Area Urban League, Communities for a Better Environment, and Disabilities Rights Advocates are some examples of organizations captured in the keyword search that did not fit our criteria. And one of our key focal organizations in San Francisco, Coleman Advocates, did not appear in our original search because it was incorporated in a neighboring county. This oversight has since been corrected as Guidestar has updated the database.

We were also able to obtain a list of all of the nonprofit organizations operating in San Francisco and Oakland in 2000 from the National Center of Charitable Statistics, and we used this comprehensive list to check against both the snowball sample and Guidestar lists (Gammal et al. 2005). NCCS captures only organizations that file a 990 form; nonprofits that have religious affiliations or have an operating budget of under $25,000 are exempt from this requirement.

We found, as did Andrews and Edwards (2004), the 990 to be an unreliable source for identifying the nature and focus of nonprofit organizations' activities and budgets.

2. We examined these organizations further through interviews, media searches, and review of academic reports on youth organizations.

3. For example, Zald and Denton (1963) describe how the YMCA has evolved over time from an organization primarily serving lower-class and recent immigrant clients to providing facilities and programs for middle-class youth.

4. Some organizations have different founding and ruling dates—the former being the years in which the organizations were established and the latter being the years in which organizations received their 501(c)3 status. Youth Together, for instance, was founded in 1996 but got 501(c)3 status in 2003. We note cases in which this is an issue.

5. As with all cooptation mechanisms (Selznick 1949), this effort sometimes worked as planned but also erred in both directions—sometimes serving as an ideology masking manipulation of locals by elite groups, on the one end, or, at the other, serving to fuel radical groups who captured programs and funds for their own ends (Krause 1968; Moynihan 1970).

Notes to Chapter 5

1. www.sfcasa.org

2. Appendix A provides the name, organizational affiliation, title, and date of interview for all respondents. Unless otherwise noted, all quotes come from interviews.

Notes to Chapter 6

1. All numbers and figures noted in the text were current as of our data collection period, 2003 to 2005.

2. PICO website, www.piconetwork.org.

3. OCO Small Schools Conference, October 10, 2003.

4. Saul Alinksy founded the Industrial Areas Foundation (IAF) in 1940 to organize Chicago's working class. Known for his militant tactics, Alinksy wrote *Rules for Radicals* and *Reveille for Radicals,* which detail his central beliefs about community organizations as political institutions: that they should have "indigenous leadership and citizen participation; financial independence; and a commitment to defend local interests while avoiding divisive issues" (Warren 2001, p. 44). Alinsky, like PICO, based his organizing efforts on communities' existing institutions, including churches (Warren 2001, p. 45).

5. PICO website, www.piconetwork.org/ab_history.asp.

6. Appendix A provides the name, organizational affiliation, title and date of interview for all respondents. Unless otherwise noted, all quotes come from interviews.

7. OCO website, www.oaklandcommunity.org/issues.html.

8. BayCES is part of a national school reform network, The Coalition of Essential Schools.

9. The ballot measure provides $9.5 million to the Oakland Police Department to hire new police officers and $6.2 million for violence prevention programs (PICO Network 2005).

10. OCO is also a PICO organization.

11. From Coleman Advocates list of "Principles We Support," www.colemanadvocates.org, emphasis added.

12. Brodkin 1989, p. 8.

13. The concept of archetype is examined in Chapter 2.

14. Different staffing arrangements are associated with quite different incentive systems. Clark and Wilson (1961) usefully contrast organizations relying on paid staff with organizations dependent on volunteer efforts. The former, labeled "utilitarian" organizations, use material rewards, for example salaries or wages, to motivate participants to pursue organizational objectives. Of course, in the case of professional organizations, many of the rewards (and controls) experienced by participants are more internalized, being related to the identities embraced by workers and their associated commitments. On the other hand, organizations relying on volunteers employ what are termed by Clark and Wilson "purposive" incentives: Participants are rewarded to the extent that their efforts enable the organization to achieve goals of value to themselves. Although such organizations enjoy an obvious advantage—the strong linkage of organization's and members' interests—they also present a severe challenge to their leaders. Because participants are rewarded only if organizations conduct successful campaigns, organizational leaders need to assure a continuing string of victories. Under most conditions, this is a tough demand: It is hard to win all the time. As a consequence, leaders must seek to cultivate alternative rewards—for example, by producing "interesting" activities or meetings, by giving social recognition and rewards to lay leaders, and by using rhetoric that can substitute "moral victories" for actual achievements.

15. Coleman has moved toward a more community-organizing, constituent-driven model since our data collection ended. Its thirty-year history of advocacy in San Francisco, however, has been characterized by the model we describe here.

16. Discussion at OCO Board Meeting, November 11, 2003.

17. Additionally, although they all advocate for children and youth, only Coleman has elected to report lobbying expenses for grassroots lobbying, but none for legislative lobbying, and this was well below the percentage allowed by the IRS. Coleman has also had a 501(c)4 unit in the past, reinforcing its professionally directed advocacy structure.

18. There are only three foundations that support all three case organizations, but there are several others that fund at least two. Foundations and corporations typically have specific programs or interests they want to support. SFOP, for example, receives several donations from large banks because of their organizing around housing issues.

19. PICO website, www.piconetwork.org/ab_history.asp.

Notes to Chapter 7

1. Coleman website, www.colemanadvocates.org; "Mission and Principles."
2. Discussion at OCO Board Meeting, November 11, 2003.

Notes to Chapter 8

1. Appendix A provides the name, organizational affiliation, title, and date of interview for all respondents. Unless otherwise noted, all quotes come from interviews.
2. Today more than 50 percent of the entire budgets of nonprofits performing legal and social services come from government funds, and more than 800,000 nonprofits registered in 2000, up 33 percent from 1994 (Duitch 2002).
3. San Francisco Child Advocacy Network Budget Strategy Meeting, June 8, 2004.
4. Portions of this section draw on our earlier publication (Scott et al., 2006).

Notes to Chapter 9

1. This section draws on the typology put forth by Hirschman (1991). He details three arguments that reformers must rebut: perversity, futility, and jeopardy theses. Each thesis asserts from a different perspective that reformers will fail.
2. Appendix A provides the name, organizational affiliation, title, and date of interview for all respondents. Unless otherwise noted, all quotes come from interviews.
3. California's Proposition 140, passed in 1990, restricts state legislators to six years in the Assembly and eight in the Senate. Term limits make this local education and policy experience a valuable asset when newly elected representatives arrive in Sacramento because time for "on-the-job" learning in the capital is compressed.
4. "The Sunshine Ordinance was adopted by the voters of the City/County of San Francisco in November 1999 and went into effect in January 2000. The City/County of San Francisco already had a Sunshine Ordinance; however, the new one strengthens the previous one. The Sunshine Ordinance is an ordinance to insure easier access to public records and to strengthen the open meeting laws. The Sunshine Ordinance also outlines a procedure for citizens to follow if they do not receive public records they have requested" (www.ci.sf.ca.us/site/bdsupvrs_index.asp?id=22269).

References

Aizer, A. (2008). Neighborhood violence and urban youth. Working Paper 13773. Cambridge, MA: National Bureau of Economic Research.

Alameda County Probation Department. (2005, October). *Monthly statistical report.* Oakland, CA: Author.

Alameda County Public Health Department. Community Assessment, Planning, and Education Unit. (2004). *Oakland health profile 2004.* Oakland, CA: Author.

Aldrich, H. E. (1979). *Organizations and environments.* Upper Saddle River, NJ: Prentice-Hall.

Aldrich, H. E., & Ruef, M. (2006). *Organizations evolving* (2nd ed.). Thousand Oaks, CA: Sage.

Andrews, K., & Edwards, B. (2004). Advocacy organizations in the U.S. political process. *Annual Review of Sociology, 30:* 479–506.

Annie E. Casey Foundation. (2004). *City and rural Kids Count data book.* Baltimore, MD: Author.

Annie E. Casey Foundation. (2005, 2008). *KIDS COUNT data book.* Baltimore, MD: Author.

Armstrong, E. A. (2002). Crisis, collective creativity, and the generation of new organizational forms: The transformation of lesbian/gay organizations in San Francisco. *Social Structures and Organizations Revisited, 19:* 361–95.

Arthur, W. B. (1994). *Increasing returns and path dependence in the economy.* Ann Arbor: University of Michigan Press.

Astley, W. G. (1985). The two ecologies: Population and community perspectives on organizational evolution. *Administrative Science Quarterly, 30:* 224–41.

Bardach. E. (1977). *The implementation game: What happens after a bill becomes law.* Cambridge, MA: MIT Press.

Baumgartner, F. R., & Jones, B. D. (1991). Agenda dynamics and policy subsystems. *The Journal of Politics, 53*(4): 1044–74.

Béland, D. (2005). *Social Security: History and politics from the New Deal to the privatization debate.* Lawrence: University Press of Kansas.

Benford, R., & Snow, D. A. (2000). Framing processes and social movements: An overview and assessment. *Annual Review of Sociology, 26*(1): 611–39.

Bennett, W. J., Dilulio, J. J., and Walters, J. P. (1996). *Body count: Moral poverty . . . and how to win America's war against crime and drugs.* New York: Simon & Schuster.

Berry, J. M. (1989). *The interest group society* (2nd ed). Glenview, IL, and Boston, MA: Scott-Foresman/Little, Brown.

———. (1995). The advocacy explosion. In S. Theodoulou & M. Cahn (Eds.), *Public policy: The essential readings* (pp. 317–24). Englewood, NJ: Prentice Hall.

———. (2001). Effective advocacy for nonprofits. In E. J. Reid & M. D. Montilla (Eds.), *Exploring organizations and advocacy. Nonprofit advocacy and the policy process,* Volume 2. Washington, DC: The Urban Institute.

Blash, L., Shafer, H., Nakagawa, M., & Jarrett, S. (2005). *Getting behind the headlines: Families leaving San Francisco.* San Francisco: Public Research Institute, San Francisco State University.

Blau, P. M., & Scott, W. R. (1962). *Formal organizations: A comparative approach.* San Francisco: Chandler.

Blitstein, R. (2006, May 3). A study in size. *San Francisco Weekly.* Available online at: www.sfweekly.com/2006-05-03/news/a-study-in-size/.

Boris, E., & Mosher-Williams, R. (1998). Nonprofit advocacy organizations: Assessing the definitions, classifications and data. *Nonprofit and Voluntary Sector Quarterly, 27*(4), 488–506.

Bremner, R. H. (Ed.). (1974). *Children and youth in America: A documentary history, Volume III: 1933–1973.* Cambridge, MA: Harvard University Press.

Brodkin, M. (1989). *Making children a priority of our local communities: 15 Years of advocacy in San Francisco.* San Francisco: Coleman Advocates for Children and Youth.

The Brookings Institution. (2003, November). *Oakland in focus: A profile from Census 2000.* Available online at www.brookings.edu/reports/2003/11_livingcities_oakland.aspx.

Brooks, F. (2005). Resolving the dilemma between organizing and services: Los Angeles ACORN's Welfare Advocacy. *Social Work 50*(3, July): 262–70.

Buchanan, W. (2004, December 16). State official lists 7 schools to close in '05; Parents, teachers jeer administrator, lambaste decision. *San Francisco Chronicle,* Bay Area section. Available online at: http://sfgate.com/cgibin/article.cgi?f=/c/a/2004/12/16/BAGK4ACOEC1.DTL.

Campbell, J. L. (2004). *Institutional change and globalization.* Princeton, NJ: Princeton University Press.

———. (2005). Where do we stand? Common mechanisms in organizations and social movements research. In G. Davis, D. McAdam, W. R. Scott, & M. N. Zald (Eds.), *Social movements and organization theory.* New York: Cambridge University Press.

Carnegie Corporation of New York. (1989). *Turning points: Preparing American youth for the 21st century.* New York: Carnegie Council on Adolescent Development.

———. (1992). *A matter of time: Risk and opportunity in the nonschool hours.* New York: Carnegie Council on Adolescent Development.

Carson, E .D. (2001). How are the children? In C. J. DeVita & R. Mosher-Williams (Eds.), *Who speaks for America's children? The role of child advocates in public policy.* Washington, DC: The Urban Institute Press.

Carson, R. (1962). *Silent spring.* Boston: Houghton Mifflin.

Child, C. D., & Grønbjerg, K. A. (2007, March). Nonprofit advocacy organizations: Their characteristics and activities. *Social Science Quarterly, 88*(1): 259–81.

Cigler, A., & Loomis, B. (1998). *Interest group politics.* Washington, DC: Congressional Quarterly.

Clark, P. B., & Wilson, J. Q. (1961). Incentive system: A theory of organization. *Administrative Science Quarterly 6,* 129–66.

Clemens, E. S. (1993). Organizational repertoires and institutional change: Women's groups and the transformation of American politics, 1880–1920. *American Journal of Sociology, 98:* 755–98.

———. (1997). *The people's lobby: Organizational innovation and the rise of interest group politics in the United States, 1890–1925.* Chicago: University of Chicago Press.

Clemens, E. S., & Cook, J. M. (1999). Politics and institutionalism: Explaining durability and change. *Annual Review of Sociology, 25:* 441–46.

Coleman Advocates. (2001). *San Francisco's declining child population.* Summary of the Proceedings of the Children's Caucus. Sponsored by Coleman Advocates, Fall 2001.

———. (2003). An open letter to Mayor-elect Newsom. December 23.

Community Crime Prevention Associates. (2001, August 15). *Oakland Fund for Children and Youth Evaluation Report FY2000–01.* Oakland, CA: Author.

Connell, J., Gambone, M., & Smith, T. (1998). *Youth development in community settings: Challenges to our field and our approach.* Philadelphia: Institute for Research and Reform in Education.

Costello, J., Toles, M., Spielberger, J., & Wynn, J. (2000). History, ideology and structure shape the organizations that shape youth. In N. Jaffe (Ed.), *Youth development: Issues, challenges and directions* (pp.185–232). Philadelphia: Public/Private Ventures.

Covington, S. (2002). In the midst of plenty: Foundation funding of child advocacy organizations in the 1990s. In C. J. DeVita & R. Mosher-Williams (Eds.), *Who speaks for America's children? The role of child advocates in public policy* (pp. 39–80). Washington, DC: The Urban Institute Press.

Crawford, L. (2005, October). Where have all the children gone? *San Francisco Magazine,* 94–104, 118–19.

Davis, G. F., McAdam, D., Scott, W. R., & Zald, M. N. (Eds.). (2005). *Social movements and organization theory.* New York: Cambridge University Press.

DeLeon, R. E. (1992). *Left coast city: Progressive politics in San Francisco, 1975–1991.* Lawrence: University Press of Kansas.

Delgado, G. (1986). *Organizing the movement: The roots and growth of ACORN (Labor and Social Change).* Philadelphia, PA: Temple University Press.

Deschenes, S. (2003). Lessons from the middle: Neighborhood reform for youth in San Francisco. Unpublished dissertation, Stanford University.

Deschenes, S., Cuban, L., & Tyack, D. (2001). Mismatch: Historical perspectives on schools and students who don't fit them. *Teachers College Record, 103*(4): 525–47.

Deschenes, S., McLaughlin, M., & Newman, A. (2008). Organizations advocating for youth: The local advantage. *New Direction for Youth Development,* 117.

Deschenes, S., McLaughlin, M., & O'Donoghue, J. (2006). Nonprofit community organizations in poor urban settings: Bridging institutional gaps for youth. In W. W. Powell & R. Steinberg (Eds.), *The nonprofit sector: A research handbook,* 2nd ed. New Haven, CT: Yale University Press.

DeVita, C. J., Montilla, M., Reid, E., & Fatiregun, O. (2004). *Organizational factors influencing advocacy for children.* Report to The Foundation on Child Development. Washington, DC: Urban Institute.

DeVita, C. J., Mosher-Williams, R., & Stengel, N. A. J. (2001). Nonprofit organizations engaged in child advocacy. In C. J. DeVita & R. Mosher-Williams (Eds.), *Who speaks for America's children? The role of child advocates in public policy.* Washington, DC: The Urban Institute Press.

DiMaggio, P. J. (1983). State expansion and organizational fields. In R. H. Hall & R. E. Quinn (Eds.), *Organization theory and public policy* (pp. 147–61). Beverly Hills, CA: Sage.

———. (1991). Constructing an organizational field as a professional project: U.S. art museums, 1920–1940. In W. W. Powell & P. J. DiMaggio (Eds.), *The new institutionalism in organizational analysis* (pp. 267–92). Chicago: University of Chicago Press.

DiMaggio, P. J., & Powell, W. W. (1983). The iron cage revisited: Institutional isomorphism and collective rationality in organizational fields, *American Sociological Review, 48:* 147–60.

Djelic, M. L., & Quack, S. (2004). *Globalization and institutions.* Northampton, MA: Edward Elgar.

Duitch, S. (2002). *Speak up: Tips on advocacy for publicly funded nonprofits.* New York: The Center for an Urban Future.

Einbinder, S. (2000). *Advocacy for children by nonprofit organizations: A case study of the California Children's Policy Council.* Summary from the Nonprofit Sector Research Fund projects and findings, available at www.nonprofitresearch.org/newsletter1531/newsletter_show.htm?doc_id=4643

Evan, W. M. (1966). The organization set: Toward a theory of interorganizational relations. In J. D. Thompson (Ed.), *Approaches to organizational design* (pp. 173–188). Pittsburgh, PA: University of Pittsburgh Press.

Evans, P., Rueschemeyer, D., & Skocpol, T. (Eds.). (1985). *Bringing the state back in.* Cambridge, England: Cambridge University Press.

Fesler, J. W., and Kettl, D. F. (1991). *The politics of the administrative process.* Chatham, NJ: Chatham House.

Fligstein, N. (2001a). *The architecture of markets: An economic sociology of twenty-first century capitalist societies.* Princeton, NJ: Princeton University Press.

———. (2001b). Social skill and the theory of fields. *Sociological Theory, 19:* 105–25.

Foster, L. K., Gieck, B., & Dienst, A. (2005). *Involving youth in policymaking and coordinating youth policy: State-level structures in California and other states.* Sacramento: California Research Bureau.

Friedland, R., & Alford, R. R. (1991). Bringing society back in: Symbols, practices and institutional contradiction. In W. W. Powell & P. J. DiMaggio (Eds.), *The new institutionalism in organizational analysis* (pp. 232–63). Chicago: University of Chicago Press.

Fruchter, N. (2001, July/August). Challenging failing schools. *Shelterforce Online.* Retrieved from www.nhi.org/online/issues/118/Fruchter.html.

Fung, A. (2003). Associations and democracy: Between theories, hopes, and realities. *Annual Review of Sociology, 29:* 515–39.

Galaskiewicz, J., & Bielefeld, W. (1998). *Nonprofit organizations in an age of uncertainty.* New York: Aldine de Gruyter.

Gammal, D. L., Simard, C., Hwang, H., & Powell, W. (2005). *Managing through challenges: A profile of San Francisco Bay Area nonprofits.* Palo Alto, CA: Stanford Project on the Evolution of Nonprofits, Center for Social Innovation.

Gibson & Associates. (2005a). *Oakland Fund for Children and Youth: Needs assessment report.* Oakland, CA: Author.

———. (2005b). *Oakland maps: Interpretation of trends and gaps for the Oakland Fund for Children and Youth.* Oakland, CA: Author.

Giddens, A. (1979). *Central problems in social action: Action, structure, and contradiction in social analysis.* Berkeley: University of California Press.

———. (1984). *The constitution of society.* Berkeley: University of California Press.

———. (1998). *The third way: The renewal of social democracy.* Cambridge, England: Polity Press.

Ginwright, S., & James, T. (2002). From arrests to agents of change: Social justice, organizing, and youth development. *New Directions for Youth Development, 96.*

Gormley, W. T., & Cymrot, H. (2006). The strategic choices of child advocacy groups. *Nonprofit and Voluntary Sector Quarterly, 35*:102–22.

Graddy, E. A., & Morgan, D. (2005, March). Community foundations, organizational strategy and public policy. Unpublished ms., School of Policy, Planning, and Development, University of Southern California. Research Paper 23.

Granovetter, M. (1973). The strength of weak ties. *American Journal of Sociology, 78:* 1360–80.

Greenwood, R., & Hinings, C. R. (1993). Understanding strategic change: The contribution of archetypes. *Academy of Management Journal, 38:* 1052–81.

———. (1996). Understanding radical organizational change: Bringing together the old and the new institutionalism. *The Academy of Management Review, 24*(4): 1022–54.

Hair, E. C., Moore, K. A., Hunter, D., & Kaye, J. W. (2002). Youth development outcomes compendium. Unpublished paper, Edna McConnell Clark Foundation.

Hammack, D. C. (1989). Community foundations: The delicate question of purpose, in R. Magat (Ed.) *An agile servant: Community leadership by community foundations* (pp. 23–50). New York: Foundation Center.

Hannan, M. T., & Carroll, G. R. (1995). An introduction to organizational ecology. In G. R. Carroll & M. T. Hannan (Eds.), *Organizations in industry: Strategy, structure and selection* (pp. 17–31). New York: Oxford University Press.

Hannan, M. T., & Freeman, J. (1977). The population ecology of organizations. *American Journal of Sociology, 82:* 929–64.

———. (1989). *Organizational ecology.* Cambridge, MA: Harvard University Press.

Hawkins, D. J., & Catalano, R. F. (1992). *Communities that care.* San Francisco, CA: Jossey-Bass Publishers.

Hawley, A. (1950). *Human ecology.* New York: Ronald Press.

Heredia, C.D. (2006, June 26). Considering health care options. San Francisco *Chronicle.* Retrieved from www.sfgate.com/cgibin/article.cgi?f=/c/a/2006/06/26/BAGM7JK9E21.DTL

Hertz, J. (2002). *Organizing for change: Stories of success.* Retrieved from http://comm-org.utoledo.edu/papers2002/hertz/home.htm.

Hirschman, A. O. (1991). *The rhetoric of reaction.* Cambridge, MA: Belknap Press of Harvard University.

Hoffman, A. J. (1997). *From heresy to dogma: An institutional history of corporate environmentalism.* San Francisco: New Lexington Press.

Hoffman, J. A. (1999). Institutional evolution and change: Environmentalism and the U.S. chemical industry, *Academy of Management Journal, 42:* 351–71.

Hojnacki, M., Baumgartner, F. R., Berry, J. M., Kimball, D. C., & Leech, B. L. (2006, August/September). *Goals, salience, and the nature of advocacy.* Paper presented at the annual meeting of the American Political Science Association, Philadelphia, PA.

Huskey & Associates. (2004). Alameda County, California: Comprehensive study of the juvenile justice system. Hayward, CA: County of Alameda.

Hwang, H. (2006). *Professionalization in nonprofit management.* Unpublished manuscript, Center for Social Innovation, Graduate School of Business, Stanford University.

Imig, D. (2001). *Social movements and the public policies they lead and follow: The case of American children's policy.* Memphis, TN: The University of Memphis. Available online at: www.seweb.uci.edu/users/jenness/Imig.html.

Jenkins, J. C. (2006). Nonprofit organizations and political advocacy. In W. W. Powell & R. S. Steinberg (Eds.). *The nonprofit sector handbook,* 2nd ed., pp. 307–32. New Haven, CT: Yale University Press.

Johnson, J. B. (2005, August 31). U.S. census finds more are poor but numbers lacking health care remains steady. *San Francisco Chronicle,* A2.

Kingdon, J. W. (1984). *Agendas, alternatives, and public policies.* Boston: Little, Brown.

Knight, H. (2005a, November 8). Ackerman offers to quit early but union won't give her concessions—closures discussed. *San Francisco Chronicle,* Bay Area section. Retrieved online at www.sfgate.com/cgibin/article.cgi?f=/c/a/2005/11/08/BAGIEFKN7C1.DTL.

———. (2005b, October 22). Gates money pulled from small schools. San Francisco *Chronicle,* B1.

Krause, E. A. (1968). Functions of a bureaucratic ideology: Citizen participation. *Social Problems, 16:* 129–43.

Laumann, E. O., & Knoke, D. (1987). *The organizational state: Social choice in national policy domains.* Madison: University of Wisconsin Press.

Laumann, E. O., Marsden, P. M., & Prensky, D. (1983). The boundary specification problem in network analysis. In R. S. Burt & M. J. Minor (Eds.), *Applied network analysis* (pp. 18–34). Beverly Hills, CA: Sage.

Lawler, E. J., Ridgeway, C., & Markovsky, B. (1993). Structural social psychology and the micro-macro problem. *Sociological Theory, 11*(3, November): 268–90.

Lawrence, P. R., & Lorsch, J. W. (1967). *Organization and environment: Managing differentiation and integration.* Boston, MA: Graduate School of Business Administration, Harvard University.

Lee, B. & Lounsbury, M. (2004, August). Movements and markets: Establishing organic food as a high quality product market. Paper presented at the Annual Meetings of the Academy of Management.

Lerner, R. M. (2005, September). Presentation to the National Academies of Science/Institute of Medicine/National Research Council Workshop on the Science of Adolescent Health and Development. Washington, DC.

Lipset, S. M. (1996). *American exceptionalism: A double-edged sword*. New York: W. W. Norton and Company.

Lopez, A. (2001). *Households and families in the ten largest cities of the San Francisco Bay Area*. Available online at: http://ccsre.stanford.edu/reports/report_3.pdf.

Lounsbury, M. (2005). Institutional variation in the evolution of social movements: Competing logics and the spread of recycling advocacy groups. In G. F. Davis, D. McAdam, W. R. Scott & M. N. Zald (Eds.), *Social movements and organizational theory* (pp. 73–95). New York: Cambridge University Press.

Lounsbury, M., Ventresca, M. J. & Hirsch, P. M. (2003). Social movements, field frames, and industry emergence: A cultural-political perspective on recycling. *Socio-Economic Review, 1:* 71–104.

Macallair, D., & Males, M. (2004). A failure of good intentions: An analysis of juvenile justice reform in San Francisco during the 1990s. *Review of Policy Research, 21*(1): 63–78.

MacDonald, G. B., & Valdivieso, R. (2000). Measuring deficits and assets: How we track youth development now and how we should track it. In N. Jaffe (Ed.), *Youth development: issues, challenges and directions* (pp. 149–84). Philadelphia: Public/ Private Ventures.

March, J. G., & Olsen, J. P. (1989). *Rediscovering institutions*. New York: The Free Press.

Mayer, S. E. (1994). *Building community capacity: The potential of community foundations*. Minneapolis, MN: Rainbow Research.

Mayor's Office of Criminal Justice and Juvenile Probation Department. (2006). *Juvenile justice local action plan: 2006 update*. San Francisco: San Francisco Juvenile Justice Department.

McAdam, D., McCarthy, J. D., & Zald, M. N. (1988). Social movements. In N. J. Smelser (Ed.), *Sociology*. Newbury Park, CA: Sage.

———. (1996). Introduction: Opportunities, mobilizing structures, and framing processes—Toward a synthetic, comparative perspective on social movements. In D. McAdam, J. D. McCarthy, & M. N. Zald (Eds.), *Comparative perspectives on social movements: Political opportunities, mobilizing structures, and cultural framing*. New York: Cambridge University Press.

McAdam, D., & Scott, W. R. (2005). Organizations and movements. In G. F. Davis, D. McAdam, W. R. Scott, & M. N. Zald (Eds.), *Social movements and organization Theory* (pp. 4–40). New York: Cambridge University Press.

McCarthy, J. D., & Castelli, J. (2002). The necessity for studying organizational advocacy comparatively. In P. Flynn & W. A. Hodgkinson (Eds.), *Measuring the impact of the nonprofit sector*. New York: Kluwer Academic/Plenum Publishers.

McKersie, W. S. (1999). Local philanthropy matters: Pressing issues for research and practice. In E. C. Lagemann (Ed.), *Philanthropic foundations: New scholarship, new possibilities*. Bloomington: Indiana University Press.

McLaughlin, M. W. (n.d.). *Community counts: How youth organizations matter for youth development.* Washington, DC: Public Education Network.

———. (1987). Learning from experience: Lessons from policy implementation. *Educational Evaluation and Policy Analysis, 9*(2): 171–78.

———. (2006). Implementation research in education: Lessons learned, lingering questions and new opportunities. In M. I. Honig (Ed.), *New directions in education policy implementation: Confronting complexity.* Albany: The State University of New York Press.

McLaughlin, M. W., with M. Irby and J. Langman. ([1994], 2001) *Urban sanctuaries: Neighborhood organizations in the lives and futures of inner-city youth.* San Francisco: Jossey Bass, 1994.

Michels, R. (1949). *Political parties,* E. and C. Paul (Trans.). Glencoe, IL: Free Press. (First published in 1915)

Minkoff, D. (1994). From service provision to institutional advocacy: The shifting legitimacy of organizational forms. *Social Forces, 72*(4): 943–69.

———. (2002). The emergence of hybrid organizational forms: Combining identity-based service provision and political action. *Nonprofit and Voluntary Sector Quarterly, 31:*

Moore, M. (1988). What sort of ideas become public ideas? In R. B. Reich (Ed.), *The power of public ideas* (pp. 55–83). Cambridge, MA: Ballinger.

Morris, A. (2000). Reflections on social movement theory: Criticisms and proposals. *Contemporary Sociology, 29:* 445–54.

Moynihan, D. P. (1970). *Maximum feasible misunderstanding.* New York: Free Press.

Munch, R., & Smelser, N. J. (1987). Relating and micro and macro. In J. C. Alexander, B. Gieson, R. Munch, & N. J. Smelser (Eds.), *The macro-micro link,* pp. 356–387. Berkeley: University of California Press.

Musto, D. D. (1975). Whatever happened to "community mental health"? *The Public Interest, 39:* 53–79.

National Academy of Sciences. (1982). *Making policies for children: A study of the federal process.* Washington, DC: National Academy Press.

National Commission on Excellence in Education. (1983, April). *A nation at risk: The imperative for educational reform.* A Report to the Nation and the Secretary of Education. Washington, DC: U.S. Department of Education.

National Research Council and Institute of Medicine. (2002). *Community programs to promote youth development.* Committee on Community Level Programs for Youth. J. Eccles & J. A. Gootman (Eds.). Board on Children, Youth, and Families, Division of Behavioral and Social Sciences and Education. Washington, DC: National Academy Press.

Newman, A. R. (2007). *A case for a right to education for equal citizenship.* Unpublished dissertation, Stanford University.

Noam, G. (2002). Introduction. *New Directions for Youth Development,* 93.

Oakes, J., & Rogers, J., with M. Lipton (2006). *Learning power: Organizing for education and justice.* New York: Teachers College Press.

Peterson, P. E., Rabe, B. G., and Wong, K. T. (1986). *When Federalism works.* Washington, DC: Brookings.

Pfeffer, J., & Salancik, G. R. (1978). *The external control of organizations.* New York: Harper & Row.

PICO Network. (2005, April 19). Retrieved July 10, 2006, from www.piconetwork .org/news/oakland_community_organizations_5.html.

Pierson, P. (2004). *Politics in time: History, institutions and social analysis.* Princeton, NJ: Princeton University Press.

Pittman, K., & Cahill, M. (1992). *Pushing the boundaries of education: The implications of a youth development approach to education policies, structures and collaborations.* Paper presented at the Summer Institute of the Council of Chief State School Officers.

Pittman, K., Irby, M., & Ferber, T. (2000). *Unfinished business: Further reflections of a decade of promoting youth development.* Takoma Park, MD: The Forum for Youth Investment.

Pittman, K., & Wright, M. (1991). *Bridging the gap: A rationale for enhancing the role of community organizations in promoting youth development.* Commissioned paper for the Center on Youth Development and Policy Research.

Piven, F. F., & Cloward, R. A. (1971). *Regulating the poor.* New York: Pantheon.

Porter, M. E. (1980). *Competitive strategy.* New York: Free Press.

Powell, W. W. (1990). Neither market nor hierarchy: Network forms of organization. *Research in Organizational Behavior, 12:* 295–336.

Pressman, J., & Wildavsky, A. (1973). *Implementation.* Berkeley: University of California Press.

Public/Private Ventures. (2000). *Youth development: Issues, challenges and directions.* Philadelphia: Author.

Putnam, R. (2000). *Bowling alone.* New York: Simon and Schuster.

Rainey, H. G. (1991). *Understanding and managing public organizations.* San Francisco: Jossey-Bass.

Rao, H., Monin, P., & Durand, R. (2003). Institutional change in Toque Ville: Nouvelle Cuisine as an identity movement in French gastronomy. *American Journal of Sociology, 108*(4): 795–843.

Reid, E. (2001). Building a policy voice for children. In C. J. DeVita & R. Mosher-Williams (Eds.), *Who speaks for America's children? The role of child advocates in public policy* (pp. 105–33). Washington, DC: The Urban Institute Press.

Reid, E. J. (2000). Understanding the word "advocacy": Context and use. *Structuring the inquiry into advocacy.* Nonprofit Advocacy and the policy process. A seminar series. Volume 1. Washington, DC: The Urban Institute. Retrieved October 1, 2008, from www.urban.org/UploadedPDF/structuring.pdf.

Rodham, H. (1973). Children under the law. *Harvard Education Review, 43:* 4.

Ruef, M., Aldrich, H. E., & Carter, N. M. (2003). The structure of organizational founding teams: Homophily, strong ties and isolation among U.S. entrepreneurs. *American Sociological Review, 68:* 195–200.

Rutherford, P. (2004). *Weapons of mass persuasion: Marketing the war against Iraq.* Toronto, Ontario, Canada: University of Toronto Press.

Salamon, L. (Ed.). (2002). *The state of nonprofit America.* Washington, DC: The Brookings Institution Press.

Schneider, A., & Ingram, H. (1993). Social construction of target populations: Implications for politics and policy. *American Political Science Review, 87*(2): 334–47.

Scott, W. R. (2008a [1995]). *Institutions and organizations: Ideas and interests,* 3rd Ed. Thousand Oaks, CA: Sage.

———. (2008b). Lords of the dance: Professionals as institutional agents. *Organization Studies, 29:* 219–38.

Scott, W. R., & Davis, G. F. (2007). *Organizations and organizing: Rational, natural and open system perspectives.* Upper Saddle River, NJ: Pearson/Prentice Hall.

Scott, W. R, Deschenes, S., Hopkins, K., Newman, A., & McLaughlin, M. (2006). Advocacy organizations and the field of youth development: Dynamics of early stages of field structuration. *Nonprofit and Voluntary Sector Quarterly: 35*(4).

Scott, W. R., Ruef, M., Mendel, P. J., & Caronna, C. A. (2000). *Institutional change and healthcare organizations: From professional dominance to managed care.* Chicago: University of Chicago Press.

Self, R. O. (2003). *American Babylon: Race and the struggle for postwar Oakland.* Princeton, NJ: Princeton University Press.

Selznick, P. (1949). *TVA and the grass roots.* Berkeley: University of California Press.

———. (1957). *Leadership in administration: A sociological interpretation.* Berkeley: University of California Press.

Sewell, W. H. Jr. (1992). A theory of structure: Duality, agency, and transformations. *American Journal of Sociology, 98:* 1–29.

Shirley, D. (1997). *Community organizing for urban school reform.* Austin: University of Texas Press.

Siler, T. (2005, March 25). School clinic sets standards in health care. Retrieved July 10, 2006, from www.npr.org/templates/story/story.php?storyId=4569392.

Skocpol, T. (1992). *Protecting soldiers and mothers: The political origins of social policy in the United States.* Cambridge, MA: The Belknap Press of Harvard University Press.

———. (1995). *Social policy in the United States.* Princeton, NJ: Princeton University Press.

———. (1999). Advocates without members: The recent transformation of American civic life. In T. Skocpol & M. P. Fiorina (Eds.), *Civic engagement in American democracy* (pp. 461–509). Washington, DC: Brookings Institution Press.

———. (2003). *Diminished democracy: From membership to management in American civil life*. Norman: University of Oklahoma Press.

Skocpol, T., & Dickert, J. (2001). Speaking for families and children in a changing civic America. In C. J. DeVita & R. Mosher-Williams (Eds.), *Who speaks for America's children? The role of child advocates in public policy*. Washington, DC: The Urban Institute Press.

Smith, J. (2005). Globalization and transnational social movement organizations. In G. F. Davis, D. McAdam, W. R. Scott, & M. N. Zald (Eds), *Social movements and organization theory* (pp. 226–48). New York: Cambridge University Press.

Smith, S. R., & Lipsky, M. (1993). *Nonprofits for hire: The welfare state in the age of contracting*. Cambridge, MA: Harvard University Press.

Snow, D. A., & Benford, R. D. (1988). Ideology, frame resonance, and participant mobilization. In B. Klandermans, H. Kriesi, & S. Tarrow (Eds.), *From structure to action: Social movement participation across cultures* (pp. 197–217). Greenwich, CT: JAI Press.

Snow, D. A., Rochford, E .B. Jr., Worden, S. K., & Benford, R. D. (1986). Frame alignment processes, micromobilization, and movement participation. *American Sociological Review, 51*:464–81.

Stinchcombe, A. L. (1965). Social structure and organizations. In J. G. March (Ed.), *Handbook of organizations* (pp. 142–93). Chicago: Rand McNally.

Stone, C., Orr, M., and Worgs, D. (2006). The flight of the bumblebee: Why reform is difficult but not impossible. *Perspective on Politics, 4*(3): 529–46.

Stone, C. N. (2001). Civic capacity and urban education. *Urban Affairs Review, 36*: 595–619.

Stone, D. (2002). *Policy paradox: The art of political decision making*. Scranton, PA: W. W. Norton & Co.

Sundquist, J. L. (1969). *Making federalism work*. New York: Russell Sage Foundation.

Sutton, J. (1988). *Stubborn children: Controlling delinquency in the United States, 1640–1981*. Berkeley: University of California Press.

Thompson, J. D. (1967). *Organizations in action*. New York: McGraw-Hill.

Tilly, C. (1978). *From mobilization to revolution*. Reading, MA: Addison-Wesley.

U.S. Bureau of the Census. (2000). State and county quickfacts. Available online at: http://quickfacts.census.gov/qfd/states/06000.html.

Ventresca, M. J. (2002). When states count: Institutional conflict and the global field of official statistics, 1800–2000. Unpublished manuscript.

W. T. Grant Foundation. (1988). The *forgotten half: Pathways to success for America's youth and youth families*. Washington, DC: W. T. Grant Commission on Work, Family and Citizenship.

Walker, T. (December 15, 1998a). New Oakland system has politicians maneuvering. *The San Francisco Chronicle,* A19.

———. (November 10, 1998b). Power sharing in Oakland: Jerry Brown and city manager on joint mission to save city. *The San Francisco Chronicle,* A1.

Warren, M. R. (2001). *Dry bones rattling: Community building to revitalize American democracy.* Princeton, NJ: Princeton University Press.

Weatherley, R., & Lipsky, M. (1977). Street-level bureaucrats and institutional innovation: Implementing special education reform. *Harvard Educational Review,* 47:171–97.

Wildavsky, A. B. (1988). *The new politics of the budgetary process.* Glenview, IL: Scott, Foresman.

Williamson, O. E. (1975). *Markets and hierarchies: Analysis and antitrust implications.* New York: Free Press.

Wilson, J. Q. (1973). *Political organizations.* New York: Knopf.

———. (1989). *Bureaucracy: What government agencies do and why they do it.* New York: Basic Books.

Wolfe, R. E. (2006). Community foundations as agents of local social change. Unpublished dissertation, School of Education, Stanford University, Palo Alto, CA.

Wolpert, J. (1999). Communities, networks, and the future of philanthropy. In C. T. Clotfelter & T. Ehrlich (Eds.), *Philanthropy and the nonprofit sector in a changing America.* Bloomington: Indiana University Press.

Wood, R. L. (2002). *Faith in action: Religion, race, and democratic organizing in America.* Chicago: University of Chicago Press.

Wynn, J. R. (2000). The role of local intermediary organizations in the youth development field. Discussion Paper SC-03. Chicago: Chapin Hall Center for Children, University of Chicago.

Yee, S. M. (2008, Spring). Developing the field of youth organizing and advocacy: What foundations can do. In S. Deschenes, M. McLaughlin, & A. Newman (Issue Eds.), *Community organizing and youth advocacy: New directions for youth development.* San Francisco: Jossey-Bass.

Yogis, J. (2006, September). What happened to blacks in San Francisco? *San Francisco.* Retrieved from www.sanfranmag.com/story/what-happened-black-san-francisco.

Zald, M. N., & Denton, P. (1963). From evangelism to general service: The transformation of the YMCA. *Administrative Science Quarterly.* 8; 214-34.

Zald, M. N., & McCarthy, J. D. (1987a). "Social movement industries: Competition and conflict among SMOs." In M. N. Zald & J. D. McCarthy (Eds.), *Social movements in an organizational society: Collected essays* (161–180). New Brunswick, NJ: Transactions Books.

——— (Eds.). (1987b). *Social movements in an organizational society.* New Brunswick, NJ: Transaction Publishers.

Index

Not reviewed
by the BCCB